PRESSURE POLITICS
IN AMERICA

S. J. Makielski, Jr.
Department of Political Science
Loyola University

New Orleans, Louisiana 70118

University Press of America™

Copyright © 1980 by

University Press of America, Inc.

P.O. Box 19101, Washington, D.C. 20036

Library of Congress Cataloging in Publication Data

Makielski, Stanislaw J
     Pressure politics in America.

     Includes index.
     1. Pressure groups--United States. I. Title.
JK1118.M33   322.4'3'0973   80-5529
ISBN 0-8191-1129-5
ISBN 0-8191-1130-9 (pbk.)

TABLE OF CONTENTS

PART I: STRUCTURE AND DYNAMICS

Chapter

Chapter

Chapter

LIST OF TABLES

Table

LIST OF ILLUSTRATIONS

Illustration

PART I

STRUCTURE AND DYNAMICS

CHAPTER I

INTRODUCTION

Fifteen angry homeowners confront a weary city planning commission. The lawyer for the homeowners has just finished his statement. A woman takes the floor. "You people don't care, do you? You don't care at all about what happens to us?"

The lawyer murmurs to her, trying to calm her. The faces of the planning commissioners flush with irritation.

At the same time, in Washington, the assistant information officer of a major corporation orders another martini for the senior researcher of a federal regulatory agency. They are on friendly terms, playing tennis together on weekends. The information officer says, "Tom, I read the draft report. It's a fine piece of work, really fine."

He reaches into his briefcase. "Look," he goes on. "Those figures you've got in section two, check them against these, will you? I think you're off-base there, just a little. But you look it over for yourself."

Later that evening, in the same city, two young women and three young men finish proofreading their report on a popular toy for young children, a toy which has blinded three infants and scarred six others. Their consumer protection organization wants the toy taken off the market, and the report should prove their point. Now that the work is done, they wonder when it should be released to the press. Sunday? Sunday is a

1

"good news day," parents have the leisure to
read the papers and they are thinking about their
kids. Still, the story might get buried, rele-
gated to page 21 if there is a flood of other
big stories. Monday, then? Editors need fresh
material for the Monday edition. . . .

The lawyer for a civil rights group rubs
his hands together nervously. In a few minutes
he will be called upon by the justices of the
state supreme court to present his brief as an
amicus curiae (a friend of the court). Although
the case involves sex discrimination, although
it will no doubt be appealed to the United States
Supreme Court, it is important to win a favorable
decision here and now. The issues could possibly
affect the welfare of black Americans in similar
cases and lately the U.S. courts have shown a
reluctance to overrule state court decisions.
He clears his throat and stands to address the
court.

As different as these four events are,
they have two important elements in common. In
each instance, citizens are exercising their constitutionally guaranteed right to "petition the
government." And, in each case, a group is applying pressure to government in an effort to gain
some advantage, to further a cause, to shape how
government makes policy.

The essence of modern pressure group
politics is the intimate relationship of organized pressures to the day-to-day decisions and
processes of government. At almost any time,
some place an official of government feels the
effects of organized group pressures. As one
scholar has phrased it, "Since early in the history of the Republic, organized interest groups
have wielded a strong degree of power. Such
exercise of power . . . has been perhaps the feature of political power most characteristic of

2

American democracy."[1] That is, the activities
of pressure groups are as much a part of the political process as the elections that gain the
attention of newspaper and television reporters.
And, because so often group pressures are applied
quietly, if not secretly, it is even more vital
that they be understood.

The Myths of Pressure Group Politics

At the outset, it is important to point
out some of the myths that surround pressure group
politics, because they are so widely held and
so effectively bar real understanding of how pressure politics works in America.

Myth Number One: Pressure groups operate
through bribes, corruption, and "undue influence."
Like many myths, there is enough truth in it to
give this common belief widespread credibility.
The public is periodically treated to the spectacle of officials corrupted by the money and
favors of ruthless lobbyists. In the early decades
of this century, again in the 1920s, in the 1930s,
under the Truman and Eisenhower administrations,
and once more in the "Watergate" and post-Watergate
scandals, it was all too apparent that the greed,
lust, and hunger for power of elected and appointed
officials could be exploited by skilled manipu-
lators.[2] The same sad tale regularly unfolds itself in state and local governments.

The likelihood, however, is that of the
tens of thousands of pressure groups in the United
States, only a small percentage resort to pay-
offs, call girls, and blackmail to get what they
want. They do not because they do not need to.
Usually an enterprising pressure group can find
a legislator, an administrator, or a judge who
is sympathetic to the group's interests. If there
are no officials actively sympathetic, there are
often those who will respond to group power,

realizing that if they fail to listen to the
group's demands they will suffer politically.

Many groups do not resort to undue influence because of the risk of exposure, the dangers attendant on publicity and even trial and
conviction of the group's leaders. As important,
relatively few pressure groups have large sums
of money to dispense lavishly without careful
consideration of what they expect to gain by doing
so.

Myth Number Two: Pressure groups are
the agents of the "special interests," the wealthy,
powerful elites of American society. As with
the first myth, there is a large ingredient of
truth here. The higher the economic status,
the more likely a person is to belong to a pressure group, and without question the major business corporations, associations of high status
professions such as doctors and lawyers, and
the middle class are more active in pursuing
their interests before governmental agencies
than are the "little people."[3] One of the significant developments of the last two decades,
however, has been the rapid growth of groups
devoted to protecting newly expressed interests:
blacks, Chicanos, native Americans, consumers,
and the citizen. Further, it must be remembered
that some of the most powerful of all pressure
groups--the unions--draw their strength from
the working man and have been in opposition to
business interests for nearly a century.

At least one community organizer, Saul
Alinsky, made a national reputation by training
and assisting lower-class people in the craft
of pressuring government.[4] Others have turned
such unlikely raw materials as welfare recipients
into active pressure groups.

To say as much should not obscure the
realities of pressure group politics, however.
There are important differences in the power of

4

various groups, in the ability to extract concessions from government and to block or modify
the public decision-making process. The reasons
for these power differentials will be a major
theme of this book.

Myth Number Three: There is something
fundamentally undemocratic about pressure groups.
There has been a long tradition of nervousness
about a society that divides itself along lines
of interests, especially when those interests
are collectively advocated. James Madison in
discussing the problems of government argued:

A zeal for different opinions concerning
religion, concerning government, and many
other points . . . ; an attachment to different leaders ambitiously contending for
pre-eminence and power; or to persons of
other descriptions whose fortunes have
been interesting to the human passions,
have, in turn, inflamed them with mutual
animosity, and rendered them much more
disposed to vex and oppress each other
than to cooperate for their common good.

He continued, "The regulation of these
various and interfering interests forms the principal task of modern legislation and involves
the spirit of party and faction in the necessary
and ordinary operations of the government."[5]

This troubled view of pressure groups
has persisted down to the present. Michael
Parenti writing in 1974 of the effect of the
American constitutional system said,"[the Founding Fathers] understood what some theorists today seem to have forgotten: that the diffusion
of power among various segments of government
. . . leads to the compartmentalized groups
which can resist and deter popular desires."[6]

It is easy to conclude that the very
nature of pressure group politics stands in opposition to the concept of a democratic order.

5

The issues are complex enough that they can be
touched on only briefly here (see Part III for
a more extended discussion). It must be kept
in mind, however, that pressure groups are one
way, and an important way, by which various
problems are brought to the public's attention.
Were it not for environmentalist groups like
the Sierra Club and the Audubon Society we would
know much less about and have done far less about
the threat to our natural environment. Had it
not been for the National Association for the
Advancement of Colored People, black Americans
might still have fewer legal and economic rights
than they have today. Were it not for the long
struggle of the labor unions, many working Americans would be paid less, toil longer hours, and
work in more dangerous conditions.

Pressure groups, then, in pursuing their
own often narrow "interests" frequently raise
questions that are of a far more general concern
and get those questions placed on a local, state,
or national agenda where action is sooner or
later taken. In this respect, pressure groups,
like political parties or elected office-holders,
help to perform a representative function.

Saying that pressure groups help to raise
and express issues is, however, not the same
as saying that pressure group politics as we
now know it is anything close to sufficient for
a democratic order. As we shall see, there is
much about group politics that excludes participation by others and which may help to confuse,
dampen, or even prevent the expression of additional interests.

An understanding of the nature of group
politics, then, requires the ability to focus
on the paradox of powerful, elitist interests
pursuing highly narrow goals at the same time
other dedicated groups seek the more general
goal of social betterment. To see one while
ignoring the other gives only a distorted view
of contemporary group politics.

6

Policy and Access

The task which pressure groups set themselves is to gain leverage over what government
does, to influence public policy. The general
term which political scientists use for this
process of influence is "gaining access." Like
most general terms, access covers a wide range
of phenomena. It can mean that a group is simply
able to convince a policy-maker to listen to
its arguments. It can mean the group establishes
a regular relationship with the policy-maker,
one in which the legislator or administrator
turns to the pressure group for information,
guidance, or even instructions. Access can mean
the group becomes "institutionalized" into the
policy process: it actually becomes a functioning part of government. Grant McConnell has
shown, for example, that the various county
units of the Farm Bureau Federation are integral
to the workings of the soil conservation program.[7]
Various state regulatory boards require by law
that specific interests be formally present on
the boards, and the recently created federal
health review agencies must have health service
"producers" (doctors and hospital administrators)
sit on the governing bodies of the agencies.

Access may also mean that a pressure
group gains its influence through a direct exchange of favors, as when the American Milk Producers Association won a favorable decision from
the U.S. Department of Agriculture by making
a sizeable contribution of money to the 1972
Nixon campaign.[8] And it can mean that a pressure group virtually owns the policy-maker through
an established pattern of bribery and corruption,
and perhaps blackmail and intimidation.

The degree of access a group has, and
the kind of access, is a crude index of the power
of the group, but the story is more complicated
than that. "Classic" interest group theory
assumed that government, and the men and women

7

in government, were little more than intermediaries in the conflict between struggling private
pressure groups.[9] Legislators were seen as merely
waiting until some balance of power was worked
out between private interests, and then writing
the results into law. Recent research has shown
that this view of group politics portrayed as
a one-way street what is really far more complex.
Policy-making in the American system involves
a wide array of decision-makers: legislators,
executives, bureaucrats, and judges, and federal,
state, and local officials as well as pressure
groups and their lobbyists.[10] Each of these
"actors" has a different base of power and may
or may not be subject to pressure group influence.
Occasionally, a group's "access" to the policy-
making process may in reality be a matter of
the group depending on the favors of a strong
political figure who uses the group to his own
ends.

        The danger in studying pressure groups
is one of over-reacting. It is easy to assume
pressure groups are all-powerful, as the classic
group theorists did, or to go to the other extreme and assume that groups have no power at
all. The more accurate portrayal would be that
while public policy is not entirely and solely
the product of the group struggle, neither is
it completely free of the effects of pressure
group influence. And sometimes, in some policy
areas at least, group power may indeed be the
dominant, controlling influence in what government does.

                The Nature of the Problem

        Our examination, then, must proceed with
an open mind. Two initial questions must be
answered: first, what is the structure and nature
of modern pressure groups in the United States?
Second, what do these groups do in the political
arena and how do they do it?

The answers to these questions prepare
the way to approach the third and larger question:
What is the significance of pressure group politics for American democracy at present and in
the future? It is hoped that such an examination
and review will give us a clearer sense of how
the political system operates in reality.

In answering these questions, two important themes recur. First is the way the
structure of the American political system affects and has helped to foster pressure group
politics. Federalism, the separation of powers,
checks and balances, and an electoral system
based on a federal system all provide pressure
groups with opportunities that more unitary
systems do not.[11] Equally, the structure of
the political system has affected the structure
of the groups themselves, which in turn influences
their behavior.

A second theme is that despite the volumes
of research and the considerable analysis and
thought given to pressure groups, we often cannot give a simple, direct answer to the question,
"How powerful are they?" Trends and patterns
can be detected, but there is frequently contra-
dictory evidence. We are more apt to know what
we do not know than to have final, complete
answers.

We can safely say, however, that understanding the pressure group, what it is, why
it is, and what it tries to do is as necessary
to gaining a full picture of American politics
as is understanding party politics, constitutional law, or the procedures of state and
national legislatures. As we begin to fill in
that picture, we are in a better position to
raise the fundamental questions about the direction and potential of American democracy.

9

References for Chapter I

[1]Grant McConnell, Private Power and American Democracy (New York: Alfred A. Knopf, 1966), p. 3. McConnell's book is one of the most thoughtful studies of the role of pressure groups.

[2]Joan Joseph, ed., Political Corruption (New York: Pocket Books, 1974) has a good series of articles describing the major scandals from the beginning of the nation through Watergate. Larry L. Berg, Harlan Hahn, and John R. Schmidhauser, Corruption in the American Political System (Morristown, N.J.: General Learning Press, 1976) attempt to come to grips with the nature, persistence, and impact of corruption on the nation's politics.

[3]Sidney Verba and Norman H. Nie, Participation in America: Political Democracy and Social Equality (New York: Harper and Row, 1972), pp. 176ff.

[4]Saul Alinsky, Reveille for Radicals: A Pragmatic Primer for Realistic Radicals (New York: Random House, 1971).

[5]James Madison, "Federalist No. 10," in The Federalist, Modern Library Edition (New York: Random House, n.d.), pp. 153-54.

[6]Michael Parenti, Democracy for the Few (New York: St. Martin's Press, 1974), p. 193.

[7]McConnell, Chapter 7.

[8]U.S. Senate Select Committee on Presidential Campaign Activities, Report (New York: Dell, 1974), Volume II, Chapter VI.

[9]See G. David Garson, "On the Origins of Interest Group Theory," American Political Science Review 68 (December 1974): 1505-19,

for a good review and critique of classic group
theory.

[10]Thomas R. Dye, Understanding Public
Policy, 2d ed. (Englewood Cliffs, N.J.: Prentice-
Hall, 1975). See also James E. Anderson, Public
Policy-Making (New York: Praeger, 1975).

[11]Richard H. Leach, American Federalism
(New York: W. W. Norton, 1970) is a good introduction to federalism. Daniel Elazar, American
Federalism: The View from the States, 2d ed.
(New York: Thomas Y. Crowell, 1972) is a controversial, but thought-provoking, discussion
of the political and governmental nature of
the American federal system.

CHAPTER II

THE BASES OF GROUP POLITICS

In the political struggle, strong forces
push some individuals to join with others to
seek political power. The results are parties
and groups. Experience shows that the pressure
group provides advantages the party system does
not, especially in terms of shaping public policy.
In turn, pressure groups are influenced by their
interest base, public policy, and the structure
of the American system.

Politics and Groups

Every citizen in a democratic society
faces a fundamental choice: whether to act
politically as an individual or to join forces
with other persons of like opinions or goals
to pursue their common concerns collectively.
This choice is more than a theoretical exercise,
since it raises large questions about the degree
of participation, the costs and rewards of participation, and the probable effects of individual
action.[1]

Careful research has proven that most
people, most of the time, prefer to act as self-
identified members of one of the two major political parties. Although there has been a
steady decline in the proportion of adult Americans who vote in presidential elections, still
about 62 percent of the electorate think of
themselves either as Republicans or Democrats.[2]

And, as Table 1 shows, the act of voting
is the most common political act of the American
citizen. The table also proves that "political

13

TABLE 1

SELECTED POLITICAL ACTIVITIES OF AMERICANS

Activity	Percent Participating
Vote in Presidential elections	72
Vote in local elections	47
Active in an organization concerned with community affairs	32
Have contacted a government official about an issue or problem	20
Have formed a group or organization to solve community problem	14

SOURCE: Sidney Verba and Norman H. Nie, *Participation in America: Political Democracy and Social Equality* (New York: Harper and Row, 1972), p. 31.

man" is a relatively rare species, if by that phrase we mean a citizen who is aware of political events, eager to let his leaders know about his feelings on the current issues of the day, and pursuing his political interests through the ballot box, petitions, face-to-face meetings with officials, and organizing to make his wishes known. The vast majority of the citizenry is relatively inert, waiting to be triggered into action by an election or a conflict that directly touches their concerns.

Although the political parties still hold the loyalties of office-seekers, party workers, and "strong identifiers," the traditional two-party system is haunted by serious problems.[3] The disenchantment of a large segment of the public is demonstrated by the steady increase of voters who think of themselves as "Independents," but there has also been a decline in the attachment of even those people who continue to label themselves Democrats or Republicans, especially among younger voters.[4]

Part of the decline of the political parties can be explained by the role the party plays in American life. In theory, the purpose of the party is to act as an "interest aggregator," that is, as a vehicle for bringing together diverse blocs of people, helping them to compromise their conflicts within the party mechanism and to settle on mutually satisfactory nominees for office and a program the nominees will carry out once elected.[5] By doing so, the theory goes, the political party provides an institutional outlet for conflict while resolving disputes in a stable and sensible fashion.

The process of interest aggregation has, however, the effect of blurring or even ignoring the deeply-felt concerns of many people. By virtue of the necessity to gain a plurality of the votes cast, party leaders are understandably reluctant to take strong positions on issues for fear of angering more voters than they will win over. It would be only a slight exaggeration to say that party leaders and office-seekers instead of wanting to "run on the issues" are eager to do anything to avoid the issues, especially those that threaten to divide the electorate.

For many citizens, however, the issues are precisely what they do care about. Union members, fearful that efforts to control inflation might limit their power to negotiate for higher wages, want to know what nominees for office plan to do about high prices. Members of the Catholic Church and other religious groups want to know where office-seekers stand on legalized abortion. Business executives worry about how vigorously government intends to pursue consumer protection measures or pollution controls.

Given the reluctance of the American political party to take strong positions on issues, it is not surprising that some citizens turn to others who share their feelings in an effort to force political leaders to give attention to their desires. The result is what is commonly called a pressure group. If the role of the party is to attempt to aggregate interests, the role of the pressure group is to express, to articulate, interests.

From Interest to Pressure Group

Because each of the two major parties has historically brought together diverse interests at the expense of complicated compromises and blurred issues, they act as efficient routes to public office and the power that goes with office. For others, however, winning control of the machinery of government is less important than having government act in certain ways: provide tax breaks to business, assist farmers,

16

pass and enforce civil rights laws, control exploitation of the environment, and a host of
other goals. The concern is with public policy,
what government does or does not do. As political
scientists put it, these people have a political
interest, that is, a conscious attitude about
some desirable condition which they hope to bring
about through their efforts.

It is obvious that most people have
several interests, ranging from lower taxes to
better schools, from a more "rational" foreign
policy to "doing something" about high crime
rates. As two scholars have noted, "The personal
agendas of citizens are fantastically varied. . . .
If what concerns him is general--war, high prices,
the quality of schools, traffic problems, property taxes--there remains an almost infinite
variety of personal sets of public issues."[6]

Generally, these interests lie dormant
unless they are aroused by a hard-fought political campaign in which one candidate or the other
appeals to what he believes is a popular issue.
More often, as noted, office-seekers will attempt
to stay away from issues and the interests underlying them except when it is very clear a majority
of the voters support a particular position.

In other instances, however, the interest
is strong enough to bring people together of
their own volition. They discover they share
a common interest and begin to interact on the
basis of that interest, that is, to discuss it
among themselves and to seek some way of advancing or protecting their interest. When this
much has occurred, an interest group has come
into being, that is, a collection of more than
two people who interact on the basis of a commonly shared concern.[7]

An important point needs to be made here.
Groups are a common phenomenon in human behavior.

17

Most of us participate in groups of some kind:
family, street corner gangs, office coffee clubs,
church socials, fraternal organizations, or simply
friendship groups. The basis of these groups
is also a set of commonly shared attitudes, such
as affection, recreation, status, and the basic
human urge to associate with one's fellows. Social groups such as these, however, are not the
same as interest groups. The term interest group
is usually reserved for groups which place demands on their environment.[8] For example, if
the office secretaries' social group were to
ask the supervisor for an extended coffee break,
it has stopped being a social group and become
an interest group.

When an interest group goes one step
farther and turns to the political system to
press its demands, it becomes a political interest group, or as it is frequently called,
a pressure group. There is, thus, an important
distinction that must be made among social groups,
interest groups, and pressure groups.[9]

It should be noted that this process
is not an inevitable evolution. Many, probably
most, social groups never become interest groups.
Many interest groups never become pressure groups.
Further, it is not necessary for a group to exist
as a social group before it becomes an interest
group or a pressure group.

To illustrate the process, it is useful
to see it at work in a real instance.

The Sommerset Homeowner's Association

Sommerset is a clearly defined neighborhood of eighty-seven homes in a rapidly growing
city. It is bounded on the east by a declining
working class neighborhood, where many of the

18

homes are rental property, have been broken up
into apartments, or have given way to small businesses. On the west there is a solid middle-
class area, separated from Sommerset by a wide
main traffic artery. On the north, there is
another middle-class area, more recently developed, containing a number of new apartment
complexes. To the south, Sommerset is protected
by a major city park.

All eighty-seven homes in Sommerset are
owned by their occupants, most of whom are older
people. Since 1967, six younger families have
bought homes in the area, attracted by the large
lots, spacious homes, and quiet environment,
despite there being no school nearby and no convenient mass transit facilities or churches.

During 1971, the staff of the City Planning Commission undertook a major revision of
the city's comprehensive plan. Troubled by the
lack of housing for young families, the staff
searched for areas suitable for apartment complex
growth, partly as an effort to prevent further
flight of the middle class to the city's suburbs.
In examining the city's neighborhoods, the planning staff observed that population pressures
were shifting in the direction of Sommerset,
that the area to the east of Sommerset was already going over to "mixed uses," and in their
revision of the plan recommended that the east-
ern half of Sommerset (including about forty
homes) be redesignated to permit apartment house
and convenience shopping development.

As the change for Sommerset was only
a small part of the total package of revisions,
no one in the Sommerset area was aware of the
proposed redesignation until, as required by
law, the Planning Commission advertised public
hearings on a neighborhood by neighborhood basis.
The proposal came as a rude shock to the residents of Sommerset. Most had lived in their
homes for decades. The young families which

19

had moved in had bought because the houses were, comparatively speaking, real bargains. All had assumed that the neighborhood was "established," and the only changes would be individual families moving in or out in the natural course of events.

Although there were patterns of friendships among neighbors, no basic groups knit the neighborhood together. Most had friends who lived elsewhere in the city; all went to church or to social gatherings outside the neighborhood, and so, while everyone knew everyone else's face, nothing had previously brought all the families together.

Despite the shared dismay, for a period of two weeks nothing was done to resist the change. Then, one of the families invited their next-door neighbors in to discuss what could be done. All agreed to expand the meetings by contacting the people they knew and thus "snowball" the discussion.

After a week of intense discussion, during which the date for the Planning Commission hearings drew closer, it was found that all the families were anxious to do something to protect the neighborhood. A meeting was held in the largest available home, and it was agreed to set up a group to be called "The Sommerset Homeowner's Association" to fight the proposed change. Officers were elected, dues collected and used to hire an attorney to represent the group before the Planning Commission.

As it happened, the Association was successful in blocking the change. Upon examination, the "case" of the Sommerset Homeowner's Association shows a typical defensive reaction to a proposed change. Each of the families had a clear "interest" in their homes and their economic and emotional investment in the neighborhood, but until the proposed redesignation was

20

publicized, nothing had happened to activate
that interest. When the catalyst appeared, the
homeowners progressed swiftly to group status
and then to pressure group status.

Although in this case a pressure group
came into being to oppose a governmental action,
in other cases groups are formed to do battle
with other pressure groups which the former see
as threatening to their interests. As one scholar
noted, for example,

the growth of large enterprises created
new frictions commonly described as between big business and the public; on
closer inspection, they often turned out
to be frictions between two sorts of
business . . . that led to demands for
governmental intervention by one or the
other of the contending groups.[10]

In the same way, railroad owners and operators
organized to oppose the growing power of unions
in the 1870s and 1880s.[11]

Action by government, activities by
other pressure groups, or even changes in social
and economic climate (such as a growing awareness
of environmental or racial issues) all can have
the effect of heightening an awareness of a
dormant interest to the point that those sharing the interest will seek each other out and
band together to protect or promote that interest. The result often is the formation of
a pressure group turning to government as a
useful tool to further the group's interests.

The Nature of Interests

Because interests are the cement which
binds a group together and the motivating power
which impels a group into politics it is

21

necessary to realize that the term includes an often bewildering array of concerns. It is fairly simple to categorize interests as "economic," "ideological," and so forth, but it should be realized that the categories often conceal as much as they explain.[12]

It is, for example, possible to speak of a union member and a business executive both being motivated by economic interests. The working man probably sees economics in highly personal terms: the size of his paycheck, his fringe benefit package, and the comfort and safety of his working conditions. The business executive, however, has an economic interest that does include his personal compensation but also reaches beyond to a fascinating game of competition among corporations for market position, the expansion of his own division within the corporation, and the struggle between costs and profits in which dollars are, basically, only counters for keeping score. To say, then, that each is motivated by "economics" risks obscuring the nature of the conflict that may exist between them.

With this vital cautionary note in mind, it is useful to discuss the major types of interests that bring groups into the political arena.

Economic Interests

A fundamental concern of large numbers of pressure groups is, simply, material gain. Since the founding of the Republic, government has been a rich source of subsidies, contracts, and financial advantage. During the early 1800s, for example, many state governments allowed private corporations to operate turnpikes, toll bridges, and ferries, thus assuring speculators a chance to fleece farmers and merchants who needed to move their goods on these "public"

22

thoroughfares. Under Alexander Hamilton, as
the first Secretary of the Treasury, bankers
and businessmen who held government bonds were
guaranteed they would receive principle and interest on their investment. During the mid-
nineteenth century, railroad companies were the
recipients of enormous grants of land and money
from federal, state, and local governments amounting to a virtual guarantee of rich profits to
stock and bond holders. More recently, farmers
have received direct agricultural subsidies,
contractors and suppliers have benefited from
federal and state road and airport building projects, universities from direct grants, and even
some minority groups from economic development
assistance.[13] Defense research and development
and space probes have had the effect of creating
major industries largely dependent on government
contracts. Similarly, a little heralded but
significant industry of consultants has come
into being to conduct surveys, make evaluations,
and recommend program innovations for federal,
state and local government agencies.

        And there are many affected indirectly.
Some of these are the small businessmen who benefit from nearby government installations, land-
owners whose property increases in value as a
result of public works projects, store owners
helped by convenient municipal parking lots,
hotel and restaurant proprietors whose profits
increase when a new sports arena is built under
government sponsorship.

        The list could be expanded without ex-
hausting the realities. Equally as significant,
as governments become increasingly involved in
efforts to provide for the health and safety
of the public, each new program almost inevitably
affects an economic interest, and often several
such interests. The effort to reduce air pollution generated by automobiles has been opposed
by car manufacturers and has led to increased
gasoline consumption at a time when petroleum

is more precious. Car owners, producers, and
oil interests thus were affected by government
requirements aimed at a pressing national problem.

In short, "economic" interests appear
in virtually every operation of government. Because people--whether businessmen, laborers,
consumers, or taxpayers--can readily see the
material effects of changes in government policy,
it is rare indeed for a governmental action not
to evoke economically oriented pressure groups
on one side or another of an issue.

Social Interests

Although economics is the most powerful
motivating force in pressure group politics, at
least in the sheer number of groups, social values
also produce a wide range of group activity.
Social values are those which touch on a person's,
or group's, sense of community, relations with
other people, valued "objects" such as home,
place of residence, or social position, and sense
of self-esteem. As seen in the case of the Sommerset Homeowner's Association, social values
were the major interest at work. There was an
economic interest, but equally, or more importantly, there was a concern with preserving "the
quality of the neighborhood." Resistance to
school and housing integration is often based
on social values. Related to such issues, but
of a different order, are the struggles over
strongly held beliefs on social issues such as
birth control, sex education, and legalized
abortion. All precipitate powerful reactions,
and the groups representing these feelings, such
as churches, women's liberation groups, and
parent-teacher associations, are fighting for
what they feel to be significant social values.

As with the expanding role of government
in the economy, governmental programs which

24

touch on social value systems have had the effect of enlarging the range of involvement of socially-oriented groups. Urban planning, family planning for the poor, court decisions on abortion, anti-discrimination laws in housing, schools, and public facilities, and aid to private schools among other government actions, have been sought and opposed by socially-oriented groups.

Ideological Interests

Although only a thin line separates social interests from ideological interests, the line is an important one. Ideological interests are generally directed toward specifically political concerns, that is, the role and processes of government in America.[14]

Ideologically oriented groups generally have a reformist bent. Some, such as various right wing organizations, hope to redirect American political processes away from the welfare state to a return to rugged individualism; others, such as the "Old Left" and the "New Left" hope to move the country toward socialist or more radical approaches to government.[15] A number, however, are less concerned with some utopian vision of society than the desire to "open the system" and to encourage widespread citizen involvement and interest. The list includes groups such as the League of Women Voters and Common Cause.

Environmentalist organizations and consumer groups would also be included among ideological pressure groups. Although the latter tend to focus on matters of economic concern, their interest is not material gain for themselves but to establish standards of fair pricing, fair advertising, and product safety as a means of protecting "the average buyer" from the confusing and occasionally buccaneering practices of modern

marketing techniques. Both environmentalists
and consumer organizations try to pressure governments into a more positive role in protecting
the public from what is viewed as "exploitation,"
in the one case of the natural environment, in
the other of the buying public.

As logical as it may seem to classify
groups by their interests, it must be noted that
a pressure group is a human institution, bringing
together individual wants and purposes which,
in the mind of the person involved, often are
not so clearly defined as they may first appear
to the outside observer. A business group, whose
interest seems obviously material gain, upon
examination could be pursuing a mixture of interests, economic, ideological, and even social.
Its members may be concerned with their profit-
loss statements, but they possibly are struggling
to preserve their vision of the "free enterprise
system" from the encroachments of "creeping
socialism." To assume their evocation of these
ideological values is merely public relations
risks overlooking a powerful motivating force
for some or all of the members of the group.

Interests and Public Policies

Although it is possible to categorize
groups broadly on the basis of their interests--
economic, social, or ideological--the activities
of pressure groups also touch on and are related
to specific types of public policies. An economic
group may, for example, seek direct subsidies
for its members, as does the domestic maritime
industry, or it may attempt to persuade government to use its powers to shift benefits from
one group to another, as in public employment
programs which tax one segment of the population
to provide jobs for the unemployed.

Theodore Lowi has suggested one useful
means of classifying public policies.[16] The

four major types, by Lowi's scheme, are: distributive, redistributive, regulatory, and constituent
policies. Distributive policies are those which
provide direct (and usually economic) benefits
to a group. Government subsidies, whether to
farmers, corporations, cities, school districts,
or hospitals, are the most common examples. Tax
policies can have the same effect, however. Many
states provide new or expanding industries with
tax reductions, and the federal government uses
tax credits to industry in an effort to stimulate
the economy.

Redistributive policies, as their name
suggests, shift benefits from one group to
another, or from one segment of the population
to another. Public housing, free or low-cost
medical care, aid to schools with a large proportion of disadvantaged children, and unemployment
compensation are all redistributive policies.
While the examples just given are ones in which
the direction of redistribution is from the more
affluent to the less, the reverse can occur as
well. A regressive tax (one that proportionately
taxes the poor more than the well-to-do) is a
form of "reverse redistribution." The sales
tax, property tax, and many state income tax
schedules have this effect.[17]

Regulatory policies are designed to control behavior. Frequently they are attempts
to prevent behaviors that are considered to be
economically or socially dangerous. Anti-trust
laws, "blue sky" laws (which forbid the false
advertising of corporate stocks), anti-
pornography regulations, speed limits, bans
on public nudity or drunkenness, and occupational
safety laws are all examples of regulatory policies. Some regulatory policies may actually
be aimed at protecting what is considered to
be an important interest. Land use zoning, for
instance, can preserve the quality of residential
neighborhoods; laws forbidding child labor came
into being to prevent children from being

27

exploited by industry; the original justification
for regulating the airways was to prevent one
radio station's programs from drowning out another's.

Finally, constituent policies are those
which affect the relation of the citizen to
government. Laws and regulations governing
voting, "sunshine" laws (which require the meetings of government agencies to be open to the
press and public), freedom of information laws
(which provide citizens with access to government
files), reapportionment of electoral districts,
establishment of an "ombudsman" (a person or
agency charged with hearing and investigating
citizen complaints), and "little city halls"
are constitutent policies which by their existence and conduct can shape the opportunity of
the average citizen to influence governmental
behavior.

Table 2 gives some examples of interest
base and policy type, matched with examples of
groups which might pursue a particular policy.
A thoughtful examination of the table suggests
some important conclusions and hypotheses.

First, a group or set of groups need
not limit its interest base or policy concerns
to one category. In the table, for example,
civil rights groups are concerned with open housing and with voting rights. The same would be
true for corporations, in the sense that they
are as concerned with pollution controls as they
are with tax credits.

This multiple policy focus indicates
some of the complexity of modern pressure group
politics. At one point in its history, the
NAACP, as a civil rights group, focussed almost
entirely on voting rights for blacks. Today
it concerns itself with school integration, job
discrimination, public employment programs, and
open housing, as well as voting rights. In

28

TABLE 2

POLICY AND INTEREST: SOME EXAMPLES

Policy Type	Interest Base	Policy Example	Group Example
Distributive	Economic	Tax credits to industry	Corporations
	Ideological	Free abortion clinics	Feminist groups
Redistributive	Economic	Public welfare	Welfare groups
	Social	Open Housing	Civil rights groups
Regulatory	Social	Zoning	Homeowners groups
	Ideological	Pollution control	Environmentalists
Constituents	Ideological	Voting rights	Civil rights groups

short, the term "special interest" group may only rarely be applicable to contemporary groups.

Second, the table suggests that the relationship between pressure group and government is perhaps more intricate, and dynamic, than classic group theory often assumed. Public policies come into being, sometimes through the efforts of pressure groups; once in existence the policies stimulate the organization of new groups. This, at least, was the pattern of welfare policy.[18]

Third, it must be noted that the "boundaries" among the four types of policies are not all that distinct.[19] What could be a distributive policy for one group can be redistributive to another. Government price supports to farmers have a distributive effect for them, but for the taxpayer (whose dollars pay for the supports) and the consumers (who may ultimately pay more for their groceries), the effect is redistributive: their dollars are being transferred to the farmers' pockets. In much the same way, a regulatory policy may actually be distributive or redistributive. The U.S. Civil Aeronautics Board, in "regulating" competition among established airlines, prevented new airlines from coming into being. One result was that the ticket prices paid by passengers were higher than they might have been.[20] Regulation in this case redistributed money from traveller to airline.

We might hypothesize that pressure group conflict and activity is most intense where different types of policy overlap. It seems likely that it is these areas of overlap that the broadest array of interests--and the groups representing them--are touched. An issue such as "coastal zone management" (whether and how the areas adjacent to the open waters are to be controlled by governmental decisions) is partly regulatory (what uses are to be permitted) and

30

partly distributive (who is to benefit from the uses permitted). And as an issue, coastal zone management evokes reactions from ideological and economic interests including environmentalists, business groups alarmed by greater government "intervention," oil companies, fishing and hunting groups, real estate developers, land owners, and state and local officials.

The important point, however, is that public policy viewed in the pressure group context takes on a more complex character. A "simple" matter of setting aside certain areas for movie theaters showing X-rated movies, for example, can turn out to be extraordinarily complicated in the face of aroused economic, social, and ideological interests.

Public policies, then, are one of the important bases of pressure group politics. A policy proposal may be the triggering mechanism that converts interest group into pressure group; a group may feel it is impelled to become active politically to protect some distributive, redistributive, or regulatory policy it feels is especially beneficial to it; or a group may seek changes in constituent policies because it believes it is being left out of the decision-making processes of government. In each instance, it is the interaction between policy and interest which establishes the relationship of the group to the political system.

Geographic Bases

For some pressure groups there is another dimension to their interests, that is, a sense of jurisdiction or geographic area of concern. As in the case of the Sommerset Homeowner's Association, the group's interest is defined by a specific area, a kind of "turf" that the group feels it must defend.

31

Particularly in state and local politics, this sense of territoriality affects the degree to which a group will feel impelled to engage in pressure activities. One neighborhood may stand by indifferently while another is gutted by a major highway project. One part of a city may fight fiercely to protect its historic buildings without being concerned with demolitions occurring elsewhere.

Even economically oriented groups are frequently based on specific geographic areas, such as a downtown businessman's association, suburban shopping center retailers, and associations of merchants or professionals centered on one street or avenue, such as the Fifth Avenue Association of New York City. Formal governmental jurisdictions provide the simplest and perhaps most common geographic bases: cities, towns, counties, and even states. Thus there will be a city (or county) real estate association, Young Men's Business Club, Chamber of Commerce, and Chapter of the Sierra Club or of the Audubon Society. At the state level there will be the medical society, the bar association, the state chapter of the American Institute of Architects, the state council of the AFL-CIO, and the state chapter of the NAACP among others. Many of the "state-wide" organizations will, of course, also have local branches.[21]

One importance of the geographic base of pressure groups lies in the way it defines and limits interests, leading many interest groups to remain quiescent until they feel their "territory" is threatened.

The geographic base of groups has another important dimension, however. The American political system is itself largely geographically organized: the states, cities, counties, and electoral districts within them are the physical power bases of most elective officials and are

often the units with which public administrators
must work in carrying out policies. As Grant
McConnell has pointed out, "the political geography" of the American federal system affects the
power of pressure groups and their chances to
have their interests reflected in policy decisions.[22] A numerically small group can wield
a disproportionate influence if its membership
is concentrated in key geographic areas. As
a simple example, were black Americans spread
uniformly throughout the area of the nation,
their 12 percent of the total population would
have little impact. Concentrated in certain
key cities and states, blacks are able not only
to elect legislators and executives but to make
demands through their group leaders, demands
which at least some policy-makers feel they must
respond to. Farmers have long enjoyed a similar
advantage, as have unions in "blue collar" cities
and suburbs.

        The federal system in combination with
group interests and the geographic distribution
of group members also affects the policy process.
Much so-called "pork barrel," the distribution
of public works projects, by the U.S. Congress
and state legislatures is a response to geographically based groups seeking the material benefits
of public construction and installations. In
recent years, the distribution, redistribution,
and regulation of energy resources among various
sections of the country has become a focus of
intense struggle among economic and ideological
interests. Political geography is, then, another
influence which shapes the base of interests
and the outcome of struggles over policy decisions.

                Politics and Interests

        The pressure group can accordingly be
viewed as an important alternative to the political

                        33

party as a way of participating in politics.
The alternatives are not mutually exclusive,
of course. As we have seen, most Americans
choose not to be members of pressure groups but
to participate as voters.

The pressure group does, however, act
as a significant political vehicle for those
who feel some important interest is being affected and who feel the need for collective
action to protect or advance that interest. But
the relationships among pressure group, participation, and public policy is not a simple one.
The "bases" of group politics is a complex interaction between interests, policy, and geographic base. Illustration one outlines the
pattern of interaction in a somewhat simplified
form.

Stated in summary, interest and political
geography are closely interwoven, as are public
policies and geographic bases. In turn, public
policy is both influenced by and influences a
group and its interests: what a group seeks
and whether for that matter it is involved in
politics at all is affected by what policies
governments pursue or fail to pursue.

This basic interaction "model" is a fundamental of group politics. It helps to explain
the origins of groups, the form they take, the
power that groups wield, and even the strategies
that they follow when the enter the political
arena.

ILLUSTRATION ONE

BASES OF GROUP POLITICS

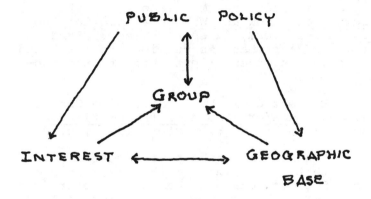

35

References for Chapter II

[1]There are a number of useful works on
political participation. One of the most valuable is Sidney Verba and Norman H. Nie, Participation in America: Democracy and Social Equality
(New York: Harper and Row, 1972). See also
Roger Cobb and Charles D. Elder, Participation
in American Politics: The Dynamics of Agenda-
Building (Boston: Allyn and Bacon, 1972).
Lester W. Milbraith and M. L. Goel, Political
Participation: How and Why Do People Get Involved in Politics?, 2d ed. (Chicago: Rand
McNally, 1977) summarizes previous research and
analysis and is an excellent guide to the sub-
ject.

[2]Everett Carll Ladd, Jr., with Charles
D. Hadley, Transformations of the American Party
System (New York: W. W. Norton, 1975), p. 259.

[3]A number of works have concerned themselves with the "decline" of the American party
system. See, for example, David S. Broder, The
Party's Over: The Failure of Politics in America
(New York: Harper and Row, 1971) and Walter
Dean Burnham, Critical Elections and the Mainsprings of American Politics (New York: W. W.
Norton, 1970). Ladd and Hadley also come to
a cautiously pessimistic conclusion, at least
as far as seeing the "old system" continue.

[4]Norman H. Nie,Sidney Verba, and John
R. Petrocik, The Changing American Voter (Cambridge, Mass.: The Harvard University Press,
1976), Chapter 4.

[5]Gabriel Almond and G. Bingham Powell,
Comparative Government: A Developmental Approach
(Boston: Little, Brown, 1966) coin the phrases
"interest aggregator" and "interest articulator"

36

to apply to parties and pressure groups respectively (pp. 75 and 102).

[6]Verba and Nie, p. 105.

[7]James Q. Wilson, Political Organization (New York: Basic Books, 1973) has noted that the precise origins of organized interests is obscure (pp. 195-97). The process may not necessarily be as logical and rational as outlined here.

[8]David B. Truman, The Governmental Process: Political Interests and Public Opinion (New York: Alfred A. Knopf, 1951), pp. 53-54.

[9]Political scientists will frequently refer to "interest groups" knowing that in context it will be understood they mean pressure groups.

[10]V. O. Key, Jr., Politics, Parties, and Pressure Groups, 5th ed. (New York: Thomas Y. Crowell, 1964), pp. 76-77.

[11]Grant McConnell, Private Power and American Democracy (New York: Alfred A. Knopf, 1966), p. 39. Wilson has commented, "A threat is a more powerful incentive for organization than an opportunity" (p. 148). Note the behavior of the residents of Sommerset.

[12]There is a rich literature on ways of defining interests. A useful guide is Constance Smith and Ann Freedman, Voluntary Associations: Perspectives on the Literature (Cambridge, Mass.: Harvard University Press, 1972), Chapter 1. See also Robert H. Salisbury, "An Exchange Theory of Interest Groups," in Interest Group Politics in America, ed. Robert H. Salisbury (New York: Harper and Row, 1970), pp. 32-67; Almond and Powell, pp. 75-78; John Guinther, Moralists and Managers: Public Interest Movements in America (New York: Doubleday, 1976). Among the various

ways of classifying groups or their interests
are: broad category of interest (as done here);
membership base (women, blacks, doctors, consumers); behavior (protest, terrorist, moderate);
broad goals (reformist, reactionary, system-
supportive); and benefits allocated to members
(direct individual benefits, group benefits,
intangible rewards). Each method of classification has its values and uses. An ideal system
would no doubt take into account all these factors (and perhaps others) but thus far the complexities of interests, groups, and pressure
group behaviors have defied precise systems of
categorization.

[13]McConnell, Chapters 7, 8, and 9 discusses some of these groups and their interests.

[14]The term "ideological" is used more
broadly here than to refer to a logically consistent and holistic view of the political order
and political values.

[15]See Geroge Thayer, The Farther Shores
of Politics, 2d ed. (New York: Simon and Schuster,
1968) for a discussion of both right- and left-
wing groups. Andrew S. McFarland, Public Interest Lobbies (Washington, D.C.: American
Enterprise Institute, 1976) discusses some consumer and environmental organizations, such as
the Nader organizations and the Sierra Club.
He also examines Common Cause and the League
of Women Voters.

[16]Theodore Lowi, "American Business,
Public Policy, Case Studies, and Political
Theory," World Politics 16 (July 1964): 677-
715. Lowi added constituent policies to his
scheme in "Four Systems of Policy, Politics,
and Choice," Public Administration Reveiw 32
(July/August 1972), pp. 298-310.

[17]Gerhard Lenski, Power and Privilege
(New York: McGraw-Hill, 1966), p. 311.

[18]Wilson, pp. 64-68, describes the rise of the National Welfare Rights Organization in response to an already existing policy. S. J. Makielski, Jr., Beleaguered Minorities: Cultural Politics in America (San Francisco: W. H. Freeman, 1973) discusses this pattern in relation to minority groups.

[19]Mark V. Nadel, "The Hidden Dimension of Public Policy," Journal of Politics 37 (February 1975): 2-34.

[20]AP Wire Dispatch, 5 March 1977. The U.S. General Accounting Office estimated that passengers could have saved between $1.4 billion and $1.8 billion a year during 1969-1974 had the CAB allowed greater competition.

[21]Chapter III discusses organization in greater detail.

[22]McConnell, pp. 105-6.

CHAPTER III

ORGANIZATION AND DYNAMICS

Characteristically, pressure groups become highly organized, with specialized roles
through which members carry out the group's goals.
Organizational form is often a response to the
environment the group must work in and its membership base. In turn, organization as a process
creates certain dynamics within the group, some
of which may be stressful.

Group Membership

To become a "member" of one of the major
political parties, all a person has to do is
to think of himself as a Republican or Democrat.
In many states, of course, it is possible to
register under a party label, but there is no
other requirement for membership. One important
characteristic that sets the pressure group apart
from the political parties is that virtually
all pressure groups have established membership
criteria that must be met in order to formally
belong to the group.[1] These membership criteria
in effect set members apart from non-members
and, depending on how rigorous the requirements
are, insure some degree of homogeneity in the
interests brought under the group's rubric.

For many groups the membership criteria
may be no more than a willingness to pay dues.
Some may require dues and the signing of a statement of agreement with the broad purposes and
goals of the group. Other groups, especially
professional and business groups, will require
that the prospective member be licensed in the

profession or actively engaged in business. A
layman, for example, would not be admitted to
membership in the American Medical Association,
or a college professor to the downtown retail
merchant's association.[2]

While relatively few pressure groups
have the kind of rigorous membership criteria
of, for example, the Daughters of the American
Revolution which requires a prospective member
to document descent from an active participant
in the American Revolution or of the several
Ku Klux Klans which for all practical purposes
require members to be Protestants of Anglo-Saxon
descent, most do demand formal application, dues,
and often sponsorship by someone who is already
a member.

Effects of Membership Criteria

Two effects flow from membership criteria.
One is that the group is insured that an active
interest is present in the member. He or she
has had to overcome an obstacle to become a member and cares enough about the group's interests
to be willing to make a sacrifice of time and
money to gain membership.[3] Thus, the mildly
concerned are separated from the actively interested. From a political standpoint, the
group's leadership can feel that it speaks for
people who genuinely share the attitudes of the
group and who intend to act on the basis of
that interest.

A second and related result of membership criteria is the creation of a definable
"power base" for the pressure group. The membership rolls provide a clear statement of who the
members are. In American politics, where it
is rarely certain what "the people" think on
any given issue, the pressure group spokesman
can claim that he at least does speak for an

organized, active, and identifiable constituency.[4]

The underlying assumption of membership
criteria is that they separate the true activists
from the "mass public." On the face, this assumption would seem to be a safe generalization,
but there is surprisingly little hard data to
test the generalization. There is, in fact,
some reason to believe that not all the members
of a particular pressure group are as strongly
motivated as membership in the group might lead
the observer to believe.[5]

A psychological "map" of reasons for
group membership would include a wide variety
of influences. For example, a qualified young
woman might join the Daughters of the American
Revolution because of a strong desire to preserve
the nation's heritage. In this case, her interest and sympathy with the group's goals are
the impelling forces toward membership. She
might, however, only in a very vague way share
these attitudes, but seek membership because
one or more of her friends are also members and
persuade her to join. In this situation, other
factors are playing a major, and perhaps the
crucial, motivating role. Finally, she may have
no interest whatsoever in the stated goals of
the group but be convinced that it is socially
useful to her to belong to such a high status
organization. Here other factors play the over-
whelming role in producing membership.[6]

Although pressure group spokesmen would
prefer that public officials and the general
public believe that all group members are dedicated, alert, and aggressive activists, even
a superficial acquaintanceship with most pressure groups would indicate that this is rarely
so. But, if a person does go to the trouble
to hurdle the barriers of membership criteria,
why should commitment to the group be so qualified?

43

One reason has already been offered: membership does not necessarily come as a product of shared attitudes. Two other explanations can be suggested. First, many people who belong to one group belong to more than one group, that is, they are "joiners." A young woman may belong to the D.A.R., the Junior League, the League of Women's Voters, and her church social. She may also work part- or full-time or have a family to raise. In her circumstances, there is simply a limit to her time and physical and emotional energies. Whatever her <u>attitudes,</u> her interest, she simply may be unable to express them in steady activist <u>behavior.</u> And,available data do show that those who join one group are apt to be members of more than one.[7]

Second, some group theorists have argued that "cross-pressuring" dilutes individual commitment to a group.[8] A Roman Catholic woman concerned with women's liberation can be caught in a cross-pressured situation since many feminist groups are strong advocates of legalized abortion; the Catholic church is a strong opponent. Cross-pressuring, in short, occurs when, in the same individual, two strongly felt attitudes are in conflict. "Classic" group theorists argued that in such situations the cross-pressured person is faced with an insoluble dilemma and hence is reduced to passivity.

As theoretically persuasive as the concept of cross-pressures is, it has been argued in response that it is an unlikely phenomenon in group politics. People tend to join groups that are psychologically compatible.[9] Thus, the Catholic woman mentioned above would seek out a feminist organization that shared her views of abortion; a member of the American Legion would not join a peace group; a man who belonged to the Ku Klux Klan would certainly not join the NAACP.

44

It seems probable that where cross-pressuring occurs, it manifests itself prior to active group membership, that is, at the attitudinal level. As such, cross-pressures probably do inhibit some Americans from acting on their interests by joining a group representing one or another of those interests. Cross-pressuring may also come into play when a group widens or changes its goals. A union, originally concerned with better working conditions for employees, that opposed the war in Viet Nam risked alienating those members who belonged to veteran's organizations.

The contemporary view of cross-pressures is, however, that it is substantially less significant than earlier theorists held. Nonetheless it exists as a potential, especially for groups which are expanding their concerns beyond the original interest or geographic base.

Varieties of Membership

The cumulative impact of various motives for group membership, of other demands on an individual's time, and of cross-pressuring is to produce various levels of commitment to the group itself within the membership. If to these factors is added the individual variation in how strongly a person feels about an issue or an interest over time, the "profile" of group membership no longer appears as one of equally dedicated and strongly motivated activists. Illustration two suggests the pattern of membership roles produced by these variations in a typical group. In the center is the "activist cadre," those who are most deeply committed to the group's interests and who will generally do most of the group's work: sitting on committees, holding office, doing the housekeeping chores and often acting as the recruiters and spokesmen for the group. Closely tied to the

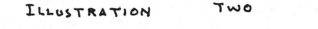

ILLUSTRATION TWO

STRUCTURE OF GROUP MEMBERSHIP

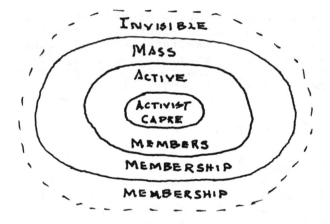

INVISIBLE
MASS
ACTIVE
ACTIVIST
CADRE
MEMBERS
MEMBERSHIP
MEMBERSHIP

activist cadre are the active members: people
who also are deeply committed to the group's
interest, but who for reasons ranging from other
commitments to the recency of their membership
are not part of the core cadre. They are a pool
of activists, however, who in times of crisis
or involvement in major issues will provide essential manpower and political support.

At the outer fringes are the "mass members," those who belong to the group but whose
commitment is less deep for all the reasons already mentioned. The membership dues and their
presence on the group's roster are political
resources, but it is probable that they can be
energized only at times when the group faces
the most burning issues and, even then, some
may remain inactive.

The lines between these three main types
of member roles are often blurred, and a group
member can float from one category to another
depending on what the group itself is doing and
the attitudes and commitments of the individual
member. Further, the proportion of each type
per group seems to vary, although the activist
cadre is almost always a small, even a tiny,
percentage of the total membership.

There is a fourth type of "member,"
those who are not formal members but who share
the interests and goals of the group, and either
fail to or are prevented by circumstances from
actually joining the group. Called "fellow
travellers" by Truman,[10] they can perhaps more
accurately be thought of as "invisible members."[11]
Although not members of the group, they are "a
potential pool of new members, a possible source
of public support in times of stress and
crisis. . . . "[12] For many pressure groups,
the invisible membership is a vital political
resource, increasing the formal membership of
the group substantially in realistic political
terms. Many intellectuals, for example, are

47

strong supporters of the union movement; many
non-doctors will rally around the American
Medical Association to prevent governmental intervention in the medical professions; large
numbers of whites contribute money, moral, and
political support to civil rights organizations.

The fourfold category of pressure group
membership highlights an important paradox in
the political base of modern pressure groups.
On the one hand, their formal membership is
rarely as homogeneous and cohesive as either
group propaganda or casual observation indicates.
On the other, many if not all pressure groups
have a broader base to draw upon in their invisible membership than the formal membership
indicates. Obviously, the principle problem
with an invisible membership is that it is an
unknown quantity: it may or may not make its
support felt during a political struggle. Thus,
no matter how inert the formal mass membership
of a group is, it amounts to a better known
quantity in the political equation and thus a
more reliable one.

Formal Organization

It would be an unusual pressure group
indeed that remained simply an undifferentiated
group of people intereacting more or less at
random. Like most other groups, pressure groups
develop and formally establish roles, tasks,
and specialization among their members.

Micro-Organization

At the micro-level, this organizational
pattern consists of selecting officers, creating
committees, and to the extent the group can
afford it, hiring a permanent staff. In effect,

the group creates an apparatus that gives it
continuity, direction, and a research and analysis capability. A downtown retail businessman's
association, for example, regularly chose a
president, a president-elect (to succeed the
president the next year), and a treasurer. In
addition it had a committee on rules and by-
laws, whose primary task was to determine membership criteria; a committee on finance concerned
with land use and parking regulations in the
central business district; and a committee on
education concerned with public relations. In
turn the three officers plus the committee chairmen made up the executive committee which met
at a minimum of twice a month to coordinate committee activities, write agendas for both the
committees and general meetings, and, in fact
to determine what the organization was to do
and when. These seven men were an inner circle
within the activist cadre of the organization,
some of whom gave as many as twenty hours a week
to the work of the group.[13]

The group also had rented office space,
a full-time executive director and a full-time
secretary. A lawyer acted as counsel to the
group, having been chosen by the committee on
rules and by-laws. The executive director
served as secretary to meetings of the committees
and the group as a whole, did research, prepared
draft reports, maintained the group's files and
records, and carried on most correspondence.

The formal organization of this association is fairly typical. Many pressure groups
do not have the funds for a full-time or a part-
time staff; often these chores are done on a
volunteer basis by the officers. Others will
have staffs as large as small corporations. Many
have complex committee systems, including not
only permanent or "standing" committees but "ad
hoc" special committees set up to perform one
task and then dissolve. Increasingly today large

49

pressure groups will have specialized "political
action committees" modelled after the labor union
practice which are especially concerned with
political strategies and tactics, including influencing elections, contacts with elected and
appointed public officials, and maintaining
records on voting behaviors and the political
strengths and weaknesses of legislators, judges,
and executives. Public relations has been and
continues to be a major concern conducted either
by an internal committee and staff or contracted
out to a professional consultant firm.

These organizational arrangements are
a means by which the group's activities can be
efficiently directed to fulfilling the group's
goals. In effect, activist members become experts in the subject matter of their committees;
staff support, where it exists, frees group
members for making decisions rather than doing
research and writing, and because there is a
relatively small number of people involved out
of the total membership activities can be coor-
dinated and directed by the leaders.

In these respects, organization carries
a group to a higher level of complexity and purpose. The group is no longer simply people interacting in formal, established, and purposeful
ways.[14]

Organization has its hazards, of course,
not the least being the threat of over-
bureaucratization. Too many committees, too
many officers, too many rules and procedures
lead to delays, multiple veto-points, and constant coordination problems.

The micro-organization of a pressure
group usually reflects fairly accurately its
interest base. Its committee system generally
parcels out those tasks the group has determined
to be the long-standing and most pressing issues.
The creation of ad hoc committees or "task

forces" usually shows that new interests or issues are emerging which previous structures are poorly designed to meet.

All formal organizational schemes are modified by "informal organization," that is, a pattern of roles and interactions that by-pass the paper organization.[15] Informal organization comes into being partly because of personal likes and dislikes: this person finds he can "work well" with someone but cannot with someone else. In some cases, informal organization comes into being to overcome the delays and problems inherent in a heavily bureaucratized organization. In other cases, informal organization may be a product of power struggles: one faction attempting to gain control over the crucial decisions of the organization against the resistance of another.

In the case of the downtown retailer's association discussed above, for example, an embryonic informal organization was building to by-pass the finance committee chairman. Some of the executive board distrusted him, believing him to have personal political ambitions and to be a "publicity hog." Two of his committee members chafed at his slowness in calling committee meetings to discuss pending tax legislation before the state legislature. It was generally acknowledged that both these committee members aspired to the committee chairmanship and thus admission to inner circle of the executive committee. In response to these urges, the chairman of both the development committee and the education committee worked to have committee tasks assigned to their committees rather than finance, in the apparent hope that the finance committee chairman would eventually step aside in disgust. Whether this tactic worked or not, it still meant that the pressing business of the organization was handled by the more aggressive committees.

A second factor influences the formal micro-organization of a pressure group: the need to accommodate power and factional divisions. The advantage of a multiplicity of committees is that various shades of attitudes toward the basic group interest can be represented through the committee system without precipitating struggles for dominance within the organization as a whole. Where the interest and geographic base of the group is fairly homogeneous, the group leadership can comfortably manage with a tight, neat, and small formal structure. In those cases where a group is attempting to encompass a broad span of attitudes and even several interests, greater organizational complexity results. Power struggles still occur, but they are at least partially confined to the various committees and each committee or officer acts as a check on the others.

There is a third factor at work in influencing group organization. The complexity of public policy discussed in Chapter II forces some degree of specialization on active pressure groups. Even homeowners groups, which typically are fairly small and compact, often find that to "protect" their neighborhoods they need committees or individuals who concentrate on a wide variety of topics, such as taxation, land use regulations, streets and highways, parks and recreation, schools, and newer programs like historic preservation and federally sponsored community development policies. All are policies which potentially redistribute or regulate activities which can touch the group's geographic interest base. In brief, organizational decisions do not occur in a vacuum; the interaction of policy, group, and interest imposes formal or informal structures on the group.

It is possible to say, then, that the micro-organization of a pressure group is in part a reflection of internal power balances, and in part a response to public policy. But,

it must be constantly kept in mind that formal
organization is modified by the realities of
informal organization.

Macro-Organization

And, pressure group organization is also
complicated by the federal system. The "macro-
organization" of a pressure group, that is, its
overall form, is a product of the geographic
bases of so many group interests, reinforced
by the geographic base of the American governmental system. Some groups are "unitary"; others
are some combination of these.[16]

Illustration 3 gives the basic structural
outlines of the major types of macro-organization.
The structures are based on the relationship of
the members to the overall organization. In
the unitary type, members as individuals are
the basic components of the group. No inter-
mediary organizations stand between individual
and the group as a whole. This is the common
pattern of most local pressure groups.

In the federation, the group as a whole
is made up of subsidiary groups each of which
in turn is a unitary group. The national AFL-
CIO is a federation, for example, composed of
the unions which belong to that body. It is
not possible to be a member of the AFL-CIO without belonging to one of the unions affiliated
with national organization.

Other groups in effect combine the unitary and federated patterns in a chapters-members
system. A person can belong to the state or
national organization directly and, simultaneously,
belong to state or local chapters of the same
organization. This is a pattern common to certain professional organizations, such as the

ILLUSTRATION   THREE

FORMS   OF   GROUP ORGANIZATION

(1)
UNITARY

(2)
FEDERATION

(3)
CHAPTERS - MEMBERS

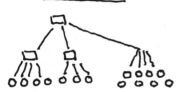

(4)
TRADE ASSOCIATION

KEY:

☐ = ORGANIZATION

O = INDIVIDUALS

American Institute of Architects which also has
state and local chapters. The Audubon Society
and the Sierra Club also have state and local
chapters. In general, however, one cannot belong
to a chapter without first having membership
in the national organization.

The trade association is separated from
other types of pressure group organizations in
that individuals are not members but organiz-
tions are, and unlike the federation which is
an organization of organizations but ultimately
resting on individual members, at no point in
the structure does the trade association have
individual members. As its name suggests, the
trade association is almost always made up of
business firms engaged in like activities, such
as oil production, steel manufacture, or coal
mining.[17] Some trade associations, however,
do not limit themselves to one industry, such
as the National Association of Manufacturers,
but nonetheless conform to the trade association
membership pattern.

Why does one pressure group follow a
certain pattern of macro-organization and another
a different pattern? There seem to be no adequate answers. The best explanation is, apparently, that organizational patterns are rooted
in the individual histories of each group, the
product of early leadership decisions as to whom
the group could most effectively draw into its
ranks, and, as membership grew or remained stable
how best to structure that membership effectively.
Many chapters-members groups seem to have grown
out of what were originally unitary groups. As
the membership in particular geographic areas
expanded, more localized issues appeared, encouraging these members to want an organization
near at hand but still associated with the larger
entity. The result, logically, was the charter-
ing of chapters. The Sierra Club has followed
this pattern. However, the American Farm Bureau
Federation grew out of a reverse process: the

emergence of local groups which ultimately coalesced into a national organization.[18]

The variations on the organizational theme are so numerous that no blanket explanation will cover all cases. It can safely be said, however, that the geographic base of most interests interacting with a federal system that is also geographically based has contributed to, if not caused, the complex structure of American pressure groups.

Like the loose structure of the American political party, the macro-organization of pressure groups operating at the state or national level is a form of accommodation to the diversity of attitudes which can exist even under the rubric of a common "interest." This diversity is perhaps best illustrated by a case study.[19]

<u>The Metropolitan Real Estate
Boards Association</u>

New York City is unique among other American cities in that the municipality contains five counties within it.[20] Although the counties of New York, Kings, Bronx, Queens, and Richmond today have at best limited governmental functions they do serve as geographic bases for a number of business and professional associations. Among these are the county real estate boards, themselves unitary organizations acting as spokesmen for their members before the city and state governments.

In 1937, the five boards from the counties came together to create the Metropolitan Real Estate Boards Association, the purpose of which was to be a political action arm for the real estate interests. The presidents and executive secretaries of each of the county boards made up the membership of the association. It never

hired a staff and rotated the chairmanship among
the county presidents on an annual basis.

Over the next twenty years the Association was able to act effectively as a spokesman
for its constitutent members on a number of
issues, especially those concerning land use
and building regulations which might increase
operating costs of both developers and landlords.
There were, however, basic tensions within the
organization. In the first instance, the membership of the New York Real Estate Board out-
numbered the total membership of all the four
other boards combined. Further, despite a shared
attitude of resistance to zoning and other laws
that might hamper real estate development, the
New York members took a more compliant attitude
toward changes in those laws, in part because
as larger businesses they had the legal and
technical capability to cope with the complexities of the new laws. The sheer size (3000
members) and strategic location of the board
in speaking for the heart of the city also gave
the New York members an advantage over the other
members of the Association.

Two results flowed out these differences
between the New York board and the others. One,
the New York board was able to and did bargain
more successfully with government decision-makers.
Second, there was a tendency for the New York
board to grow restive under the positions taken
by the Metropolitan Real Estate Boards Association which, because of the composition of the
organization, tended to defend the interests
of the other four counties.

Although an overt split was avoided in
the period from the founding of the Association
to 1960, two or three times serious difficulties
emerged. Then in 1960 a new zoning law was proposed, one much more stringent than any previously offered. The chairman of the City Planning
Commission was himself a successful realtor and

a member of the New York county real estate community. He was, thus, sensitive to the nuances
and diversities within the city's real estate
interests.

In the ensuing struggle, the Planning
Commission chairman was able to play on the
natural divisions that already existed by offer-
ing concessions to the New York Board while
virtually freezing out the more hostile other
boards. Although the Metropolitan Real Estate
Boards Association struggled manfully to maintain a solid front, ultimately the New York
board broke with the Association, without advance
warning, thus leaving the realtors' campaign
against the new zoning law in a shambles, the
real estate community speaking with divided
voices, and the Association without its largest
and most influential constituent organization.

In this case, "shared attitudes" and
even common goals had been brought under one
organizational heading, but the organization
itself was unable to compensate for the shadings
of difference that may exist within shared attitudes. It is, of course, possible that the
differences built into the Association could
have been reconciled had its opposition not been
so knowledgeable or skillful, but the essential truth remains the same: there are limits
to which formal organization can successfully
respond to the variations in the interest bases
of its component parts. And, it is important
to note again the impact of geographic base on
interests.

Change and Stress

Pressure groups, like most human institutions, rarely remain unchanging. Change generally
stems from the interaction of two forces: change
in the environment and decisions within the group.

58

Often the latter is a response to the environmental change; occasionally, however, a group decision will stimulate changes in the environment.

For a pressure group usually the most crucial changes in the environment are an expansion of governmental activity or the rise of a competing pressure group. The two are often related: the slow but steady rise of the union movement forced businessmen with increasing frequency into either trade associations or other forms of groups in an effort to block the labor movement's effort to have government regulate labor-management practices. In a like manner, when certain trade associations were able to win tax or regulatory advantages, other firms sought to create associations to gain the same benefits.[21] In effect, organization does have a tendency to stimulate organization among other interests and counter-organization among competing interests.

In other instances, however, a pressure group may make "internal decisions," the decision to be more aggressive politically, or to shift its attention from local or state policies to the national scene. The Sierra Club, once a California-based "conservation" group, for example, became a national "environmentalist" group.[22]

In either circumstance, a change in environment or in internal policy, the group involved may find itself forced to enlarge its membership base and to reorder its microorganization. As a group expands the number of its members it typically encounters painful factional problems. The larger the group, the more likely there will be differences in attitude ranges and the intensity with which interests are held among members. These differences may manifest themselves through sub-groups (factions), who will struggle to see their goals become the dominant ones in the group.[23] "Newcomers" may resent the power of the "old-timers" and the power of those in the activist cadre who have taken the leadership positions for themselves. Interaction within the group itself will tend to become increasingly depersonalized, occurring through news letters, mass mailings, and a once-a-year convention rather than on a face-to-face basis. The "national-chapters" form of macro-organization does help to alleviate many of these problems by providing for "local" flexibility and more intimate patterns of interaction.

The problem is, stated succinctly, that the massive pressure group loses some of its effectiveness as an interest articulator and becomes increasingly an interest aggregator. It faces the dilemma of political action in a mass democratic society: large numbers and a large geographic base can be political advantages, but both heighten the probabilities of internal dissensions and factionalism, requiring the group to act more and more as an agency of internal compromise and conflict resolution.[24]

The problems are serious enough that at least one theorist has argued that there is an inherent limit on the size of pressure groups.[25] In effect what seems to be a single pressure group is really a number of pressure groups operating temporarily under one rubric. The logic of the argument is more persuasive than the reality, however. There are simply too many large national organizations that have survived for too long to accept the idea that many pressure groups have yet attained their inherent limits.[26] The point is valid, however, in that for a group to maintain its solid front, to avoid shattering factionalism and even the dissolution of the group, it must find a means of mediating between shadings of attitudes, differing geographic interests, and the risks and benefits of change.

Even given these structural problems, however, organization is a means by which group interests can be converted into successful group pressures. Organization, in short, is a way of operationalizing group attitudes. Organization musters the numbers, skills, and energies of people sharing a common attitude and translates them into direction and action. Each type of macro-organization is a device for accommodating complexity and diversity within a given interest, and the accommodation is carried forward to the micro-organization of the group. Under stress, these arrangements may falter or even fail, but at least as often they provide the essential vehicle through which leadership decisions are made and political power is exerted.

References for Chapter III

[1] Judith G. Smith, ed., Political Brokers: Money, Organizations, Power, and People (New York: Liveright, 1972) has an excellent collection of essays on various pressure groups and their membership criteria.

[2] Some groups will give "honorary memberships" to persons who have performed services for the group.

[3] There are major exceptions to this generalization. In "closed shop" situations, a person must be a union member to gain employment, regardless of one's feelings about the goals of the union movement.

[4] Grant McConnell, Private Power and American Democracy (New York: Alfred A. Knopf, 1966), pp. 104-7 notes the importance of an identifiable constituency as a power resource. See also Sidney Verba and Norman H. Nie, Participation in America: Political Democracy and Social Equality (New York: Harper and Row, 1972), Chapter 2.

[5] S. J. Makielski, Jr., The Politics of Zoning: The New York Experience (New York: Columbia University Press, 1965), p. 154.

[6] James Q. Wilson, Political Organizations (New York: Basic Books, 1973), pp. 33-34 points out that members can be committed to a pressure group for any number of reasons, ranging from the direct, concrete benefits they hope to receive, to the pleasures of associating with others, to a sense of being engaged in a worthwhile cause. See also Lester W. Milbraith and M. L. Goel, Political Participation: How and Why Do People Get Involved in Politics?, 2d ed. (Chicago: Rand McNally, 1977), p. 8.

62

[7]Louis S. Loeb and Daniel M. Berman, American Politics: Crisis and Challenge (New York: Macmillan, 1975), p. 92. V. O. Key, Jr., Politics, Parties, and Pressure Groups, 5th ed. (New York: Thomas Y. Crowell, 1964), p. 502. National surveys have indicated the higher a person's socio-economic-status the more likely he is to belong to more than one group. Charles R. Wright and Herbert H. Hyman "Voluntary Association Memberships of Adult Americans: Evidence from National Surveys," in American Political Interest Groups: Readings in Theory and Research, ed. Betty Zisk (Belmont, Calif.: Wadsworth Publishing Co., 1969), p. 307.

[8]David B. Truman, The Governmental Process: Political Interests and Public Opinion (New York: Alfred A. Knopf, 1951), p. 157.

[9]Stanley Rothman, "Systematic Political Theory: Observations on the Group Approach," in Readings in Political Parties and Pressure Groups, eds. Frank Munger and Douglas Price (New York: Thomas Y. Crowell, 1964), pp. 72-91.

[10]Truman, p. 114.

[11]S. J. Makielski, Jr., Beleaguered Minorities: Cultural Politics in America (San Francisco: W. H. Freeman, 1973), p. 28.

[12]Ibid.

[13]Elected officerships tended to rotate among these seven men. Chapter IV discusses the role of group leaders.

[14]Wilson, p. 13, points out that organizational roles influence the behaviors of people within organizations.

[15]Informal organization has been the subject of a substantial body of research and theory.

63

Daniel Katz and Robert L. Kahn, The Social Psychology of Organizations (New York: John Wiley and Sons, 1966), pp. 350 ff. have a valuable discussion of the importance of informal organization.

[16]Truman, p. 115.

[17]McConnell, p. 58, shows that the great period of growth of trade associations occurred immediately before World War I as a response to public policies aimed at regulating industry.

[18]Key, pp. 26-27; McConnell, pp. 76-77.

[19]Makielski, The Politics of Zoning, pp. 137-41.

[20]Each county is coterminous with a borough, and vestiges of borough government continue to exist.

[21]McConnell, pp. 58-59.

[22]Andrew S. McFarland, Public Interest Lobbies (Washington, D.C.: American Enterprise Institute, 1976), pp. 84-85.

[23]Albert O. Hirschmann, Exit, Voice, and Loyalty (Cambridge, Mass.: Harvard University Press, 1970).

[24]Wilson, p. 275.

[25]Mancur Olson, Jr., The Logic of Collective Action: Public Goods and the Theory of Groups (New York: Schocken Books, 1968).

[26]Wilson, p. 129. See also McFarland, pp. 36-39, who points out that one of the problems with Olson's analysis is an assumption that only direct, material benefits cause people to belong to groups.

CHAPTER IV

LEADERS AND LEADERSHIP

It is generally accepted that almost all pressure groups are dominated by a clique of insiders, made up of the activist cadre. This is the often quoted "iron law of oligarchy" which holds that in a political organization power gravitates into the hands of a few who then use that power to maintain themselves in a position of control.[1] As far as it goes, the iron law of oligarchy does appear to describe a reality, but as is often the case, it also simplifies the role and functions of group leaders. Although not necessarily typical of every pressure group, an examination of the Southern Christian Leadership Conference under its most famous leader helps point up some of the dynamics of group leadership.[2]

Dr. King and the SCLC

The Southern Christian Leadership Conference (the SCLC) had its origins in the struggle by southern blacks to win some measure of freedom from the oppression of a legal and social system that required them to sit in the backs of public buses, to use "colored only" restrooms and restaurants, to expect to be denied jobs reserved for whites, and to live a life of daily slights and humiliations. In late 1955, the Reverend Martin Luther King had been in a new position as pastor of a black church in Montgomery, Alabama for only one year. He was relatively unknown, and while much of his education had been concerned with social injustice there was little or no systematic political thought or political experience in his background.

65

Two circumstances brought Dr. King into the world of pressure politics. The precipitating event was the refusal of Mrs. Rosa Parks to move to the back of the bus on December 1, 1955 as the law required all black passengers to do. She was duly arrested and charged with the offense. As it happened, Mrs. Parks was a woman of some standing in the black community, and the word quickly passed among black leaders. These men and women had already been attempting to pressure the white community for some concessions through the local chapter of the NAACP and other organizations. They decided the Parks case was dramatic enough to provide an opportunity to overcome one of the most humiliating symbols of white domination.

The other circumstance was the often intense rivalries within the black community of Montgomery. What was needed was a new organization bridging all factions and a new face to act as spokesman for the group. The Reverend Ralph Abernathy suggested the creation of the Montgomery Improvement Association to meet the first need. Dr. King admirably met the second.

The struggle over Montgomery's public transportation policies was a long and bitter one. During the course of it, Dr. King gained a first-hand acquaintance with the need for careful organization and the difficulties of conducting negotiations with an intransigent opposition. He was also forced to examine his own philosophical and political beliefs, and to attempt to give a voice to the poverty-stricken, often illiterate, almost always frightened blacks of the city, many of whom had very little in common with a well-educated "middle class" leader. That the struggle was eventually successful is evidence enough Dr. King at least partly solved these problems, but it is clear the effort strained his physical and emotional energies severely, even with Dr. Abernathy handling much of the organizational detail.

Nonetheless, victory brought him national
and international acclaim and he was invited
to lead the budding SCLC headquartered in Atlanta,
Georgia. The hope of the SCLC was to put together a south-wide organization which would
press for improved opportunities for blacks.
The expansion to a broader geographic, and in
effect membership, base posed grave problems,
however. How was such an organization to be
structured? What broad strategic goals would
it seek? How would it select its targets and
what would be its tactics?

Internal stresses quickly manifested
themselves. Young and militant black students
wanted their own organization and to pursue
direct action. Many older blacks preferred
"appeals to reason" and gradualism. The SCLC
attempted to solve the problem by encouraging
the creation of the Student Non-Violent Coordinating Committee (SNCC) as a young person's arm
of the SCLC and, eventually, setting up two
divisions within SNCC: one devoted to direct
action and one devoted to the more moderate goal
of voter registration.

This organizational solution was at best
partial, however: an attempt to paper over the
deeper philosophical and strategic problems facing the organization. Dr. King had already
addressed himself to these issues. At the philosophical level he had turned to black Christianity
energized by a sense of social justice. The
folk spiritual elements of black Christianity
struck a responsive chord in the hearts of many
blacks. The sense of social justice reached
out to educated black leaders and no small number
of liberal whites. At the strategic level, black
Christianity's sense of patience and humility
was entirely compatible with Dr. King's understanding and American restatement of Ghandhi's
passive resistance. The result was a program
of "non-violent revolution," a system in which
members of the SCLC would appeal to the reasonable

and decent elements of the white community, if
necessary by quietly accepting physical punishment, imprisonment, and humiliation as the prices
of forcing confrontation with white prejudice.

Although the strategic solution was in
theory more complete than the organization solution, like the latter it faced opposition. While
appealing to many blacks and whites, passive
resistance also seemed to many to emphasize
passivity over resistance. As a result King
often found his hand forced in selecting tactical targets. The Selma campaign was in no
small part forced on him by the younger militants; events in Birmingham outstripped his
leadership. He was able to give only limited
direction to the Chicago campaign.

By the time of his assassination in 1968,
both Dr. King and the SCLC represented only one
of several approaches to the black liberation
movement. The SCLC had lost much of its original
youthful vigor: many of the activist cadre were
reluctant to support Dr. King's Poor People's
March on Washington.

From the perspective of the 1980s it
is easy to be critical of King's leadership of
SCLC; it is necessary, however, to keep in mind
that Dr. King and the SCLC played a vital role
in setting the movement for equal opportunities
for all Americans into motion. For our purposes,
it is more important to note that while Martin
Luther King was the personal embodiment of the
SCLC and that he and a relatively small number
of people making up the activist cadre were the
leadership of the SCLC, by no means did the iron
law of oligarchy work in this case. King and
the other leaders of the SCLC made the formal
decisions, but often these decisions were forced
upon them by the nature of the group's membership
and its goals. Even his philosophy of political
activism, consciously or not, was adapted and
formulated to speak for that membership. He

provided the words, the logic, the concepts,
but the necessity for those words and logic
sprang from the group itself. As exceptional
a pressure group as the SCLC under King's leadership was, it is probably safe to hypothesize
that a similar dynamic relationship exists between the leaders and membership elements of
most other pressure groups.[3]

Roles and Functions of Leaders

    Like the leaders of all other organiza-
tions, pressure group leaders must devote a
substantial amount of their time and effort to
"housekeeping" activities, that is, managerial
chores. These chores include seeing to it that
the committee system is working, membership dues
are being paid, files and records are kept up
to date, meetings are scheduled, and the group's
public relations are being attended to. To a
great extent, tasks like these can be delegated
to other officers or to the staff if the group
is sufficiently prosperous to be able to afford
staff help. But, even with delegation, the task
is rarely much lighter, it only takes on a different cast: the management and supervision
of other people. As most executives know, as
much as 80 percent of their time is given over
to "people problems," handling disputes between
people, encouraging laggards, hiring and firing
staff, checking on the work of others, keeping
morale high, and staving off discontent. In
large and bureaucratized groups, these leadership
tasks can grow to fill all the individual leader's
available time. In smaller groups, often the
leader must perform much of the routine work
himself.

Maintaining the Organization

The language of organization theory refers to these managerial tasks as <u>organization maintenance</u>. While the least dramatic of all leadership tasks, it is certainly one of the most important, because it is concerned with keeping the organization itself in proper running order so that it is capable of acting as an effective political influence.[4] The role of the group's leadership in organization maintenance is to act as caretaker of the group: to insure that the organization's structure is in fact doing what it is supposed to be doing to maintain or advance the members' interests, that it is keeping, and possibly strengthening, its ability to act in the political arena, and that the group is not being sapped of its strength by arguments between committee chairmen, for example, or poor staff work, or indifferently kept records and poorly run meetings.

Particularly in competitive group settings, where there are a number of other pressure groups struggling for the attention of governmental officials, the well maintained group is vital to success. It will have the ability to withstand the stresses of a long drawn-out struggle, it will have the staff able to do quick research accurately, and it will have the money and manpower available to press its claims. Alone, of course, good management is insufficient for political victory, but without it, a group however large and wealthy is apt to be politically helpless against better organized and maintained opponents.

Speaking for the Group

Because modern pressure groups are complex organizations often embodying a wide range

of commitments to the group's goals, it is politically desirable that the group be able to
speak with a single and coherent voice. And,
one of the vital roles of group leadership is
to act as group spokesman. Although the task
on its face may seem simple enough, rarely is
it so. The leadership must decide what it is
going to say and to whom.

The "what" (or content) of the message
requires knowing what the group's goals really
are, how they may be most persuasively stated,
and what the group is willing to do or proposes
to do if its goals are not satisfied. Because
there are different levels of commitment to the
group's interests within the group, the leadership has to decide how "hard a line" it is willing
to take. As group spokesman, for example, Martin
Luther King committed the SCLC to non-violence
and a willingness on the part of the group members to be imprisoned to advance their goals.
More militant blacks, especially in the late
1960s, felt non-violence failed to express the
anger and depth of commitment of many blacks
willing to resort to "revolution" to achieve
equality. In effect, Dr. King had said that
his pressure group would press hard to achieve
its goals, but there was a limit on the form
that pressure would take. As already pointed
out, many SNCC militants felt this was an in-
accurate and unwise statement of black needs.

Closely related to content is the whom
or audience of the message. Illustration four
shows in schematic form the audiences that a
group may attempt to address. As a pressure
group, naturally a primary target will be those
public decision-makers whose actions affect the
group's interests. These may be legislators,
executives, or administrators. Here the group
spokesman is attempting to state why the group
favors or opposes a particular decision and he
may express the message in terms of the consequences that will occur if the public official

71

THE   GROUP LEADER   AS   SPOKESMAN

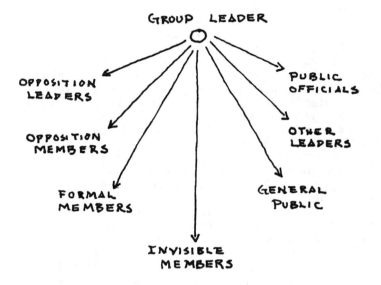

GROUP   LEADER

OPPOSITION
LEADERS

OPPOSITION
MEMBERS

FORMAL
MEMBERS

INVISIBLE
MEMBERS

PUBLIC
OFFICIALS

OTHER
LEADERS

GENERAL
PUBLIC

fails to act in the group's interests. These are often the "bottom line" negotiating sessions: the group will support the official at the next election if the official votes for or against a particular bill, for example.

Messages directed to the general public or to a group's invisible membership usually involve attempts to create a "favorable climate of opinion," perhaps to muster support outside the formal membership of the group for its goals or even to recruit new members. Dr. King addressed his books and speeches to the American public in an effort, often successful, to generate support for the SCLC in its struggles with southern white leaders. The content of these messages usually is broader and more general than that directed toward public officials.

Pressure group leaders may also speak to their opponents. If the message is aimed at opposition or rival leaders, it too may involve efforts to negotiate, to settle differences outside of governmental action. Often these messages may be a statement of an intent to do battle, in effect a warning that if an opposing group intends to pursue some goal it will meet with resistance. Labor unions, for example, may announce their intention to fight business groups seeking special tax breaks for business. A message of this kind can be an invitation to negotiate and compromise before the struggle begins by making clear that some particular group feels its interests are being touched upon.

Messages directed at rival groups' memberships are aimed at undercutting the rival leaders' base of support. If effective, it is hoped that a struggle can be averted or negotiations can be forced on the opposition.

One of the most important targets of the leader as group spokesman is his own membership.

He must remind the members of the issues at stake,
their need to support their leaders, and the risks
of factionalism or indifference in the political
struggle. Speaking to the group members is
actually a form of organization maintenance:
in part keeping the members informed, in part
attempting to maintain solidarity and support.
In this case, the content of messages are apt
to be heavy with reminders of what the group
interests are and what is to be gained (or lost)
in the political process.

Clarifying Interests

        Related to the role of spokesman is that
of interest clarifier. That is, one of the tasks
of the group leader is to specify and make clear
to both the group's members and its other audiences what it is the group seeks. One of the
most important contributions of Dr. King to the
SCLC was to formulate in clear and unambiguous
terms the commitment and style of that group
in the civil rights movement. In a similar
fashion, union, business, conservation, farm
and other interest group leaders attempt to make
their respective group's goals and approaches
clear.

        Often the clarification process involves
stating general goals in specific operational
forms. A taxpayers league, for example, concerned
with "good and efficient government" will need
its leaders to translate these broad aims into
concrete programs, such as better financial controls in government, the adoption of civil service or rational budgeting processes. During
the Depression of the 1970s, the leaders of the
AFL-CIO phrased their concern for rising unemployment in terms of specific governmental jobs
bills which would generate greater employment.
Interest clarification serves a dual purpose:
it gives the group's members a clear objective

74

to strive towards and thus a common interest to rally around. It also provides the leaders with a means of measuring--and hailing--their own success. Once, and if, the objective is won, the leadership can point proudly to the victory.

Further, in broader political terms, interest clarification allows other groups and officials to begin to negotiate over concrete issues. "More jobs for minorities," for example, while an effective rallying cry for group members and the invisible membership, needs to be restated into how many jobs, in what kind of occupations, paying what kinds of salaries.

Because interest clarification involves stating the goals of the group to its own members and to "the outside world," it is one of the more difficult, and dangerous, decision-making processes group leaders are involved in. One risk was pointed up in Dr. King's relationship with the black community: in clarifying the goals and methods of the SCLC he lost substantial support among young blacks. As modern pressure groups attempt to absorb larger and larger memberships, the leaders face the threat of failing to articulate the interests of sizable segments of their memberships or even in stating the issues in a way that group members feel run counter to their concerns (as in the case of the Metropolitan Real Estate Boards Association in Chapter III). In this respect, the modern pressure group leader suffers some of the anguish of the modern political party leader: too much interest clarification may alienate substantial bases of support, but too little provides no basis for committed support. The problem is deciding what is "too much" and what is "too little."

Making Decisions

In part, the foregoing roles are summarized by the phrase decision-maker. Obviously, a crucial role of group leadership is simply to make decisions: to decide how the group is to be best maintained, what needs to be said to whom, and what are the crucial issues facing the group and how they can be best clarified.

These are basic policy or strategic decisions. In addition, however, the typical group leader faces a wide range of lesser tactical decisions: questions of timing, of negotiation, of whether to commit the group to an all-out struggle on some particular issue. In each case, a mistake can make the difference between group success and failure and often there are no clear guidelines or precedents to help the leader in making his decisions.

These four roles in effect add up to the basic function of pressure group leadership: to summarize, reflect, and act on behalf of the group's interests. Leadership provides a coherence and direction to group interests that means, in theory at least, the group acts to present its interests in ways that are most effective in achieving the satisfaction of those interests. To the extent group leadership is ineffective, the group will itself be ineffective because almost without exception a pressure group acts through its leadership.

Group Leaders

If we accept the importance of leadership in pressure group politics, the next question is: who are the group leaders?

76

General Characteristics

The most general answer is that group leaders are the activist cadre or some number of the activist cadre. As a consequence, the leaders of a pressure group would usually be those most intensely committed to the group's interests and goals (which as leaders, of course, they have a hand in defining and specifying). It does not follow that the group leaders are always altruistically motivated, however. They may stand to benefit the most from the group's achieving its goals, and they may even have higher political aspirations.[5] Not a few business people use their local business organizations as vehicles for gaining the publicity that leads to elective office, and many black leaders have followed a similar path. Further, to be a group leader is to have some power and the satisfactions that go with power. It would not be surprising to discover that many if not most pressure group leaders seek and hold their positions for a mixture of reasons, some of which may be unconscious to themselves.

In terms of more specific attributes, the likelihood is that pressure group leaders will tend to be male, white, middle class to upper middle class, and at least in their mid- to late-thirties in age.[6] These are, of course, the social background characteristics of those most likely to belong to pressure groups, and, as one might expect, the leaders of these groups are like their memberships. There are important deviations from this generalization: the rise of various minority groups and women's groups since 1960 has meant that, especially at the local level, the population of pressure group leaders is sprinkled with more black, brown, and female faces than would have been the case two decades ago. Further, there appear to be subtle shifts even within older groups: local chapters of the NAACP, for example, often had white leadership. Today this would be the exception rather than the rule. Blacks and women now occasionally make their appearance in the activist cadre of economically oriented pressure groups: perhaps as "tokens," but nonetheless there and, by being there, no doubt able to exert some influence on the group's decision-making processes.

To go beyond these generalizations risks pure speculation. There appear to be no recent studies which attempt to analyze group leadership on any comparative basis. The great variety and complexity of American pressure groups make such studies extremely difficult. At best we can say that now, as before, pressure group leaders look much like the groups from which they are drawn, except they are probably a little better educated, more politically aware, and more aggressive than the general membership of the group they are leading.

Plural Leadership

It must also be noted that at least in a large number of cases, a group is led by more than one person; that is, group leadership is frequently plural, with two or three or more persons performing the roles and functions of leadership. This was true of the SCLC, despite the vital role played by King as the principal figure of that group.[7] Usually one person bears the formal title of president, chairman, director, or whatever, but at the same time the leadership roles are shared among others, perhaps because it is extremely difficult and rare for one person to be effective as an organization maintainer, a group spokesman, an issue clarifier, and the sole decision-maker.

Plural leadership moreover has the advantage of combining several viewpoints, which at least helps to guarantee that various shadings of attitudes are represented in leadership deliberations. It is for this reason that so often pressure groups rely on elaborate committee systems. And there is the further insurance that responsibility is shared, especially if something goes wrong.

For those groups which can afford a staff, the staff is for all practical purposes a part of the group's leadership structure.[8] This is so simply because the staff is most likely to be on top of the day-to-day details of what the organization is doing, has been hired for its expert skills, and thus must be called upon for the technical advice necessary to make tactical and policy decisions. For those groups which use public relations consultants or professional lobbyists, these assistants are also virtually members of the group's leadership, for the same reasons the staff is.[9]

Within the formal leadership structure of a group, moreover, often there are patterns of informal leadership, just as there is informal organization. The president of a group may well be a mere figurehead, someone chosen because he or she is popular with the membership or presents a good image to the public while the real leader is someone else occupying a minor office or committee post but who, by skill and force of personality, actually dominates group decision-making. In general, informal leadership follows the lines of informal organization: just as formal organization requires a leadership structure, so does informal organization. But, it is safe to guess that in such situations the group is going through a period of change, at the end of which the informal leaders may well emerge as the formal leaders or as having broken away from the group because their take-over effort failed.

79

Leadership Styles

It must be remembered that leaders, whether working in virtual solitude or as members of a plural leadership structure, are individuals. As such, there is a tendency for the political leader to bring his own "style" to the way he carries out his roles. Style is, admittedly, an ambiguous term, but it can be thought of as the particularly personal way an individual combines and fulfills the roles that all leaders must assume.[10] Martin Luther King, while concerning himself with organizational maintenance, much preferred to devote most of his attention to interest clarification and acting as spokesman. When he succeeded to King's post, Dr. Ralph D. Abernathy acted as spokesman but far more emphasized his interest in maintaining the organization, as he had during the years when King was the leader of the group.

Max Weber, the sociologist, has given us the classic categories of leadership styles.[11] Based on his study of social institutions and historical patterns, Weber defined leaders as being either "charismatic" or "bureaucratic."

The charismatic leader is one who evokes in his followers a profound, even passionate, emotional attachment.[12] He is apt to be thought of (and perhaps think of himself) as being almost god-like. His appeal is not to reason but to feelings. Particularly in times of crisis, uncertainty, and deep social stress, the charismatic leader is able to act effectively because people will follow him without questioning his plans or programs, willingly accepting his dictates as an act of faith.

Weber believed, however, that charismatic leaders always gave way to bureacratic leaders, because of the tendency of groups and social movements to become more complex organizationally and thus to demand more rational approaches than the charismatic leader can provide. The bureaucratic leader is the man who is adept at handling complicated organizations, formulating programs that people will find appealing on the basis of their reasonableness, and setting in motion the cooperative and task-related activities that bring the programs to fruition. At the risk of distorting some of Weber's meaning, we could say that the charismatic leader is the brilliant spokesman and interest clarifier; the bureaucratic leader is the skilled organization maintainer and pragmatic decision-maker.

As the discussion of leadership roles suggests, it is probably safe to argue that few leaders are ever entirely charismatic or bureaucratic. A leader, or more likely the plural leadership, will combine elements of both, just as King and Abernathy working together provided a charismatic and a bureaucratic style for the SCLC.

James Q. Wilson has suggested a somewhat similar but significantly different classification of leadership styles.[13] He argues that leaders tend to be either "affective" or "instrumental."

The affective leader principally devotes his energy to maintaining the group and good relations among the group members. He is an organization-maintainer but more than that: he provides the group members with a sense of closeness and solidarity and thus effectively reduces or eliminates factional disputes. Further, he guarantees that the group will present a solid front in any political struggle. The affective leader is thus both organization maintainer and at least a bit of charismatic leader.

The instrumental leader is concerned primarily with having the group advance its interest or interests. His goal is the group's

81

successful performance of the task it has set itself. Like the bureaucratic leader, he feels the organization has a job to do and attempts to lead the group in that direction, but unlike Weber's concept of the bureaucratic leader, he may have little or no interest in the tasks of organization maintenance.

At this stage of our knowledge about pressure group leadership, we can only say that both Weber's and Wilson's analyses are valuable and thought-provoking hypotheses. Too little research has been given to group leadership to say with any confidence which typology is more correct or whether we need a new set of concepts, one which perhaps meshes the two. It should be noted that both accept that there is an interaction between leadership style and followers' needs and interests, and it seems safe to assert that this is the case.[14] The exact nature of the interaction, and the range and nature of leadership styles, remains uncertain.

The "Iron Law" Revisited

This chapter began with the "iron law of oligarchy," which is commonly held to be the most reliable description of the dynamics of pressure group leadership. It is quite true, in the sense that apparently most pressure groups are led by an activist cadre and that, moreover, it is this leadership that makes the basic decisions for the group.

If the processes of leadership selection are examined, the iron law seems to be even further borne out. At least for many small neighborhood groups, the functions of leadership go by default. Whoever is willing to do the work ends up by being in control.[15] Although for many national groups, the procedures appear to be more democratic, it is probably true that

many times elections held by mass meetings or
mail ballots are sufficiently structured if not
actually rigged that the appearances are deceiv-
ing.[16] Less is known about the operations of
large local groups or statewide groups, but
again observation leads one to believe that in
many cases the "election" of formal leaders has
already been skillfully arranged by the activist
cadre before the event occurs. Moreover, it
is not surprising that when offices change hands
the transfer is from one activist to another.
The role of the staff and of consultants only
strengthens the hands of leaders in most cases.
Since both are hired by the leadership, it would
be expecting a great deal for them to act in
ways to deliberately undercut their employers
or to threaten a status quo that provides them
with their paychecks. Once again, the iron law
seems to be born out by available knowledge.

Yet, as this chapter has suggested, the
statement may over-simplify the realities of
pressure group leadership. Two forces operate
to limit the degree to which group leaders can
be irresponsible and unresponsive toward their
memberships. The first is simply that the basic
cohesive force of a pressure group is the shared
attitude toward a particular interest. The
second is that pressure groups are voluntary
associations, that is, in most cases the members
join and choose to remain members of their own
free will.[17] These two facts operate in tandem
to limit a group's leadership. For them to move
too far away from the basic thrust of the members'
concerns in the pursuit of their own personal
goals means they risk losing their members. Especially in the United States, at a time when
groups abound, it is relatively simple for the
disaffected to either join another more satisfactory group or to create a counter-organization
of their own. Thus, one of the more oligarchical
pressure groups, the American Medical Association,
found itself during the 1960s with a diminishing
membership base and undertook to refurbish its
image and processes.[18]

As the brief case study of Dr. King and the SCLC showed, the leaders of a pressure group face, as one of their more difficult problems, the task of fathoming the often unarticulated interests of their members and expressing them organizationally and politically. When they fail to do so, not only does the group itself probably suffer political defeat but it will experience an erosion of its membership base. In brief, the pressure group leader is limited in power and style by the "voluntarism" of the pressure group system.

It must be accepted, however, that voluntarism is a far cry from the procedural safeguards of regular elections, consultation of members, and responsible reporting of actions taken and not taken. The absence of these safeguards in so many pressure groups probably suggests an important characteristic of pressure group politics. An organization based on the goal of seeking and defending its members' interests will be judged, by its members at least, as to how efficiently and effectively it promotes those interests, not by what processes, internal or otherwise, it uses to achieve its goals.

References to Chapter IV

[1]Robert Michels, Political Parties (Glencoe, Ill.: The Free Press, 1949), p. 32.

[2]The best single source on Martin Luther King's political life is David L. Lewis, King: A Critical Biography (New York: Praeger, 1970). Thomas Dye, The Politics of Equality (Indianapolis: Bobbs-Merrill, 1971), pp. 117-23, gives a capsule history of the Southern Christian Leadership Conference. Lerone Bennett, Jr., Before the Mayflower, rev. ed. (Chicago: Johnson Press, 1969) is also useful. King's own works are of course valuable: Martin Luther King, Stride Toward Freedom: The Montgomery Story (1958); Why We Can't Wait (1964); Where Do We Go From Here? Chaos or Community (1967); and Trumpet of Conscience (1968), all published by Harper and Row, New York.

[3]Ralph M. Stodghill, Handbook of Leadership: A Survey of Theory and Research (New York: The Free Press, 1974) is an excellent guide to the literature on the subject of leadership.

[4]James Q. Wilson, Political Organizations (New York: Basic Books, 1973), pp. 13-15, 216.

[5]Wilson, pp. 33-34.

[6]Wendell Bell, Richard J. Hill, and Charles R. Wright, Public Leadership (San Francisco: Chandler, 1961).

[7]Often the other leaders are thought of and referred to as "sub-leaders," but it seems that in many cases the leaders and sub-leaders act conjointly.

[8]J. Clarence Davies III, Neighborhood Groups and Urban Renewal (New York: Columbia University Press, 1966), p. 180.

[9] Robert W. Miller and Jimmy D. Johnson, Corporate Ambassadors to Washington (Washington, D.C.: American University Press, 1970), Chapter 1.

[10] James David Barber, The Presidential Character: Predicting Performance in the White House (Englewood Cliffs, N.J.: Prentice Hall, 1972) Chapter 1 lays out an intriguing analysis of leadership "style."

[11] H. H. Gerth and C. Wright Mills, eds. and trans., From Max Weber: Essays in Sociology (New York: Oxford University Press, 1958), pp. 52-54, 247-63.

[12] The term "charisma" has been corrupted by modern journalism to refer to what an earlier generation called "sex appeal" and an even earlier "star quality," that is, a person who projects an unusually attractive image to a mass audience. Note that Weber was describing a much more significant phenomenon.

[13] Wilson, pp. 216-18.

[14] S. J. Makielski, Jr., Beleaguered Minorities: Cultural Politics in America (San Francisco: W. H. Freeman, 1975), pp. 147-48. Makielski relies only on Weber's classification.

[15] Davies, p. 178.

[16] Lloyd Warner, Darab B. Unwalla, and John H. Trim, The Emergent American Society: Large Scale Organizations (New Haven: Yale University Press, 1967), p. 303. Grant McConnell, Private Power and American Democracy (New York: Alfred A. Knopf, 1966), pp. 135-37.

[17] Andrew S. McFarland, Public Interest Lobbies (Washington, D.C.: American Enterprise Institute, 1976), pp. 87-88.

[18]For the early history of the AMA see Oliver Garceau's classic, The Political Life of the American Medical Association (Cambridge: Harvard University Press, 1941). Judith Robinson, "American Medical Political Action Committee," in Political Brokers: Money, Organizations, Power, and People, ed. Judith G. Smith (New York: Liveright, 1972), pp. 70-91 recounts the more recent efforts of the AMA as a pressure group.

CHAPTER V

THE BASES OF GROUP POWER

Pressure group power--the ability of
the group to achieve its goals through the political process--stems from a combination of group
resources, the situation in which the group finds
itself, and the extent to which it is challenged
by other power forces. Although there is no
neat, satisfactory way of measuring power, there
are clearly sharp differences among groups in
the power they wield.

Power Resources

Political scientists have yet to agree
on exactly what power is or even how it can be
identified, but if in the pressure group context
we think of power as being indicated by the
group's success in achieving its goals, we can
say that it stems from at least five major variables.[1] There are: numbers, organization,
leadership skills, status and image, and money.[2]
A group that ranks high on each of these variables
has a greater probability of success than one
that is lacking in some or all, although as we
shall see even command of these resources can
be negated by other factors.

Numbers

In a democratic society, that is a society in which emphasis is placed on elections
and the expression of the "will of the majority,"

numbers are a vital political resource. A pressure group with a large membership can claim to be speaking for a significant proportion of the electorate. As such a spokesman, further, it constitutes a genuine political threat to office-holders. If its members are disappointed in the behavior of an elected official, they may punish him at the next election. There is, also, a kind of moral force in sheer numbers.[3] Most Americans consciously or unconsciously are inclined to subscribe to the line of thinking that says, "If that many people feel a certain way, there must be an element of truth and right in their position." In short, the group which can muster large numbers of people to its side has a concrete and important political advantage.

Table 3 shows the reported memberships of various national pressure groups as of 1972. Although there are clearly great differences in size from one group to another, each is an impressive, truly mass membership organization. It should be recalled further that the table does not show a group's invisible membership, those who are sympathetic to the group in general or would be on particular issues. There are, for example, probably tens of thousands of Americans who would be sympathetic to efforts by the American Legion to see veterans' benefits increased because of a sense of gratitude and patriotism. Many black and white Americans are invisible members of civil rights groups such as the NAACP and the Urban League. In this respect, then, the tabulation is conservative.

In another respect, however, the figures have to be viewed with some skepticism. Although the AFL-CIO, for example, claimed over 13,000,000 members, it must be noted that the International Brotherhood of Electrical Workers is one of the largest components of this total membership.[4] Yet, during the early 1970s, the leadership of the IBEW and the AFL-CIO were at loggerheads

90

TABLE 3

MEMBERSHIP AND STAFF SIZE OF SELECTED

PRESSURE GROUPS, 1972

Group	Membership	Staff
American Bar Association	136,451	220
National Association of Manufacturers	14,000	282
Sierra Club	135,000	70
American Legion	2,700,000	301
NAACP	450,673	125
National Urban League	50,000	1,200
Common Cause	110,000	35
American Farm Bureau Federation	1,943,181	65
National Farmers Union	250,000	25
AFL-CIO	13,500,000	600
United Autoworkers	1,500,000	n.a.
American Medical Association	219,000	1,025

SOURCE: *Encyclopedia of Associations*, 1972.

over the war in Viet Nam and the candidacy of
George McGovern for the presidency. As Chapter
III stressed, underneath numbers are the questions of the commitment of members to the asserted
goals and programs of the group, whether cross-
pressuring exists, and the degree to which the
mass membership can be activated on a political
question. That is, sheer numbers must be read
in the context of cohesiveness,[5] whether the
group members are bound together closely by their
common interests and attitudes and thus whether
the leadership is able to "deliver" on their
numbers by guiding them to take a stand on an
issue by voting, writing letters, holding mass
meetings and demonstrations, making personal
contact with government officials, or otherwise
contributing time and effort to carrying out
the group's programs.

Organization

Even with these qualifiers, however,
in the political arena numbers are a significant resource, one which governmental officials,
the media, and rival or opposing pressure group
leaders take seriously. And, the numbers must
be taken seriously because they are people in-
corporated into an organization. Although not
a great deal more needs to be added to Chapter
III on the question of organization, it must
be stressed that people in organizations have
taken a crucial step. Attitude and interest
have gone beyond a psychological predisposition
to concrete action, that is, the actual joining
of a formal group to pursue those interests.
Unorganized interests may or may not ever be
triggered into action. The very fact that they
are unorganized suggests the potential for political action is low. Organized interests,
however, are already disposed toward action and
thus are a political force in being.

92

As discussed previously, organization
is an important political resource in that it
provides the structure and the apparatus for
political action. The energies of numbers of
people are channelled and capable of concerted,
directed, and coherent action, which can be applied to a number of targets, such as executives
and legislators, in a number of places and, if
need be over an extended period of time.[6]

Money

Another advantage of organization is
that organizations are able to collect and use
money in amounts that are rarely available to
individuals. And money is a political resource
of enormous flexibility. While not the sole
key to power as many people seem to believe,
the availability of money to hire staff and consultants, including able legal advice, to use
a professional lobbyist, to conduct public relations campaigns on television, in the press,
and through specialized media aimed at the
group's membership, to entertain government
decision-makers, to make contributions to election
campaigns, and, on occasion, to send gifts and
offer bribes means that a pressure group is in
a position to work in a broad and intense way
to win its goals. As is so often the case with
political resources, possessing an abundance
of a resource does not guarantee success, but
a shortage is a real liability. So it is with
money.

For obvious reasons, pressure groups
are reluctant to reveal how much money they have
available for political purposes or even what
their total annual incomes may be.[7] Most groups
depend on membership dues--another reason why
numbers are important--with occasional appeals
for special contributions to meet the costs of

93

major political efforts. Thus, a mass membership
organization of, for example, 100,000 members
levying a $10 annual dues would receive an annual
income of $1,000,000. A substantial portion
of this sum would go to organization maintenance,
such items as office rental, utility and telephone costs, and record-keeping, but still on
any accounting the group would have a large sum
left to hire staff and conduct informational
and public relations campaigns.[8] Federations
and trade associations normally sustain themselves financially either through sharing a
percentage of the dues paid to state or local
groups within the federation or, in the case
of trade associations, receiving dues from the
membership firms. National-chapters type organizations generally expect members to pay two sets
of dues: one to the national organization and
one to the state or local group, if the local
group feels it needs its own revenue base.

It is, given the present state of information, virtually impossible to estimate accurately
the sums of money spent by pressure groups in
their various political activities. Although
the federal government and most state governments require lobbyists to register and to file
statements of expenses, the loopholes are so
numerous, the definitions of what constitutes
"lobbying" so narrow, and the laws so laxly enforced that the reports are worse than useless.[9]

The effort to probe the impact of pressure group activities in the presidential campaign
of 1972 by the U.S. Senate Watergate Committee
found that thirteen corporations had contributed
over $780,000 to the campaign, the bulk going
to President Nixon's campaign. Associated Milk
Producers, Inc., a group composed of dairy farmers, and its political action arm, Trust for
Agricultural Political Education, by collecting
just under $100 a year from its members developed

94

the capacity to spend $1,000,000 a year on federal and state election campaigns. Two other dairymen's associations had, in 1972, each a $300,000 political campaign fund.[10]

The same investigation determined that Senator George McGovern received contributions amounting to nearly $680,000 from nineteen separate unions. President Nixon received nearly $45,000 from six unions, and Senator Hubert Humphrey received nearly $177,000 from fifteen different unions. Table 4 shows how some groups donated to the 1974 Congressional elections.[11]

As impressive as these sums are, it must be kept in mind that they represent only one form of pressure group activity. Group activities before federal, state, and local administrative agencies did not come to a halt during the election years, any more than their efforts to influence public opinion on innumerable issues.[12]

In focussing on these figures, however, it would be a serious error to ignore the great differences that exist among pressure groups. Certain groups are far more affluent than others. Groups which draw their memberships from business corporations, from professionals such as doctors, lawyers, engineers, and architects, and from the "middle class" in general, such as most ideologically oriented groups, are able to charge higher dues and call for special contributions with far greater success than groups which represent minorities, the poor, and the aged, for examples.[13] Moreover, the well-maintained group will have an advantage over those whose leadership is less able: it will take greater care to see that dues are paid promptly, will keep track of those members who can be "hit" for a special levy because of their deep commitment to the group's goals, and will use the funds

TABLE 4

POLITICAL MONEY: THE 1974 CONGRESSIONAL ELECTIONS

Group Donating Money	Amount
American Medical Association Political Action Committees	$1,462,972
AFL-CIO	1,178,638
United Auto Workers	843,938
National Education Associations	398,991
National Association of Manufacturers	272,000
National Association of Realtors	260,870

SOURCE: Herbert E. Alexander, Financing
Politics: Money, Elections, and Political Reform
(Washington, D.C.:   The Congressional Quarterly
Press, 1976), p. 229.

available more efficiently. The bias, again, is
in favor of those with managerial experience
and abilities. That is, the skillful use of
money not only assures that money keeps coming
in, but that greater value, from the group's
point of view, is received for each dollar spent.

Skill

As with money, so it is with numbers
and organizations: leadership skill is required
to blend the other resources, to combine them
into an effective set of political weapons, and
to know how to use one to compensate for some
lack in any of the others. Surprisingly, there
is practically no systematic study of what "skill"
is in the world of politics.[14] Obviously, some
people are more able in politics than others,
but it is not clear why. Skill would appear
to be a combination of personality factors, experience (prior knowledge), and information
(present knowledge). Experience gives an individual a backlog of technical knowledge, such
as what rules and laws are important or binding,
as well as a grasp of how people behave in politics. Information serves to up-date his experience and amend it, if need be. Yet, as Frederick
the Great of Prussia put it, "Experience is
useless if we draw the wrong lessons from it."
The same is true of information. Studies of
various political leaders, especially U.S.
Presidents, suggest that a high degree of flexibility in treating experience, information, and
contacts with other people is at least one essential personality trait of the "skilled" leader.[15]

In more explicit terms, the "ideal" pressure group leader would have a full grasp of
his group's goals and needs, experience with
the governmental and political process, wide
contacts among public and private decision-makers,

97

and the personality to turn these potential assets
into real ones. Where individual leaders lack
any of these abilities, a staff can serve as a
substitute. As Table 3 shows, many national
pressure groups have large staffs, but it is
worth noting also that the size of a staff has
no direct relationship to the size of a group's
membership. Two of the largest staffs were
attached to two of the smaller groups (the Urban
League and the AMA). Differences can be explained in part by the intensity of group activity, leadership decisions, and the structure
of the organizations involved, as well as the
kind of activities the group is involved in.
Common Cause, for example, depends heavily on
volunteer services; labor unions often do the
same. The Urban League is active not only in
politics but in manpower training and other
educational programs for blacks, not all of whom
are by any means members of the group.

Although the staff of a group plays a
part in group leadership, the selection and use
of the staff is still a matter of skill. One
local pressure group, studied by the author,
had a five person staff, two of whom had no
particular qualifications for the jobs they were
assigned to and were given no training or help
in learning those jobs. Of the remaining three,
one who had graduate training in communications
and journalism was used principally to act as
secretary at meetings and to type up the minutes
after meetings. The fourth was a bookkeeper
and seemed to be able. The fifth theoretically
was staff supervisor, but spent most of his time
at meetings of one kind or another. In this
instance, what was in proportion to group size
a large staff turned out to be mainly a drain
on the group's resources in the form of salaries
to no especial benefit to the group. The leadership was failing in its task of organization
maintenance. Observation of the leaders indicated that they had little knowledge of how
to use a professional staff or even what a staff

of a pressure group might contribute to the group's efforts.

Leadership skill, then, while largely an imponderable and difficult to reduce to explicit terms, is a vital resource for a pressure group. Imaginative, enterprising, and aggressive leaders often can do much to overcome handicaps in other resources, as many minority groups have proven. And a group leadership which has grown stale or which was never skilled in the first instance is capable of fumbling the opportunities presented by numbers, organization, and money.

Status and Image

Another political resource that is difficult to measure yet important to group power is the status and image of the group. Some groups, regardless of the interests they are pursuing, fit more closely to the value systems of Americans than others. They thus have the appearance of legitimacy, respectability, maturity, and responsibility. A group may draw its image and status from its membership: the A.M.A. and the American Bar Association, for example, enjoy the advantage of speaking for highly regarded professions. Others may create their image by the stance they take in political affairs: the NAACP, for example, has throughout its history been the voice of moderation and pragmatism in the civil rights movement. Others may draw their status from the broad category of interests they speak for: religious groups derive much of their persuasiveness from their claim to be acting for morality and deeply held values.

Status and image, as a political resource, is difficult to evaluate because, in part, it is subject to regional fluctuations and variations

within subpopulations. Although in the northeast the NAACP would be viewed as a moderate
civil rights group, some southerners remain convinced it is a tool of the "communist conspiracy."
In one community, the political stance of church
leaders would be viewed as just that; in another,
large segments of the population would view them
as speaking with a special moral force. One
of the frustrating realities faced by contemporary pressure group leaders is the steady decline
among the public in respect for various previously high status institutions and professions.[16]
Nonetheless, some groups have a better public
image than others and this status amounts to
a substantial political advantage.[17]

At least three benefits flow from high
status for a pressure group. One is simply an
improved chance of attracting public attention
through the media in a favorable light, and thus,
possibly, increasing the group's invisible membership. When the U.S. Chamber of Commerce
speaks on economic and taxation questions, its
views will be given preferred treatment in the
media because it is a "prestigious" organization. Second, and related, high status contributes to a group's "credibility." Many
Americans continue to feel highly deferential
toward doctors. Thus, when the A.M.A. claims
to speak for doctors, these same Americans will
tend to accept its voice as authoritative. Third,
high status provides a group with leverage in
dealing with governmental decision-makers. Few
elected or appointed leaders are anxious to
challenge or anger a group that represents some
prestigious segment of the population; many are
eager to please such a group. Conversely, few
politicians are anxious to be associated with
a low status group: it is not just the respective voting strengths of the groups involved
that would lead most politicians to prefer to
be praised by the American Bar Association rather
than the Black Panther Party.

To an extent, status and image are subject to control by a group's leadership. The
leaders can insure that their research is always
solid and reliable, that their political tactics
bear up under public scrutiny and are "middle
class" and "responsible," and that, in general,
careful attention is given to public relations.[18]
Beyond these actions, however, a group's status
is largely outside its own control. A minority
group is made up of members of a minority, who
in the United States continue to be lower on
the status scale than white Protestant Americans. Unions speak for workingmen who will not
be as highly regarded as professional people.
Environmental groups are often believed to be
made up of unkempt youngsters, long-haired intellectuals, and fuzzy-minded bird-watchers (an
image in part the product of anti-environmentalist
pressure groups), all of whom have suspect images
in this country.

These five major political resources--
numbers, organization, money, leadership skills,
and status and image--are the raw materials of
pressure group power. No group possesses a
monopoly of all; few groups are richly endowed
with all throughout the group's lifespan. As
important, whether a group ranks high or low
on some political resource is largely a relative
matter, a question of the situation in which
the group finds itself.

Situational Influences of Group Power

A pressure group's power is affected
not only by the political resources which it
possesses, but the relationship of these resources
to the situation in which it is operating. In
general, a group's situation can be thought of
as being composed of two major elements: the
competitive situation of the group and the

101

historical setting.[19] Both determine to a significant extent how effective a group can be
in the political process, that is, the degree
to which a group's political resources will pay
off in terms of the group's interest. Significantly, moreover, both situational influences
are largely outside the control of the group:
they are "realities" which must be overcome,
if negative, or exploited to the fullest, if
helpful to the group.

Opposition

        Pressure group politics is largely a
struggle between two groups or among three or
more groups to control governmental policy-making.
In a competitive situation, then, a pressure
group faces opponents and, potentially, even
rivals. Where and when the opposition is strong,
much of the power of a pressure group is reduced.
It confronts, in effect, a situation of "countervailing forces," where one power source helps
to negate another opposing one.[20] It has been
argued that this process of mutually negating
forces helps to check the unbridled power of
any one group or set of interests. Thus organized labor with its numbers and money checks
the power of business interests with their money
and status. Industry and real estate interests
similarly face environmentalist groups, organized
religion in attempting to get government aid
for church schools must meet the resistance of
groups such as the American Civil Liberties Union.

        Opposition forces a pressure group to
bargain, to compromise, to moderate its claims.
On occasion, opposition may even defeat a group
which one might suppose to be enormously powerful in terms of its political resources. Moreover, it does seem to be true that the more
insistent a group is in advancing its interest,

the greater the likelihood it will encounter
an organized and aggressive opposition.[21]

The governmental decision-maker being
pressured by two powerful and contending forces
is in an advantageous position. He need fear
neither group and can listen to the advice and
information provided by both. Ultimately, he
can act as "broker," finding a compromise solution, claiming credit for resolving the conflict,
and congratulating himself for protecting "the
public interest." In this situation, the pressure group may find the tables turned on itself:
instead of applying pressure to government official, it may find itself being pressured to be
"reasonable" and to avoid taking an unbending
stance. Mayors of large cities, for examples,
have been able to make political capital by acting
as mediator in labor-management disputes, or
civil rights-private enterprise disputes.

Classic interest group theorists often
pointed to the effects of "countervailing power"
as a guarantee of democratic stability in American society.[22] As it happens, however, by no
means in every situation are power matches even
ones. One group may possess far more resources
than its opposition. It may, even, have relatively little organized opposition. Although
a sizable proportion of the public accepts and
even wants national gun control laws, there is
no "pro-gun control" pressure group with the
resources mustered by the National Rifle Association. In most of the southeast, union organizations are far feebler than their business
counterparts. And civil rights organizations,
while winning many basic legislative and judicial victories, have usually found themselves
overmatched in a straight fight with labor or
business when the interests of the latter groups
have been directly triggered.

The importance of political geography
to a pressure group must be noted once more. As
Grant McConnell has said,

It may happen that a single economic interest, such as a particular farm produce
or a particular industry is overwhelmingly
the largest in the community. In the
state, the relative importance of the particular interest will be diluted by the
existence of others; in the nation the
relative importance of the one interest
will be even less.[23]

It is not surprising, then, to find that
it is in the more populated, and the more indus-
trialized and urbanized, states that a pressure
group can expect to face the most opposition.[24]
Nonetheless, it must be remembered that in a
federal system based on geographic units, a pressure group can hold sway over particular electoral
districts and even whole communities.

Rivalry

Also affecting group power is the degree
of rivalry which a given pressure group must
deal with. Some groups are virtually the sole
spokesmen for the interests they represent, the
American Bar Association and the American Medical Association being ready examples. The same
is true of some other professions, such as the
American Institute of Architects and the American
Political Science Association. While these groups
may by no means claim every interested person
as formal members, they are in the enviable position that no other organization is a real threat
in attracting members. Few other groups are
so happily placed, however. Most confront rivals
of equal power or groups which, if more aggressive or persistent in pursuing members' goals,

104

could hope to win over some of the members of
the challenged organization. At a minimum rivals
may recruit most potential new members and thus
permanently restrict the membership base of the
group. It is not surprising, then, that some
of the fiercest pressure group struggles are
between rivals rather than opposing groups, as
with the often desperate struggles between rival
unions.

It is, of course, the voluntarism of
pressure group membership that makes rivals so
threatening. A group member who feels the leadership and policies of his original group do not
satisfy his goals can be welcomed into the arms
of a rival group. Further, rivalries mean that
the groups speaking for a particular interest
are expressing their claims through divided and
competing voices. As with opposing groups, the
governmental decision-maker is in the position
of being able to play rivals off against one
another.

With reasonably sophisticated leadership,
however, pressure groups can ameliorate the
detrimental effects of rivalries by alliance-
building, that is, coming to the terms of a
negotiated truce among rivals. This was the
purpose of the Montgomery Improvement Association
which gave Martin Luther King his initial push
into the world of pressure group politics. So,
also, the rival AFL and CIO came together in
1955. Some alliances, such as the merging of
the two great labor federations, are relatively
enduring; others may be only temporary, a response to a particular situation when leadership
can work out mutually satisfactory agreements
on one particular issue.[25]

Rivalries can be further reduced by explicit or tacit bargains. That is, rival groups
may agree, either openly or by unspoken mutual

105

assent, to allow each other unchallenged sway
in a particular geographic area or with a particular potential membership. Labor unions have
been especially willing to make such bargains,
but organized crime has also tended to follow
such a pattern. In effect, rivals express a
willingness to allow other groups to exist as
long as the one does not threaten the other.
The result is to ensure the continued existence
of all the groups involved in the bargain.

As with opposition, however, rivalries
tend to reduce the relative power of a pressure
group. Few groups in America can legitimately
claim to be the sole spokesman of all their potential members. It is estimated, for example,
that only 25 percent of all blue collar workers
are members of labor unions; and that only a
similar percentage of farmers belong to a farm
organization. With this the case, and with
membership further divided among a number of
pressure groups, any particular group is hard
pressed to claim it truly represents the "real
interests" of some segment of the population.

Historical Circumstances

Just as the competitiveness, or non-
competitiveness, of a group's situation affects
its power, the historical circumstances in which
a pressure group must work has an important effect. During the 1860s and 1870s, and again
in the 1920s, business was highly regarded by
the public and government decision-makers. In
the latter period, a President was able to say,
"The business of government is business."[26] In
effect, the status of the pressure groups speaking for business interests was high and their
opponents were at a disadvantage. Similarly,
the Populist Revolt of the 1880s, the Progressive
Era culminating in the election of Woodrow Wilson,

106

and the Great Depression all had the effect of damaging the image of business (in many cases, the wounds were self-inflicted) and strengthening farmer's organizations, unions, and other anti-business interests. It has been noted that periods of economic prosperity usually see an increase in union membership, while "hard times" have the reverse effect.[27] The 1960s, with its public concern for the crisis of the cities and its fear of domestic breakdown meant minority groups were able to assert claims and gain a hearing that ten years previously, and only a few years later, went ignored.

It is difficult to sort out what goes into an "historical era," especially in relation to the power of specific interest groups. It does seem true, however, that certain periods favor the pressing of some interests and place a burden on groups which advocate others. Pressure groups themselves work to produce such shifts in "climate," but their efforts may go unrewarded for years, or even decades, and then explode as fashionable, pressing issues. Environmentalists had, for example, long been concerned with basic trends in the use and abuse of the nation's natural resources. Then, in the 1960s, "ecology" became a top national priority, leading to the creation of a vast number of federal, state, and local programs to protect the environment and a bureaucracy to carry the programs out.

To a degree, no doubt, the historical climate is media-created. Enterprising journalists, searching for good copy, discover and publicize a problem that has gone ignored previously and focus the attention of other opinion leaders, journalists, academics, and political leaders on the issue. The "muckrakers" of the turn of the century played a key role in calling attention to the frequently savage practices of the great business enterprises. The civil rights movement was without a doubt aided enormously by television stories showing the beating of SCLC's passive resisters by white sheriff's deputies. Rachel Carson's book, Silent Spring, and Ralph Nader's Unsafe at Any Speed, helped launch the environmental and consumer protection movements respectively.[28]

Even given the power of the media, it does seem to be so that the times must be ripe for a particular set of interests to receive the attention, favorable or unfavorable, that can either dramatically enhance its power base or sharply restrict it. And, apparently one reality which modern pressure groups must deal with is the rapid shift in emphases that now is characteristic of public attention. The "farm problem" gives way to the crisis of the cities which yields to the black revolution which is replaced by poverty, in turn forced into the background by the "ecology" movement, which is rephrased as the "energy crisis." With these fluctuations, groups are tempted to strike as hard as possible while the iron is hot with a resulting ferment of pressure, conflict, and confusion concerning the issues involved.

Such fluctuations in public attention tend to encourage the emergence of rival voices to older established groups and thus to produce counter-forces to the older groups. For the group so placed, then, the new public concern for the interests it represents is not always an unmixed blessing. It may find, in fact, that it has to struggle harder to maintain its position and to claim the attention of decision-makers.

Operating together, then, the competitive situation and historical circumstances act to enhance or weaken a group's ability to use its political resources. Both situational influences are subject to some degree of control by a group's

leaders, but it appears safe to say that this
control is highly limited. A group can choose
to respond to unfavorable circumstances by remaining quiescent, in the hope that the tides
of fortune will change; it may choose to try
to anticipate unfavorable circumstances by careful attention to public relations, the group's
image, and by taking advantage of good situations
to the maximum extent; it may even choose to
breast unfavorable situations by fighting back,
but in any event the group's leaders will discover that some times are the "right" ones and
some "wrong" for the group to press its interests.

From an analytical standpoint, it is
useful to keep situational influences in mind,
because it is always tempting to focus on a
group's political resources and assume that if
it is wealthy, large, well-organized, and well-
led, it must be "unstoppable." The comparatively
poor United Farm Workers' Organization was able
to fight the far more "powerful" Teamster's Union
to a standstill in California in the effort to
organize California farm workers. During the
1930s and 1940s, the wealthy, skilled, and high
status National Association of Manufacturers
was accused of being "the kiss of death" for
any measure it supported in Congress. Despite
all its obvious political resources, the American Medical Association has been defeated time
and again on issues it considered central to
its concerns. These apparent upsets are many
times the result of situational influences modi-
fying what would appear to be enormous power
bases.

Power and Strategic Position

The political resources and situational
circumstances of a particular group add up to
what can be called the <u>strategic position</u> of the

group in the political system. As will be seen
in the following chapters, some groups hold a
better strategic position than others, for a
number of reasons, which may include their ability
to attract more skilled leaders, to have better
access to vital information, or to control at
least some of the situational influences that
bear on their circumstances. Differences in
strategic positions among groups mean that there
are important differences in the power of pressure groups, and in the power relations of groups
to government decision-makers and to the unorganized public. Interest groups theorists
long assumed that, with enough effort, any interest could make itself heard.[29] The point
may well be valid, as the experience of many
minorities has shown, but to be heard and to
be able to exert a continuing and significant
influence on the decisions of government are
two different matters. Some groups, by virtue
of their favorable strategic positions, have
a far better chance and, over a period of years,
far greater influence than others.

Just as we were able to sketch a "model"
of the bases of group politics (Illustration
one in Chapter II), we can diagram group power.
Illustration five shows in a highly simplified
form the interaction between public policy, the
major resources of pressure groups, and situational factors.

As the diagram suggests, public policy
is the target of these resources, but as with
the bases of group politics, policy interacts
with the power resources: the nature of the
public policy triggering more or fewer interests
and making some of the resources more valuable
or less so. A highly technical, difficult to
grasp regulatory policy is less likely to activate a group's mass and invisible memberships
than a sweeping distributive or redistributive
policy, for example.

110

ILLUSTRATION   FIVE
RESOURCES AND   POWER

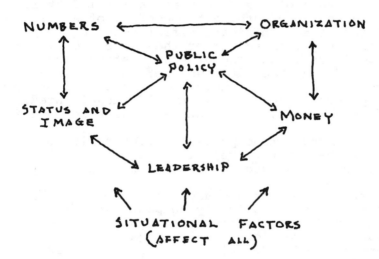

NUMBERS ⟷ ORGANIZATION

PUBLIC
POLICY

STATUS AND
IMAGE

MONEY

LEADERSHIP

SITUATIONAL FACTORS
(AFFECT ALL)

It must be remembered also that the various resources interact with each other: greater numbers generally mean more money; large numbers pose leadership difficulties which make organization all the more important. The status of a group may affect its chances to attract members and thus the money the group needs to maintain itself organizationally. Each resource must be thought of as only one step in a chain of processes that strengthen or weaken the group in influencing public policy.

As the following chapters will help show, if one were to "feed in" various groups to the model, some would appear stronger in certain resources than others. When situational factors, which largely lie outside the control of a group, are added, the significant differences in group power are highlighted. Thus the pattern of pressure politics is not one of equals struggling among each other, or at least not in every instance. It may be a situation in which one or a few powerful groups go virtually unchallenged, or, if challenged, by pathetically weak opponents.

To understand pressure group politics, the view that must be kept in mind has been well summarized by Wallace Mendelson. He said,

> Some interest groups are large, some small; some are geographically compact, some widespread, and some spotty; some have advantages of prestige, some of organization, and some of dedication--others are correspondingly handicapped. All this and more in varying degrees. The result is a layered, crazy-quilt pattern of changing interests.[30]

References for Chapter V

[1]Chapter XIII discusses the question of power in greater detail.

[2]Robert A. Dahl, Who Governs? Democracy and Power in an American City (New Haven: Yale University Press, 1961), pp. 223-69, discusses various political resources.

[3]James Madison in "Federalist No. 10," The Federalist Papers, Modern Library Edition (New York: Random House, n.d.), p. 58, makes much the same point. If a large enough number of people subscribe to some "passion or interest," he argued, then, "We well know that neither moral nor religious motives can be relied upon as an adequate control."

[4]The IBEW had a 1972 membership of 900,000.

[5]David B. Truman, The Governmental Process: Political Interests and Public Opinion (New York: Alfred A. Knopf, 1951), pp. 112-13. See also Grant McConnell, Private Power and American Democracy (New York: Alfred A. Knopf, 1966), p. 106.

[6]Theodore Lowi, The End of Liberalism: Ideology, Policy, and the Crisis of Public Authority (New York: W. W. Norton, 1969), p. 39.

[7]Judith G. Smith, ed., Political Brokers: Money, Organizations, Power, and People (New York: Liveright, 1972).

[8]Andrew J. Glass, in Smith, "Common Cause," lists Common Cause's total expense breakdown for 1970 as: Lobbying, 25%; salaries, 20%; mailings, 25%; rent and office expenses, 15%; and field organization, 15% (p. 277).

[9]The 1946 Federal law, for example,
(Title III of Public Law 79-601) required registered lobbyists to report only expenses incurred
in direct contact with Congressmen. As the
Congressional Quarterly Weekly (1975, p. 1137)
commented, "The quarterly reports lobbyists file
tend to list the trivia of their work. . . ."
And, by no means do all lobbyists register, especially at the state level.

[10]U.S. Senate Committee on Presidential
Campaign Activities, Report, Vol. II (New York:
Dell, 1974), pp. 100-15. See also Chapter IX
for a further discussion of elections and money.

[11]Herbert E. Alexander, Financing Politics:
Money, Elections, and Political Reform (Washington, D.C.: The Congressional Quarterly Press,
1976), p. 229.

[12]Almost all studies of pressure group
money focus on expenditures made in election
campaigns. It is possible, as a consequence,
that we have a skewed perspective on what groups
do with their money and how much they may spend
on all political activities.

[13]In a comparative study of pressure
groups in Canada and the United States, Robert
Presthus concluded that only between one-quarter
to one-third of all pressure groups have sufficient resources to be effective. Robert Presthus,
Elites in the Policy Process (Cambridge and New
York: Cambridge University Press, 1974).

[14]Eugene Bardach, The Skill Factor in
Politics: Repealing the Mental Commitment Laws
in California (Berkeley: University of California
Press, 1972), suggests skill is the ability to
expand one's resources. Dahl, pp. 307-8, also
has an interesting discussion of the importance
of skill in politics.

[15]See, for example, James David Barber, Presidential Character: Predicting Performance in the White House (Englewood Cliffs, N.J.: Prentice-Hall, 1972).

[16]The Harris Poll has reported a decline in public confidence for virtually all American institutions, including not only medicine, religion, and labor, but governmental institutions as well.

[17]Dahl, pp. 241-46, discusses the importance of "respectability" as a political resource.

[18]Richard Kluger, Simple Justice (New York: Alfred A. Knopf, 1976), pp. 139, 145-46ff. describes the efforts of the NAACP to attain and maintain an image of responsibility and moderation.

[19]A third situational influence, the political arena in which the group operates, is discussed in detail in Part Two. The arena is distinguished from the other situational influences in that a group consciously chooses what political arena to work in.

[20]John Kenneth Galbraith, American Capitalism: The Concept of Countervailing Power (Boston: Houghton-Mifflin, 1952), coined the term "countervailing power." He has since revised his views, arguing a convergence of power rather than a balancing of power. John Kenneth Galbraith, The New Industrial State (Boston: Houghton-Mifflin, 1967), and Economics and the Public Purpose (Boston: Houghton-Mifflin, 1973). The term continues to appear in the literature, however. See Thomas Dye, Understanding Public Policy, 2d ed. (Englewood Cliffs, N.J.: Prentice-Hall, 1975), p. 24.

[21]L. Harmon Zeigler and Hendrick van Dalen, "Interest Groups in the States," in

Politics in the American States, 2d ed., eds.
Herbert Jacob and Kenneth Vines (Boston: Little,
Brown, 1971), pp. 122-61.

[22]See especially Truman; Wallace S. Sayre
and Herbert Kaufman, Governing New York City
(New York: Russell Sage, 1960) is also a clear
statement of the "classic" position in the context of that city.

[23]McConnell, p. 104.

[24]Zeigler and van Dalen, p. 127.

[25]James Q. Wilson, Political Organizations
(New York: Basic Books, 1973), Chapter 13 has
a valuable discussion of alliance-building.

[26]Thirty years later, when the president
of a major corporation said, "What's good for
General Motors is good for America," his comment
was widely mocked and used as an illustration
of the arrogance and self-centeredness of big
businessmen. The second part of the remark was
generally ignored, "and what's good for America
is good for General Motors."

[27]Robert Salisbury, "An Exchange Theory
of Interest Groups," in Interest Group Politics
in America, ed. Robert Salisbury (New York:
Harper and Row, 1970), p. 39.

[28]Interestingly, the title of Nader's
book was drawn from an earlier work, John Keats's,
The Insolent Chariots, which made most of the
same points, but had none of the impact, that
Nader's did.

[29]Arthur F. Bentley, The Process of
Government (Chicago: University of Chicago
Press, 1908), p. 372; Truman, pp. 534-35.

[30]Wallace Mendelson, "Mr. Justice Douglas
and Government by the Judiciary," Journal of
Politics 38 (November 1976):930.

CHAPTER VI

CASE STUDY: THE CORPORATION

When in 1971, two social critics said, "Big busines is government"[1] they were repeating a theme that has appeared and reappeared in the analysis of American society for over a hundred years. The business corporation perhaps more often than any other single institution has been a source of fear, resentment, and criticism in terms of its relations to the democratic system.

It is argued that foreign and defense policy are largely shaped at the behest of corporations, that government "regulation" of business is really governmental protection of big business, that politicians from Presidents to city councilmen dance to the tune called by businessmen, and that "welfare" policies are in truth only a means of controlling the poor in specific and the public in general that they might not rise up in protest against the dictatorship of big business.[2] If only a fraction of the accusations are true, then the business corporation clearly is a major power in American society and politics.

The Corporation and Politics

The business corporation represents something of a special case in pressure group politics. This is so because while the corporation conforms to many of the generalizations in the preceding chapters, it also deviates from them in significant respects. One of these respects is in the nature of its membership. Although one could think of all the employees of a given corporation as "members" of the organization, a more realistic appraisal would be that most have

117

little if any "shared attitude" with the corporation as such.[3] They work for the enterprise, true, and no doubt become anxious if business is bad out of a fear of cutbacks and lay-offs, but their concern is not for the corporation, only their jobs. Thus the core of the corporation as a group is its top management and its middle management. A firm, such as General Motors, then, which counts its employees in the hundreds of thousands is, as a pressure group, probably not much larger than several dozen people, with a true activist cadre of perhaps not more than a dozen or so persons. Thus, the "power" of the modern corporation, to the extent that power exists, is not a function of numbers and, in fact, numbers must play only the smallest part in corporate influence as a political resource.[4]

Second, the corporation is a special case because business and government in America (as elsewhere) have been thoroughly intertwined over the years in a relationship that has grown more profoundly complicated in the last twenty years or so. It is common, of course, to speak of "the private" and "the public" sectors of the economy. The careful observer would find, however, that the boundaries, if any, are extraordinarily hard to delineate.[5] At the most superficial level, for example, he would discover that a large number of top government officials come from and eventually go back into business as their primary careers. He would find that many "professional politicians," that is men and women who spend most of their lives in elected office or working for a party organization, derive much of their income from corporate connections, often through their law firms.

At a more serious level of analysis, it would become clear, as mentioned in Chapter II, that many businesses are directly and indirectly affected by what government does, whether

118

the governmental actions are taxation policies
or public works projects. Governments, in turn,
are dependent on businesess to supply them with
many of the necessary items to carry on governmental activities, whether computers, space
exploration vehicles, bombers, or sanitation
trucks.

At the most profound level, there is
the situation in which a foreign service officer
negotiates with the government of a lesser developed country for the establishment of an
American owned business in the new nation. Is
he acting to further American foreign policy
in encouraging economic development? Or is he
really acting as a representative of American
business interests? The answer is both. And,
this answer shows the indivisibility of government and business in modern America.

It would, of course, be a mistake to
equate "business" with the "giant corporation."
By various estimates there are something like
14,000,000 business enterprises in America and
over 2,000,000 corporations. The former includes the "Mom-and-Pop" grocery store, drug-
store, farm, or shoe store. The latter includes
a large number of equally small enterprises,
ranging often from the local real estate firm
or contractor to include many banks and insurance firms scattered throughout the 20,000 local
communities of the nation. Thus, "American
business" is by no means the Exxon, General
Motors, Standard Oil, or International Business
Machines of the nation. With this qualifier
in mind, however, we must note that it is the
corporate giants which largely shape the nature
of modern business enterprise. They are not
only the largest hirers, but command the greater
share of corporate assets, are most deeply involved in what occurs domestically and in foreign
affairs, and, as it happens, have the resources
to influence governmental decision-making (see
Table 5).

119

TABLE 5

NET INCOME AND NUMBER OF EMPLOYEES OF
MAJOR CORPORATIONS, 1975

	Net Income	Number of Employees
Industrial Corporations[a]		
Exxon	$2.5 billion	137,000
International Business Machines	1.9 billion	288,647
General Motors	1.3 billion	681,000
Texaco	830 million	75,235
Mobil Oil	809 million	71,300
Commercial Banking[b]		
Citicorp	350 million	46,400
BankAmerica	303 million	65,105
J. P. Morgan & Co.	184 million	9,808
Chase Manhattan	174 million	30,130
Manufacturers Hanover	142 million	17,694

SOURCES: [a]Fortune magazine, May 1976, pp. 318-19.
[b]Fortune magazine, July 1976, p. 204.

The Nature of the Corporation

The idea of the corporation has its historical roots in the medieval city when urban dwellers managed to extract a measure of independence for their cities from the feudal nobles holding sway over them. They gained this freedom in the form of a "charter," a document that established the city as a separate entity entitled to certain rights, privileges, duties, and responsibilities. As it evolved the charter in effect and in law created a body (a <u>corpus</u>) with a life of its own and at least some legal standing as a person.

The Corporate Advantage

Two signal advantages went with the creation of a corporation. First, as a separate body, the corporation was able to own property, to borrow, buy, sell, and act just as any other person might, but with a major difference: its lifespan was as great as its charter, that is, conceivably eternal for all practical human purposes. Second, as a separate person the corporation itself was alone responsible for its actions. While human beings might own parts of the corporation, they were not subject to be held to accounting if the corporation itself broke the law, damaged someone, or even went into bankruptcy. As shareholders in the corporation they stood to gain from its activities, but risked no more than their original investment.

These two advantages meant the corporation was ideally adapted to long-term business enterprises and to ventures that might be risky enough to discourage investors unless they were assured that their liability was limited. A

substantial part of British exploration and
settlement of the New World and of Asia accordingly was undertaken by corporations rather than
groups of individuals.

    Another characteristic of the idea of
the corporation made it attractive to the businessman. It was an extremely useful way to
attract the large sums of money ("capital") often
necessary to set a major enterprise into motion.
If, for example, a man felt a new product would
sell well but needed, say, $1,000,000 for the
machinery, land, raw materials, and building
to even start manufacturing the product, he had
a limited number of ways of raising the money.
He could supply it all himself, if he were that
wealthy and willing to risk the entire sum on
his idea. He could try to convince his friends
to come in as partners. He could, perhaps, borrow it from friends or a bank, but at a cost
(interest charges). Were he to incorporate,
however, he could sell shares, perhaps in quite
small denominations, to as many people as were
willing to buy. By selling 200,000 shares at
$5.00 a piece, the money needed to carry on
the enterprise would be available. If the idea
turned out to be a failure, no one would be
seriously hurt. If a success, however, the
probabilities are good that the original $5.00
piece of the corporation would increase in value,
doubling, tripling, or more, meaning any of the
shareholders could sell their share to someone
else for a handsome return. They would, further,
as owners of the corporation, be entitled to
a proportionate amount of the business's profits.

    In theory, each person with a share of
the corporation would, as owners, also be entitled
to a voice in how the corporation was run. Unlike political systems where each person has
a vote, however, the corporate system provides
that each share has a vote. Thus, the person
owning twenty shares has twenty votes; the person with two shares has only two. Our hypothetical

122

businessman could, by buying a large number of
shares, be assured he had a major if not the
predominant voice in running the corporation.
His risk, of course, is that unless he were
willing or able to buy a majority of the shares,
someone else might do so and take control of
the corporation. Most important, however, the
capital necessary for the enterprise has been
gathered, the risk to any one investor is no
greater than he chooses to make it, each investor
stands to benefit in two ways, through direct
profit-sharing and by an increase in the value
of the shares. And, once the venture has started
there is the knowledge that since a corporation
is immortal it will continue as long as it is
profitable regardless of the individual fates
of any of the original investors.

Early Development

    Although Americans neither invented nor
were the first to make use of the corporation,[6]
the advantages of the corporation plus the economic challenges of a wealth of natural resources
and enormous undeveloped space made the United
States a happy spawning ground of corporate enterprise. In 1800, Great Britain had twenty
corporations; the United States 300.[7] Since,
in America, "sovereignty" rested with the individual states, a lively competition grew up
among the states in the granting of charters
to corporations, with Delaware ultimately emerging
as the most favorable from a business standpoint.[8]

    The nineteenth century saw a continued
growth of the number and size of corporations
encouraged by the economic boom of the Civil War
years.[9] Two structural changes began to emerge
also. Originally a corporation was seen as a
single-venture enterprise. It was established
to build one railroad, manufacture one product,
or engage in a single activity such as banking

123

or real estate development. As a person, however,
the corporation was able to buy the stock of
other corporations and thus, if it were able
to acquire enough shares, gain control of the
other corporations. With sufficient capital,
then, one corporation could successfully acquire
all its competitors and create a monopolistic
situation. The next step, which was to create
a corporation whose sole purpose was the acquisition of other corporations, led to the "horizontal
concentration" of American enterprise that in
the 1870s and 1880s produced the hated "trusts,"
single corporate enterprises that literally controlled important segments of the economy,
squeezed out or bought their competitors, and
set prices at levels often beyond what the market
was willing to bear.

     A second structural change was related
to the first. A business enterprise in most
cases was (and still is) dependent on other
businesses in carrying out its activities. It
must buy the products or raw materials of other
corporations to conduct its activities and usually
depends on others to transport and market its
products. As a consequence, control of supplies
(and their prices) and of outlets (and their
price structure) were largely out of the hands
of any given corporation. Once again, it was
found that if a corporation reached out and
acquired control of its suppliers and related
transport and outlet firms, it guaranteed stability in its operations and, not incidentally,
often increased its profits. This was so-called
"vertical integration," the combining of control
from raw material to the sale of the finished
product to the ultimate consumer or user.

     By 1900, then, there were strong thrusts
toward concentration in corporate enterprise.
Although the absolute number of corporations
increased rapidly, the control of one corporation
by another also increased.

Efforts at horizontal and vertical integration all had in common the need for large
sums of capital. It is not surprising, then,
that banks often played a crucial role in the
search for corporate control, usually at the
price of having a voice in the operations of
the final product of the series of acquisitions
and mergers. It was J. P. Morgan who mid-wifed
the creation of the first billion dollar corpo-
ration--U.S. Steel--in 1901 and when he died
twelve years later his banking firm held interests in forty-seven other corporations.[10]

Recent Developments

        In the twenty-year period following 1900
came the emergence of the corporations which
were to be the "giants" of American business:
General Motors, Ford, American Telephone and
Telegraph Company, while others in existence
grew to ever greater size, such as U.S. Steel
and the Standard Oil Companies. Although all
were battered by the Great Depression, the post-
World War II era saw their growth continue.[11]

        And, with the end of the Second World
War two other major developments took place.
The first, and perhaps most important, was the
rise of the multi-national corporation or, as
it is now called, the trans-national enterprise
(TNE).[12] As its name suggests, the TNE operates
in several nations at the same time. Although
an earlier period had seen a number of TNEs in
existence--various fruit, sugar, mining, and
other corporations, for example, operated in
Latin America as well as in the United States;
the oil companies had extended their activities
to other countries--the post war era was a time
of rapid expansion. A number of factors have
contributed to the TNE growth. The search for
low-cost labor markets, the desire to find

125

nations imposing low business taxes, the availability of high speed transportation and communications networks which eased problems of
centralized control of far-flung operations all
played a crucial role.[13]

The effects, and implications, of TNEs
are still a challenge to understanding. Their
impact in terms of spreading "lifestyles" around
the globe is enormous (Coca-Cola, for example,
is a standard beverage throughout most of the
world). In this respect, they have no doubt
contributed to the revolution of rising expecta-
tions, the desire to enjoy the material benefits
of affluence as represented by western automobiles, housing, clothing, food, and entertainment. And they have political implications that
affect both domestic and foreign policy, not
only for the United States, but for every nation
they touch.

The other major post-war development
was the rapid rise of the "conglomerate."[14]
Traditionally, most corporations were engaged
in a single activity or, where vertical and horizontal integration occurred, closely and logically
related activities. Conglomeration represented
a new dimension, however: the acquisition by
one corporation of others in fields that had
no relation to the "primary" activity of the
first. Thus a communications company might also
control an insurance company, a food processing
corporation, and a car rental firm. The justification for vertical and horizontal integration
had been to "rationalize" the market or supply
and sales processes. Conglomeration has no justification, beyond the logical one of gaining
control of enterprises which would produce profits
or a useful tax write-off.

Despite the changes that have been traced
here, once again it must be remembered that most

126

corporations are not TNEs, conglomerates, or
have undertaken either vertical or horizontal
integration. In a sense, the major developments
have been the work of exceptions rather than
the norm of corporate enterprise. Nonetheless,
it is true that the corporations which have followed these patterns have emerged as the largest,
the most affluent, and the most influential.
They are, in general, the "corporate giants"
which are the targets of the anger and fear of
their critics.

Leadership in the Corporation

If, for the moment, we accept the hypothesis that corporations are powerful pressure groups,
the obvious next questions are who runs the corporation and to what end? Surprisingly, there
is by no means total agreement on either question.[15]

As already noted, the legal theory of
the corporation has it that the shareowners (the
stockholders) are properly the ultimate source
of rulership in the corporation. Realistically,
this can rarely be the case. Many of the major
corporations have hundreds of thousands or even
millions of individual shareholders (such as
AT&T, for example). Since the principal value
of a share is its value on the stockmarket and
the claim to corporate profits (dividends) it
represents, few shareholders are concerned with
what the business they "own" is doing or why
it does it, apart from that simple economic value.
And, if dissatisfied, most will show their discontent by attempting to sell their shares to
someone else rather than seeking a change in
operations.

Illustration six represents a simplified
sketch of the structure of a typical corporation
and suggests four possible locations of corporate

127

ILLUSTRATION   SIX

STRUCTURE   OF   A   CORPORATION

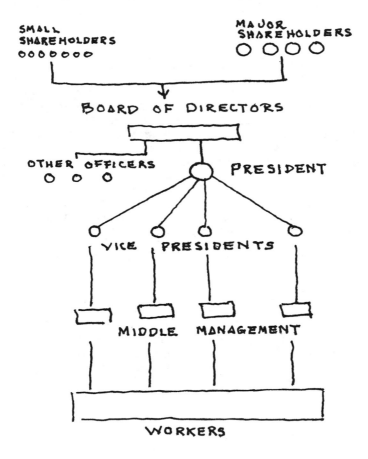

leadership. These are: the major shareholders; the board of directors (which may include some or all of the major shareholders); the top management (the officers, especially the president and the more important vice-presidents); and the "operating corporation" (middle management and the workers).

The Major Shareholders

The major shareholders, that is, individuals or institutions which own substantial blocks of stock in the company represent a logical source of control and leadership for the corporation, that is, that the "owners" are the voters and the ultimate source of authority. Supposedly, of course, one would have to own a majority of shares to be in true control. In reality, because for the typical large corporation so many of its shares are held by individuals who are basically indifferent to the operations of the company, a much smaller percentage may give a "controlling interest," that is, ownership of 20 percent or 25 percent (sometimes even less) guarantees the holder a powerful voice in corporate decision-making. The power granted by a large bloc of shares springs from the law: the voting power of those shares which mean the holder is in a position to elect directors and officers of the corporation and thus control major policy decisions (such as the acquisition of another company). Economic power stems from the threat of a dissatisfied major stockholder dumping his shares on the market and thereby depressing the value of the stock, which would damage other investors in the company. At least as serious, obvious discontent by a major shareholder circulates throughout the business community, alarming investors and creditors about the "stability" of the company.

129

Probably most people still think of major
shareholders in important corporations as enormously wealthy individuals. Once this was the
case; today, however, most major shareholders
are themselves corporations and often are financial institutions of one kind or another: mutual
funds, insurance companies, and banks. Large
blocks of shares are held by retirement plans
which in turn are controlled by one of these
financial institutions. The effect is that major
shareholders are corporations which may, in turn,
have as their major shareholders other corporations. When Mintz and Cohen argue that the real
power of the business world resides with financial institutions, then, they have a persuasive
case at hand.[16]

Power is not exercised by institutions
but by the people who are in those institutions.[17]
Thus it can be argued that one must look at who
sits on the board of directors of major corporations to determine the controlling leadership
of a corporation. Usually the board is made
up of either major shareholders or the representatives of major shareholders. They have, then,
two political advantages: they represent the
voting strength of the corporation and, as members of the board, they are the legally consti-
tuted governing body of the corporation. There
is a great deal of logic in the argument. As
it happens, there are very little data on which
to base a conclusion. Most, if not all, corporate board members are members of more than one
board; it may be assumed that each has little
interest in the affairs of any given corporation
on a day-to-day basis. It is equally safe to
say, however, that as representatives of major
shareholders who stand to gain or lose substantial amounts of money, board members will have
at least some interest in corporate policy, and
they are in theory in a position to impose their
policy preferences on the management of the
corporation.

130

Top Management

The most commonly cited locus of leadership and power in the modern corporation is top management.[18] David Finn, in fact, refers to them as the "corporate oligarchy." Top management consists of the chief executive officer (who sits on the board of directors), and the two to eight other major officers who are responsible for overseeing the vital functions of the corporation, such as finance, marketing, and manufacturing. Since these are the men who are in charge of the day-to-day details of the operation of the corporation, have at their fingertips all important information, and devote all their time to the corporation's affairs, it is argued that they necessarily determine the board's decision-making processes. They are, in short, the experts on what the corporation is doing and why and how, and since most of the board members are relatively speaking amateurs, the latter will almost always defer to the experts who must carry any decisions out. Thus, regardless of what the law says are duties of the board, it must delegate its responsibility to the men who really know what is going on. Power then comes to rest in the hands of top management.

The Operating Corporation

The fourth suggested locus of power in the modern corporation is at the lower levels of management.[19] Just as the board is a "captive" of top management in its need for information, it is argued that in the sprawling modern corporation it is physically and mentally impossible for the men at the top to keep track of and grasp what is going on in their overseas "branches," in components which are engaged in a wide variety of totally unrelated economic activities, and

131

in a rapidly changing national and world economic
situation. They, like the board, are dependent
on the advice and good sense of their subordinates and, like the board, can set down only
broad goals which others must and do turn into
actual operations.

As persuasive as the argument seems, some
analysts suggest that while this view perhaps
held for the 1950s, it is no longer so true.[20]
In effect, technology has caught up with the
delegation of authority to subordinates. Modern
financial controls allow top management to set
very specific goals and intermediate sub-goals
("managing by objective") and computers rapidly
test whether these goals are being met. Further,
the jet airplane allows a member of top management or his personal representative to fly to
the site of operations in a matter of hours or
to call a subordinate in for detailed supervision and reporting. While delegation may occur,
perhaps often as a means of testing the ability
of some "bright young fellow," any power that
is surrendered is easily regained.

Where, then, does power in the modern
corporation lie? The most sensible suggestion
would seem to be that it rests in an alliance
between top management and the financial houses
which are the spokesmen for the major shareholders.[21] In a sense, it is a negotiated agreement: the managers of the financial interests
respect and defer to the expert judgment of the
top managers who accept the need to defer to
the responsibilities of the managers of the
financial concerns.

The leadership of the modern corporation,
then, looks like the leadership of other pressure
groups. While there is a common interest, the
continued success of the corporation, there are
shadings within that set of shared attitudes.
Further, it is a plural leadership. Except in
rare cases, corporations are led by several

132

people instead of one person. The "oligarchy" pools its skills and operates with a division of labor among them, again much as other pressure group leadership teams do.

Corporate leadership claims to be motivated by corporate profits, corporate growth, and the welfare of the enterprise they lead. Some analysts accept this as a superficial characterization at best, holding that the major motivation of today's leadership is power: for themselves, gained by increasing the power of the enterprise they lead. Thus, the pattern of vertical and horizontal integration, multination expansion, and conglomeration, none of which can be economically explained by profit-motives, can be explained by the desire for power.[22]

But, it would appear the drive for power means the corporation must, in some fashion, interact with other power-wielders either as rivals or opponents, and, moreover, the quest for power means there must be some relationship with government.

The Corporation, Government, and Power

This chapter began by pointing out that government and business have long been intertwined. The relationship, more specifically, has been the intertwining of government and corporations.

Government and Business

At the national level, one of the early efforts of Alexander Hamilton as the first Secretary of the Treasury was to attempt to create a national manufacturing corporation.[23] Although

133

Hamilton's efforts had only limited success, they established a pattern that continued until close to the end of the nineteenth century. One of the most important functions of the national government was to promote industrial and corporate growth through tariff protection and subsidies of vast sums of money and vast quantities of land to railroad companies. In this respect, the United States was never a "free enterprise" economy, or at least in no way that Adam Smith would have recognized.

The rise of the great corporations in the post-Civil War years created serious problems, however. Their monopolistic practices, their frequent demands for more and more from government, and their shady political dealings encouraged a revulsion among other interests throughout the country. States had already tried to regulate the corporations they chartered, but since the larger enterprises reached beyond state boundaries and only the federal government was constitutionally entitled to regulate interstate commerce, most legislatures were helpless, a helplessness added to by the willingness of the corporations to spend lavishly to control legislators through bribes and campaign contributions.[24]

The national government moved slowly into attempts at regulating the most obvious abuses. In 1887, the Interstate Commerce Commission was created to control the worst practices of the railroads. In 1890, the Sherman Antitrust Act was passed, its intent being to preserve competition by preventing and breaking up monopolies. During the next five decades a wide variety of regulatory agencies and measures were adopted. Some came at the behest of various industries themselves, such as the Federal Communications Commission (1933) designed to reduce the chaotic competition for the airwaves by the rapidly growing radio industry, and the Securities and Exchange Commission (1934) to forestall stricter

134

regulation after the collapse of the stock market
in 1929. Others, such as the Pure Food and Drug
Act, arose out of public outcry.

Although federal regulation created a
"new climate" in which business had to operate,
the older pattern of government support of business did not vanish either. Tariffs, subsidies,
and tax incentives continued into the 1980s,
and promised to persist into the indefinite future.
And, as painful as regulation might occasionally
seem to businessmen, there is no evidence that
any major corporation has been seriously damaged
by federal or state controls. To the extent
business and government have been opponents,
it would appear that the large corporations have
generally been victors in the struggle.

Power Bases

Two factors have contributed to political
power of the corporations in America. The first
is the role of the corporations in the American
economy. While it is not necessarily so that
what is good for any one or all of the major
corporations is good for the rest of the country,
it is true that whatever is bad for them is apt
to hurt most Americans even worse. If car sales
slump, if the demand for steel declines, if
petroleum becomes difficult to obtain, the corporations involved will probably survive, but
hundreds of thousands or millions of Americans
will find themselves thrown out of work, with
a consequent drain on governmental resources
in the form of higher welfare, unemployment,
and law enforcement costs. The recession of
the early 1970s drove home with painful clarity
that even in the modern "welfare state" business
enterprise is the primary source of the welfare
of most Americans. Further, it is in substantial
measure the TNE's conversion of their money

135

assets into one currency or another that has
the most direct bearing on the "soundness" of
the dollar. When the top management of the TNEs
become seriously alarmed at the economic conditions in the country, they will tend to shift
their money assets to another "stronger" money
and banking system. Similar decisions are made
in terms of opening new plants in search for
a more beneficial taxation rate or labor supply.
And, if a TNE shifts its major production facilities to some other country, it means a loss of
present and future jobs at home (and a consequent
loss of governmental revenues).

The decisions of the giant corporations
are not simply economic decisions but are <u>political</u>
economic decisions, affecting government tax
bases, expenditure patterns, social policy, and,
if things go badly, the prestige and popularity
of those in office. The government official,
in short, must listen to the advice and complaints
of business representatives. Their advice may
be wrong; their complaints may be based on un-
truths, but he is forced to mind the fact that
if he is not attentive and his efforts to regulate or control business precipitate economic
instability, he may not only be punished at the
polls but he will be inflicting misery on large
numbers of his fellow citizens.

The central place that the large corporations hold in the domestic (and world) economy
give them a position of extraordinary bargaining
power. This position is further strengthened
by their strategic position in the sense used
here, that is, in terms of their political resources and competitive and historical circumstances.

Power Resources

In money, organization, and leadership
skills, the modern corporation is unrivalled

136

in the political arena. Although until the 1974
Election Campaign Reform Act, it was illegal
for corporations as such to contribute to federal
political campaigns, many either ignored the
law or found simple ways of avoiding the restrictions.[26] Moreover, these restrictions did not
apply to the hiring of lobbyists, public relations experts, and the expenditure of money on
legal counsel and efforts to influence public
opinion. Organizationally, the corporations
are able to work for themselves individually
and through their respective trade associations,
having as a consequence two voices to speak for
them. And, by their training and experience,
corporate leaders are masters of basic leadership skills.[27]

     Although the status and image of corpo-
rations suffer periodically, business leaders
have had the steady advantage of the image of
"success." Even when the public, the media,
and the academic world are most skeptical about
big business, there are always large numbers
of politicians who are dazzled by the power,
poise, and physical presence of top corporate
managers. Politicians, like the rest of us,
are impressed with the kind of quiet power,
elegant affluence, sophistication, and energy
of the modern business executive. Given the
other assets of corporate leadership, this personal resource is one which will necessarily
make its impact on large numbers of elected and
appointed officials in face-to-face discussions.

     Corporations, like other pressure groups,
have little control over their historical circumstances, but they have the advantage of
longevity. The corporation is "eternal"; if
the tide seems to be running against them, they
can usually wait it out. The oil depletion
allowance lost one year can be compensated for
in the future by deregulation when the energy
crisis grows more critical; the regulatory en-
thusiasm of a new agency or newly appointed

137

public administrator will dampen after a few
years of struggling with red tape, delaying
tactics, and court cases. Journalists find new
causes to pursue and public attention will shift
in that direction. The corporate form has advantages not only as a financial mechanism but
as a political one.

A final source of corporate political
power needs to be mentioned. Although U.S. Congressmen and presidents are nominally "national
leaders," in the American federal system their
political fortunes are rooted in state political
systems. Even the president must win the electoral votes of particular states, regardless
of what his popular vote may be. And particular
corporate interests bulk very large in some states.
A senator from Louisiana or Oklahoma who is not
sensitive to the needs of the petroleum industry
should not expect to hold office long. The same
would be true of senators unaware of the vital
role of the auto industry to Michigan or the
aerospace industry to Texas, Florida, and California. In each case, and many others, the state
and local party leaders will demand that politicians aspiring to national office come to terms
with the economic interests which the party leaders
must deal with. Corporate power can make itself
felt directly in Washington and indirectly through
the state political systems, and often it is
at the state level where this power is least
subject to challenge or rivalries.

The geographic base of political power
in America strengthens the corporation. Further,
it can mean that big business is extraordinarily
powerful in state and local politics. The ability
of the cities to deal with the urban problems
of housing, unemployment, racial tensions, and
a deteriorating physical plant may be determined
more by business interests than governmental
officials.[28] Similarly, at the state level,
governors and legislators can find that to act

138

against the interests of the corporation is to
risk not only losing the next election but permanently damaging the economic base of the
state.[29] If sufficiently threatened by regulatory policies, a corporation may simply choose
to relocate its branch plants or even central
headquarters.[30] And, in an age of TNEs, the
move may not be from one community to another
or one state to another, but overseas.

How Powerful?

        Obviously, the modern corporation is
a political pressure group of enormous power,
but exactly how powerful is it? Can it expect
to prevail all or even most of the times in
seeking its political goals?

        Although there is widespread agreement
that corporations are indeed powerful, this
agreement does not include the extent of that
power. Some analysts feel that for all practical
purposes the corporations "own" America, that
is, the political system functions to maximize
the goals of the corporations usually at the
cost of the public.[31] Others concede corporate
power but point out that on the record there
are countervailing forces which have in the past
limited corporate power and even inflicted sharp
defeats on them.[32] With expert opinion sharply
divided, it is unwise to jump to any immediate
conclusions. What seems to be required is further understanding and analysis. A final answer
would, it seems, have to come to grips with
several issues that thus far remain largely un-
explored:

        First, there are clearly major power
differentials among corporations. Given these
differences, how extensive are they and what
effect do they have in terms of competition

139

among corporations in the political arena (rather than simply in business affairs)?

Second, there are clearly sharp divergencies of interests among corporations. For example, airlines, trucking firms, railroads, and maritime corporations all are in some degree in business competition with each other. To what extent do rivalries and oppositions help to diminish the effectiveness of the political resources that corporations command?

Third, some analysts have argued that corporate leaders feel the world of politics is unknown terrain and would rather remain aloof from it.[33] If so, of course, a logical corollary would be that corporations do not attempt to maximize their political power but use it largely as a defensive instrument. Is this in fact the case?

Finally, how skilled are corporate leaders at politics? Leading a corporation and engaging in politics are two very different activities.[34] There is no question that most top managers are good at management, but it does not follow they would be good at politics. As has been stressed, unskilled leadership can undermine all the advantages granted by other resources, so the issue is a vitally important one in resolving the question of political power.

Before these and other questions are answered, any estimate of the real power of corporations in the pressure group system must be tentative and should be regarded as such. Until then, however, it still seems safe to say that one of the shaping influences in contemporary American politics is the growing complexity of corporate involvement in the political economy and corporations as important participants in modern pressure group politics.

140

References for Chapter VI

[1]Morton Mintz and Jerry S. Cohen, America, Inc. (New York: Dell, 1971), p. 21.

[2]There are a number of sharply critical works on the modern corporation. Aside from Mintz and Cohen, cited above, their more recent work, Power, Inc.: Public and Private Rulers and How to Make Them Accountable (New York: The Viking Press, 1976) disucsses corporate power as well as other matters. Ralph Nader, Mark Green, and Joel Seligman, Taming the Giant Corporation (New York: W. W. Norton, 1976) is also critical. John Kenneth Galbraith, The New Industrial State (Boston: Houghton Mifflin, 1973) is critical, but places corporate behavior in a larger context, viewing the relationship of business and government as one which has been mutually supportive, and equally dangerous to both.

[3]Grant McConnell, Private Power and American Democracy (New York: Alfred A. Knopf, 1966), pp. 130-32.

[4]Nader, Green, and Seligman comment, "A couple of hundred corporate managers . . . can make decisions controlling most of our industrial economy" (p. 16).

[5]Charles Merriam, Public and Private Government (New Haven: Yale University Press, 1944), p. 16, said, "The lines between public and private are not absolutes. . . . There are zones of cooperation and cohesion." This theme has reappeared in McConnell, and in Theodore Lowi, The End of Liberalism: Ideology, Policy, and the Crisis of Public Authority (New York: W. W. Norton, 1969). See also Mark V. Nadel, "The Hidden Dimension of Public Policy," Journal of Politics 37 (February 1975): 2-34.

141

[6]The year 1555 is the commonly accepted date of the first incorporation of a business enterprise.

[7]David Finn, The Corporate Oligarch (New York: Simon and Schuster, 1967), p. 21.

[8]Daniel J. Boorstin, The Americans: The Democratic Experience (New York: Vintage, 1974), pp. 414-15 describes the state competition to become the most favored "home" of corporations. Nader, Green, and Seligman (Chapter II) also have an excellent legal and political history of this process.

[9]Boorstin traces the rise and changes in the nature of the corporation, pp. 413-21. A readable and entertaining (if biased) history of the corporation in the nineteenth century is Matthew Josephson, The Robber Barons (New York: Harcourt, Brace, and World, 1934, 1962).

[10]Finn, p. 41.

[11]Robert Sobel, The Age of Giant Corporations: A Microeconomic History of American Business, 1914-1970 (Westport, Conn.: Greenwood Publishing Co., 1972) is a fine history of the period. Sobel argues that many of the giant corporations actually prospered during the Depression Era.

[12]The TNE is also often referred to as the multinational enterprise (MNE).

[13]Richard J. Barnett and Ronald E. Muller, Global Reach: The Power of the Multinational Corporations (New York: Simon and Schuster, 1974) has a fascinating study of the TNE.

[14]Anthony Sampson, The Sovereign State of ITT (New York: Stein and Day, 1973) discusses one of the most controversial of the conglomerates,

one which gained national attention for its un-
savory involvement in the 1972 election campaign.

[15]Mintz and Cohen, Power, Inc., note
the difficulty of discovering who controls the
corporation (pp. 100-1).

[16]Mintz and Cohen, America, Inc.

[17]For an intriguing "insider's" look
at a corporation, although not necessarily a
typical one, see Otto Friedrich, Decline and
Fall (New York: Ballantine, 1970). Friedrich
narrates the struggle for control over the failing Saturday Evening Post Corporation.

[18]Finn; Galbraith, The New Industrial
State; Wilbert E. Moore, The Conduct of the
Corporation (New York: Vantage, 1966); Adolph
A. Berle, The Twentieth Century Capitalist Re-
volution (New York: Harcourt, Brace, 1954).

[19]Peter Drucker, The Concept of the Corpo-
ration (New York: New American Library, 1954).
W. Floyd Warner, Darab B. Unwalla, and John H.
Trimm, The Emergent American Society: Large
Scale Organizations (New Haven: Yale University
Press, 1967).

[20]Sampson; Barnett and Muller.

[21]Richard J. Barber, The American Corporation: Its Power, Its Money, Its Politics (New
York: E. P. Dutton, 1970).

[22]Finn, p. 139. Barnett and Muller carry
this argument even further. They contend that
the TNE is an effort to replace national governments; that modern corporate executives feel
the nation-state is an out-moded concept and
lacks the rationality and stability that global
business enterprises can provide. Thus, the
long term goal of the modern corporation is to

143

take on the functions of government and stabilize
the world order.

[23]Finn, p. 23.

[24]McConnell, pp. 39, 49.

[25]Joseph A. Califano, Jr., A Presidential
Nation (New York: W. W. Norton, 1975) comments,
"Big business, particularly, is of immense sali-
ence to any president, whether Republican or
Democrat, conservative or liberal" (p. 123).

[26]William J. Crotty, Political Reform
and the American Experiment (New York: Thomas
Y. Crowell, 1977), pp. 146-47, identifies $723,000
in illegal donations from corporations in the
1972 presidential campaign. An additional sum
ranging from $12 million to $17 million was
legally donated by corporate officers to the
Nixon campaign.

[27]Robert W. Miller and Jimmy D. Johnson,
Corporate Ambassadors to Washington (Washington,
D.C.: American University Press, 1970).

[28]See, for example, Karen Orren, Corporate
Power and Social Change: The Politics of the
Life Insurance Industry (Baltimore: The Johns
Hopkins University Press, 1973).

[29]Duane Lockard, New England Politics
(Princeton: Princeton University Press, 1959)
argues that in Maine, for example, timber companies and paper manufacturers are inordinately
powerful because of their importance to that
relatively impoverished state.

[30]Some of the desperation of New York
City officials over the financial affairs of
that city can be explained by their fear that
municipal "bankruptcy" would cause many corporations to seek other homes.

[31]Michael Parenti, Democracy for the
Few (New York: St. Martin's Press, 1974); Mintz
and Cohen, America, Inc.; Henry S. Kariel, The
Decline of American Pluralism (Stanford, Cal.:
Stanford University Press, 1961).

[32]Robert A. Dahl, Democracy in the United
States: Promise and Performance, 2d ed. (Chicago:
Rand McNally, 1972); Moore.

[33]Robert A. Dahl, Who Governs? Power
and Democracy in an American City (New Haven:
Yale University Press, 1961) argues that "economic
notables" have only a limited taste for politics.
Moore takes the same position.

[34]Nader, Green, and Seligman (pp. 77-
79) note a number of mistakes made by businessmen.
Similarly, the clumsy handling of overseas bribery
by TNEs which was exposed during the mid-1970s
suggests a degree of political maladroitness
that many critics of the corporation fail to
take into account. In all fairness, it must
be noted that the CIA has shown equal clumsiness
in its covert political activities.

CHAPTER VII

CASE STUDY: ORGANIZED CRIME

While some students of American politics
have seen the corporation as a major threat to
American democracy, others especially criminologists and sociologists, have voiced alarm
at the dangers implicit in organized criminal
activity.[1] Ironically, there is solid evidence
that criminal gangs have tended to follow the
precedents set by business corporations, moving
from free-wheeling competition to a "rationalized"
system of organization in which organization,
leadership skills, a concern with public relations,
and attention to political power help to guarantee
successful operations.

Further, while organized crime is not
new to America, the first "Mafia" organization
making its appearance in New Orleans in 1875,[2]
the period 1931 to the present saw major changes
in criminal organization and tactics that have
given organized crime a new and highly modern
pressure group character. The changes mean that
organized crime is adapting to changes in the
larger society with at least as much ease as
corporations (which are, of course, partly agents
of the changes). And, if many organized crime
experts are to be believed, criminal organizations are extending their economic and political
power as they adapt.

Barriers to Understanding

There are three major barriers to understanding the role of organized crime in America.
First, there has been a widespread doubt about

147

the existence of organized crime in the contemporary sense of the word. Although most people
accepted that there were various "gangs" engaged
in gambling, pushing narcotics, controlling
prostitution, and bootlegging, the prevailing
view for a long time was that these gangs operated at the most on a city-wide basis and often
competed with each other within a single locality.
The view grew out of what most Americans were
familiar with during Prohibition, in which rival
gangs hijacked each other's liquor supplies,
murdered each other, and, all in all, did a
better job of decimating their opponents than
police forces did. Even when, in 1952, Congressional investigation (the Kefauver hearings)
revealed what appeared to be a pattern of national
and regional organization, J. Edgar Hoover, then
Director of the Federal Bureau of Investigation
and regarded with some awe as the nation's "top
crime fighter" denied that any such criminal
conspiracy could exist. Not until 1957, when
seventy-five organized crime leaders from all
over the country met at Apalachin, New York,
was Hoover publicly convinced that at least some
crime was indeed highly organized.[3] To an extent, however, the skepticism remains. Virtually
no political science textbook even mentions
organized crime as a political force in state
or local government or as an active national
pressure group.[4]

A second barrier to understanding is
our education about and attitudes toward crime
as a human activity. Those of us familiar with
popular sociology, criminology, or psychology
have tended to think of criminal behavior as
being rooted in a "deprived background." The
individual is "driven into" a life of crime by
poverty, misery, and hopelessness, and as parlor
Freudians would have it are actually acting out
self-hatred and an unconscious desire to be
punished. The idea that an individual would
go into a life of crime the same way his brother

148

or next-door neighbor might choose to become
an accountant, a doctor, or a university professor,
that is, as a career option (and a highly profitable one) seems too "deviant" to be acceptable,
but this in fact seems to be the case.[5]

This same confusion extends in a large
measure to our attitudes toward individual criminals. Most of us regard the individual mugger
or rapist with a mixture of loathing and pity,
but we have always cast a romantic aura around
some criminals: they are perhaps the symbols
of the "rugged individualism" we each would like
to believe lurks somewhere in us. Jesse James
and William (Billy the Kid) Bonney are folk heroes.
More recently, Mario Puzo's bestselling The Godfather (and the equally popular movies based
on the novel) cast the organized criminal as
a similar folk hero. Throughout the book, "the
godfather" orders a number of criminal acts committed, including murders and savage beatings,
but in each case these are acts of crude "justice,"
to assist people who are being injured by de-
praved, cruel persons who "deserve what they
get." The portrait that emerges is of a man
who is tough, powerful, and ruthless but who
is, on balance, possessed of a higher moral sense
than judges, law enforcement officials, or other
"legitimate" people. Without criticizing the
literary or entertainment value of the book (it
is not the novelist's task to preach), it should
be noted that at no point were the victims of
"the godfather's" loan-sharks, extortionists,
or "leg-breakers" portrayed.

Third, our understanding of organized
crime is limited because organized criminals,
for obvious reasons, prefer secrecy and are willing to enforce that preference with violence.
All pressure groups have areas they would rather
go unexamined, but organized crime feels this
need more intensely than any other. As a result,
much of our knowledge is based on informants

149

(often minor figures in the organization), electronic eavesdrops (also often of conversations among lesser figures), and inferences drawn from the data available. As a result, an analysis of organized crime as a pressure group must be far more speculative than of any other group.

The Nature of Organized Crime

"Organized crime" is, as a term, a partially confusing one.[6] When three people get together to plan and carry out a mugging, they are organized and committing a crime. As Donald Cressy points out, organized crime as it represents a persistent and large criminal combination means more than that; it is truly an organization in the sense that we mean it here: established specialized roles, including leadership, a staff apparatus, membership and membership criteria and designed, like the corporation, to continue over long periods of time.[7] Organized crime then refers to a formal organization that has been bureaucratized and is capable of pursuing its interests in several ways in many places over an extended time period. It is this organizational form which, in fact, gives organized crime much of its effectiveness as a pressure group.

La Cosa Nostra

Although it is common to focus attention on "The Mafia," "the syndicate," "La Costa Nostra," this organization is not the only organized crime combine in the nation, although it is probably the most significant. Other combines exist in some cases in geographic proximity to La Cosa Nostra.[8] None, however, have achieved the national scope of La Cosa Nostra.

150

The Costra Nostra ("our thing," "this thing of ours") had its origins in a traumatic war among criminal organizations in 1930-31. After substantial bloodshed, the leaders of the organizations involved decided that the literally cutthroat competition was mutually too damaging to be allowed to continue. In a series of agreements, a formal organization of nation-wide scope was created for the purpose of consolidating the gains made, limiting future internecine warfare, and making rational allocations of geographic areas and activities. The product was less a unitary organization than a federation of various "families" which had already established themselves in their respective areas.[9] Table 6 lists twenty-seven families as presented to the U.S. Senate Committee on Commerce in its hearings on "Effects of Organized Criminal Activity on Interstate and Foreign Commerce," as of 1971.[10] It is not certain that all these families were in operation at the time the federation was created.

The product of the agreement was an organization which, at the top, is led by a "commission" that "serves as a combination legislature, supreme court, board of directors, and arbitration board. . . ."[11] The membership of the commission apparently varies in size, but while not all the families are represented it exercises control over all. The purpose of the commission is to settle disputes among families, help in the selection of a new boss when a family loses its, and, if need be, make decisions concerning the punishment of those who fail to obey its wishes. In addition, apparently the commission sets membership criteria and quotas for all the families, again as a way of reducing inter-family rivalries.

The New York City area, with its six families, also has a council of the heads of the families which acts as a commission for

151

TABLE 6

CRIME FAMILIES IN THE UNITED STATES--1971

Areas of Operations
Rockford, Ill.
Springfield, Ill
San Francisco, Cal.
San Jose, Cal.
Los Angeles, Cal.
Denver, Colo.
Kansas City, Mo.
St. Louis, Mo.
Madison, Wisc.
Detroit, Mich.
Chicago-Cicero, Ill.
Buffalo-Rochester, N.Y.
Cleveland, Ohio
Florida
New England
New Orleans, La.
Upstate Pennsylvania
Pittsburgh, Pa.
Philadelphia - Camden
New York City - New Jersey - Conn. - Pa.
New York City (5)
Milwaukee, Wisc.
Montreal, Canada, and Northern New York state.

SOURCE: U.S. Senate Committee on Commerce, Report on the Effects of Organized Crime on Interstate and Foreign Commerce (Washington, D.C.:   U.S. Government Printing Office, 1972), p. 35.

the New York families. It is not certain that
other cities have similar councils.[12]

Formal Organization

The basic units of the federation are
the families. Formal leadership lies in the
hands of the boss, and he is generally an authoritarian leader. He shares some of his functions
with an "underboss," who is his assistant in
gathering information and passing on orders and
instructions, and a consigliere, a counselor,
who acts principally as an advice-giver and consultant to the boss and underboss. Beneath the
top leadership are a number of "lieutenants"
(caporegime) who are concerned with the supervision and conduct of the family's operations.
Beneath them are the "soldiers," who are the
lowest rank of formal members of the Cosa Nostra
but who themselves are usually the supervisors
of a large number of employees of the family
who actually do the work of selling numbers to
gamblers, collecting money from debtors, overseeing prostitutes, and so forth.

The family is, then, actually a managerial
enterprise, structurally not much different from
other moderate-sized business enterprises. And,
as a business enterprise, money is the principal
interest, if not the only interest of its members.

Two items set it apart from other businesses. The bulk of its money is gained illegally,
and it is willing to use violence to collect
from those who owe it money and on those members
who may be foolish enough to "betray" it. Further, because it is engaged in illegal enterprises
its relationship with government creates special
problems that other pressure groups do not have.

153

The traditional activities of organized crime have been gambling, in which Cosa Nostra members control betting on horse races, sports events, and various lottery schemes; loan sharking, that is, lending money at interest rates as high as 1,000 percent a year; and the importing and sale of narcotics. Prostitution and bootlegging appear to be declining in importance, as is outright extortion (the so-called "protection racket," which amounts to "Pay me and I won't beat you up"). The enormous profit garnered from these activities has produced another important leadership position in many families, that of "money mover."[13] The function of the money mover is to funnel the illegally gained money into legitimate enterprises, thereby "laundering" it and not incidentally protecting Cosa Nostra leaders from the bane of their existence, income tax evasion prosecutions. The money mover is an escalation of technical expertise for the Cosa Nostra since he, and his employees, must be knowledgeable in contemporary tax law, accounting procedures and ways of evaluating good investment prospects.

The threat of "treachery," that is, a member of the Cosa Nostra acting as a police informer or telling too much in the course of a grand jury investigation also has created two functional specialties within the organization: that of "enforcer" and of "executioner." The task of the enforcer is to make the necessary arrangements for a "hit" (a killing). The executioner, and his team of assistants, actually carry the task out.[14] Both jobs are temporary, that is, special assignments made to able individuals for one "contract" and both are richly rewarded, although the enforcer's more so: "The enforcer maintains internal security and discipline. . . . His, after all, was the executive talent that pulled the whole thing together and made it work."[15]

154

The complicated relationship of organized crime to the governmental system creates two other important positions in the Cosa Nostra: that of "buffer" and of "corrupter." The task of the buffer is to act as a go-between for top leaders and their subordinates and, often, apparently for lesser figures and their employees. They act so that no specific crime can be directly traced to a leader: they give the orders that they have been instructed to give. In effect, the buffer is similar to the "cut-out" in espionage work. The police are forced to go through a chain of individuals to track down who ordered a crime committed, and only one of these people need maintain silence to break the chain. The positions of enforcer and executioner are strong incentives for maintaining that silence.

The task of the corrupter is summarized in his title. It is his job to make contacts with law enforcement officers, politicians, and judges, nurture those contacts and, when and if the opportunity presents itself, corrupt the officials to the Cosa Nostra's uses.

The Cosa Nostra, like other pressure groups, has evolved an organizational structure adapted to the environment in which it operates and reflective of the interests it contains. Its federated macro-organization gives each of the families flexibility in handling local conditions and, like most other federations, it is based on geographic "jurisdictions." The national commission is a useful means of settling inter- and some intra-family disputes. At the micro-organizational level, each family has worked out a structure of internal positions which provide leadership, the allocation of resources, and the capability to carry out important tasks in maintaining the organization's integrity and handling the outside world.

These organizational changes have been further strengthened by the shift of Cosa Nostra

into "legitimate" business: gaining control
of labor union locals, becoming silent partners
in business ventures, and progressively becoming
openly the owners and operators of businesses.
The embarrassment of riches provided by illegal
operations almost has forced expansion into
legitimate enterprises.   There are inherent limits
on the number of expensive homes and automobiles
one can enjoy and on the number of illegal goods
that can be sold to the public.   Legitimate businesses, whether dishonestly run or not, provide
a source of expansion, the opportunity to launder
funds, and, as important, access to the world
of respectability and the social and political
power that goes to a man who is wealthy and re-
spectable.   And, interestingly, many crime leaders
do seem to crave respectability, if not for themselves then for their children.   This craving,
however, may not be all sentimental.   Respectability does give protective coloration to the
base of illegal activities and also means off-
spring will probably go on to the university
educations which will give them the technical
skills to handle the steadily more complex operations of the Cosa Nostra.

Other Crime Organizations

          Although La Costra Nostra is the best
organized, and most extensive criminal syndicate
in the United States, it is not the only one.
There is evidence that there are other criminal
gangs that operate at least on a city-wide level,
either with the toleration of or in competition
with the Cosa Nostra.   Thus it is said that Cleve-
land is dominated chiefly by a "Jewish syndicate,"
although other experts claim the dominance of
the Cosa Nostra there.[16]   However, it does seem
to be clear that in the ghettos of many large
cities, blacks and Puerto Ricans are each creating
their own criminal organizations in defiance and

156

imitation of the Cosa Nostra and gradually pushing the older organization out.[17] There is
probably friction and perhaps even violence as
a result; but the shift is coincidental with
the move of the Cosa Nostra into legitimate business and "white collar crime" (such as dealing
with stolen stock certificates) and so the leadership is more willing to surrender some of its
previous pre-eminence.

Ironically, the civil rights and black
(and other minorities) liberation movement helped
pave the way to the expansion of organized crime
among these groupings. By challenging the "white
establishment," whether licit or illicit, by
fostering a sense of minority pride, and by spreading organizational skills, the freedom movements
provided much of the groundwork for the crimi-
nally inclined to challenge the old line families
and gain a "piece of the action" for themselves.
Like the Cosa Nostra, these newer organizations
are racially or ethnically based, and, with the
appearance of more black or brown law enforcement officials, politicians, and administrators
there is "one of us" in government who may be
susceptible to corruption.

None of these organizations have achieved
even regional scope apparently and few, if
any, would appear to have attained the micro-
organizational sophistication of La Cosa Nostra.
Such developments are, however, probably only
a matter of time. The economic and power advantages of organization are great enough to
impel sophisticated leaders toward more refined
and more extensive structures.[18]

Organized Crime, Power, and Government

Two preconditions must exist for successful organized crime: illegal goods and services
desired by enough members of the public to produce

a profit; and a governmental system vulnerable
to the pressure of the criminal organization.
The first provides the essential political resource of organized crime: money. And money
is the tool used to find weaknesses in the political system.

Money and Numbers

        The amount of money gained by organized
crime is, of course, impossible to estimate.
The President's Commission on Law Enforcement
and Administration of Justice (1967) estimated
that gross proceeds from illegal gambling amounted
to around $20 billion a year; from narcotics
$350 million a year; and from loan-sharking pro-
fits in the "multi-billion dollar range."[19] Two
scholars, after a careful review of estimates,
place gross income at $40 billion a year with
$10 billion as net profit.[20] That is, it seems
likely that organized crime receives as profit
a sum of money equal to or greater than the total
incomes of all other American pressure groups
(corporations excepted). As with corporate
income, probably most of this money is not available for political purposes, being earmarked
to support an affluent lifestyle and for rein-
vestment, but without question an amount of money
on this scale represents an awesome political
resource.

        As a political resource, the membership
of organized crime remains something of an unknown quantity. Estimates of the total membership of the La Cosa Nostra vary between 5,000
and 10,000.[21] These figures do not include employees of one kind or another, public officials
and businessmen who because of their corruption
or money debts are virtually owned by the Cosa
Nostra, and those eagerly awaiting formal membership. The membership of various black, Puerto

158

Rican, and other crime syndicates have not even
been estimated.

Cosa Nostra families themselves vary
greatly in size. The smallest has apparently
only about twenty members; the largest 700. In
any given political situation, then, it is less
the numbers organized crime can muster than its
other political resources.

Organization and Leadership

As already noted, it is organization
which provides the various crime syndicates with
one of their most potent political advantages.
The specialized tasks of corrupter, enforcer,
and executioner mean that, as a pressure group,
the family is geared to bring its resources and
skills to bear on the political system. Further,
the roles of enforcer and executioner represent
another dimension of organized crime: its willingness to use violence and physical threats
against not only its own members but competitors
and opponents. In this respect, organized crime
is set aside as a special case when compared
with almost all other pressure groups.

Some radical minority groups have been
willing to use violence to upset "the system,"
and are organized with this purpose in mind.
Few, however, have elevated this willingness
to the organizational sophistication, ruthlessness, and skill which organized crime specialists
are willing to apply against informers, infil-
trators, those who fail to pay their debts, or
those whom they decide are threats to their
organizations. The result is that opponents
of organized crime syndicates must accept that
"political struggle" includes not only lobbying,
votes, court procedures and the other paraphenalia
familiar to domestic politics, but "war" in the
literal sense, involving possible physical harm

159

or death to oneself and to family and friends. Violence as an instrument of policy is an accepted value for the organized criminal. Moreover, the nation-wide (and international) scope of organized crime means its intended victims can be pursued regardless of where they attempt to hide themselves. As is so often the case with a willingness to use violence, the threat is more effective than the actual use. Only the most rash or the most desperate usually are willing to risk triggering the mechanisms of enforcement and execution.

As might be inferred, it seems the leadership skills of organized crime are generally of a high order. La Cosa Nostra at least does conform to the iron law of oligarchy, with a vengeance, since in virtually all cases "the boss's" word is law unless he violates the dictates of the national commission. As with most authoritarian systems, however, this oligarchical pattern presents the major problem facing the various families, that of leadership succession. In the absence of any democratic or quasi-democratic method of replacing leaders, "the old man" may hang on regardless of how weary, senile, wrong-headed, or physically incompetent he has become. The use of plural leadership helps alleviate some of these problems. The underboss and the consigliere can take up the slack, if permitted to by their chief. Often, the only solution seems to be the murder of the man to make way for younger and fresher blood, which creates the problem of internal factionalism unless consensus has been reached within the family. In the New York area, for example, there were leadership crises within the Cosa Nostra in 1957, 1960, 1964, and again in 1978-79. In each instance the difficulties were resolved only with violence.[22]

Despite these problems, organized crime leadership has been and continues to be highly

skilled, partly because leaders must prove their
merit by rising through the ranks and partly
because the money rewards for leaders are so
great competition is keen, guaranteeing that
only the "best" will gain the coveted top positions. A man will be expected to have served
ably in the crucial roles of corrupter, enforcer,
and executioner, and to have some ability as
a money-mover. Favoritism and nepotism does
occur among blood relatives and as a consequence
of marriage ties, but the greater number of
leaders still seem to be recruited on the basis
of ability.[23] The result is that the top leadership of the various families are thoroughly
familiar with all the important operations of
their groups and know intimately the needs of
their members and their organizations.

Status and Image

        Logically, status and image should be
one of the major weaknesses of organized crime
in terms of its political resources. As it happens, the problem is not so serious from their
point of view as it might seem. To large segments of the communities in which crime organizations operate, the members of the organization
are figures of success, contempt for "the system,"
and masculine virility, if not exactly hero
images. Especially among ethnic and racial working and lower-class people, the crime leaders
are men to imitate rather than hate. This image
has not been damaged by the occasional popularity
organized crime figures enjoy among members of
the entertainment world, with the consequent
blending of the vision of fabulous glamor and
the awesomely wealthy crime lord. A thoughtful
observer has to admit there is a thrill here:
the most ugly aspects of organized crime rarely
surface and for novelists and movie-makers the
bosses are almost irresistible subjects for
their craft.

161

Further "crime in the streets"--muggings, rapes, burglaries--are highly personal and common enough to seem a threat. The organizers of crime, especially crime such as gambling or loan-sharking, are far less ominous-seeming than the products of their activities, most significantly the nar- cotics addict. Few people bother to make the connection between the organizer who has deliber- ately buffered himself and the mugging that occurred just down the street.

Like other pressure group leaders, organi- zed crime leaders are attentive to public rela- tions. A common practice is the substantial donation to a charitable organization which often brings about an invitation in subsequent years to fund-raising balls and banquets. The leader thus associates himself with a worthy cause, proves he has a heart of gold, and not just in- cidentally hob-nobs with business executives, political leaders, and social elites, all for what is to him a small contribution from his (tax-free) annual income.

Cosa Nostra leaders have a reputation for being good neighbors. Their wealth allows them to buy homes in high status areas and apparently they go to some effort to ingratiate themselves with their neighbors by actively entertaining, contributing to fund-drives and churches and living what seem to be quite re- spectable lives. That they are also often able to solve neighborhood problems through their connections at city hall is an added benefit.

In combination with their choice of a place to reside, the shift into legitimate busi- ness lends an additional aura of respectability to the Cosa Nostra leader. Like other well- to-do husbands and fathers he goes to work at his general contracting firm's office, is the director of a bank, or is the busy owner of a chain of retail stores. To his non-criminal friends and neighbors he is a pillar of his

162

community, hard-working, affluent, with good connections in the right circles to get things done, and with sons and daughters in college. Older leaders may lack a certain polish and have deplorable taste in their home furnishings, but today even these signs of a "poor background" are giving way to men who blend perfectly into the world of the successful business executive and professional.

To the extent possible, then, organized crime had done what it can to overcome its status and image problems. In New York, the effort went so far as to take advantage of the newly aroused sensitivity to ethnic slights by the creation of a pressure group aimed at overcoming the image of La Cosa Nostra as an Italian-Sicilian ethnically based group. The effort was successful enough that many television programs rewrote scripts about organized crime to delete Italian-sounding names.

Unlike other pressure groups, however, organized crime needs less a positive image in the public's eye than no image at all. Public disinterest is one of its strongest assets and to the extent that public concern about crime is directed against "crime in the streets" and away from the activities of organized crime, the leadership of the criminal syndicates can be well satisfied with their status and image.[24] To some degree, there is an ironic reverse twist in organized crime's sense of its status and image. As one knowledgeable observer of crime in America put it to the author,

> Syndicate leaders aren't all that unhappy when they get blamed for a murder they didn't order committed. It maintains their credibility, you see. Every potential witness or informer, a lot of law enforcement people, every small-time punk quakes in his boots. They get reminded they too can be 'hit' and toe the line.

An image of ruthlessness has its political uses.

163

Situational Factors

The principle behind the organization
of La Cosa Nostra was to control and rationalize
the competitive situation of organized crime.
It was a means of eliminating the problems of
unfettered rivalries by, in effect, vertical
and horizontal integration, and on balance appears to have been remarkably successful. Not
all rivals have been eliminated, as already noted,
but in general tacit bargains appear to have
produced a remarkable degree of harmony in a
"business" that is so profitable to its participants. The major opponents of organized crime
are, of course, federal state, and local law
enforcement agencies and to the extent possible,
organized crime has moved to neutralize this
opposition. It may well be that organized crime
occupies the most comfortable competitive situation of any pressure group in America.

As is true of other pressure groups,
there is very little organized crime can do to
control its historical circumstances. Certain
long-term trends have probably had adverse effects, most particularly the stress on the "professionalization" of public employees, especially
policemen, the civil rights movement, and the
steady gains in the education and affluence of
the American public in general. In some measure,
these long-run trends reduce the public's demand
for the goods and services the organized criminal
has to offer, although any reductions that have
occurred do not appear to have done any real
economic damage to organized crime. The shift
into legitimate business as a means of conglomer-
ating is perhaps in part a response to these
trends, as well as being a search for respectability, added power, and a place to invest
illegally gained profits.[25]

Other trends, such as the "corporate
revolution," and the accompanying technological

164

revolutions, have been reflected in the increasing
sophistication of organized crime. In this respect, La Cosa Nostra at least seems to have had
the flexibility to adapt to changes in its environment.[26] However, technology through computer-
ized information systems and electronic eavesdrops
constitutes a major threat to organized crime
since it is upon the accumulation of information
and its collation and rapid dissemination that
income tax evasion cases, criminal conspiracy
prosecutions, and systematic adverse publicity
and harassing investigations are built. To date,
organized crime leaders have not found a totally
effective counter to modern police technology
except in the political sphere.

Governmental Vulnerability

        It was pointed out earlier that one of
the pre-conditions essential to the existence
of organized crime is a governmental system vulnerable to the pressures of the criminal organization. Crime leaders have found this condition
to exist. Up until the creation of the national
crime federation, penetration of governments
was largely ad hoc in approach. Many local-
based organizations found the great political
machines of the first third of the century more
than agreeable in making arrangements with crime
leaders. The criminal organization provided
money and, often, goon squads to be used in controlling local elections. In return, they received what amounted to a license to pursue their
activities unhampered by law enforcement agencies.
Much of the success of bootlegging during Prohibition days depended on the corruptibility
of federal enforcement agents.

        Although both Prohibition and most of
the major political machines are now matters
of history, the patterns developed then continue

165

today. Organized crime has found it can pene-
trate and control governmental operations.

The foundation of the Cosa Nostra's
pressure politics is corruption based on money.
Corruption is so essential, in fact, that one
authority argues that just as the job of "corrupter" is an integral part of the organization,
the role of "corruptee" should be considered
for all practical purposes as essential to the
organization.[27] Corruption is vital to the organized criminal because it means he can pursue
his illegal activities free of the inconvenience
of police arrests and investigations, thereby
guaranteeing the uninterrupted flow of profits.
Further, it means if he or his more important
subordinates and employees are arrested, they
know that they will not be convicted or at the
worst they will be afflicted with only minor
penalties. At least as significant, the control
over government granted by corruption heightens
the image of omnipotence: the crime leaders
are to be feared not only because they are ruthless but they control government as well; their
rivals and opponents have no place to turn for
protection.

As practiced by the Cosa Nostra, corruption
falls into one of two patterns: direct bribery
and corruption by accommodation. Direct bribery,
while crude, is effective. It is based on the
sad but reasonable assumption that in any population of public administrators and politicians
there are some who are greedy enough to violate
their public trust, imprudent enough in their
personal financial affairs to have gotten themselves into desperate straits, or coldly ambitious
enough to take "help" from anyone. The task
of the corrupter is to seek out these people
and seduce them into taking the first pay-off.
Once they have, of course, they are trapped.
They must continue to obey orders because they
themselves have now committed a crime and, if
exposed, are not guaranteed the elaborate network

166

of protection the crime syndicate provides for
its formal members. Further, once they "go to
work" for organized crime and refuse to obey
orders they are subject to being introduced to
the enforcement process: a point that is usually
made quite clear to the corruptee.

Although the police patrolman is one
of the obvious targets of corruption, he is a
relatively small fry target. Granted that if
he is on the "payroll," the numbers runner, book-
maker, and street level narcotics salesman are
guaranteed safety, the more important and desirable targets are higher-ranking police officials,
members of the prosecuting attorney's staff (or
the prosecutor himself), judges, and federal,
state, and local legislators. If, in any given
city one or two people in these positions are
corrupted, then the crime organization is politically secure. It can be certain that: police
patrolmen will be quietly told to "lay off";
the crime organization will instantly receive
information about the progress of investigations;
investigatory materials will be lost or ineptly
assembled; indictments will be quashed; charges
reduced; prosecutions fumbled so that trials
end in acquittals; judges will declare a mistrial;
sentences will be light; city councils will grant
liquor licenses; state regulatory agencies will
grant corporate charters; organized crime investigation units will be starved for funds; and
special task forces or investigating commissions
will concentrate their energies on "crime in
the streets" or "revolutionary violence" or the
"threat of subversion." The list could be extended.

In brief, direct bribery is an investment in the behavior of strategically placed
public officials, an investment that pays off
in protection from police "interference" and
in positive policy decisions that guarantee a
return on that investment, such as the governmental purchase of criminal-owned real estate
for highway development at inflated prices.

167

Corruption by accommodation is more indirect than outright bribery but can be as effective. In essence, it is a tacit or explicit
bargain that organized crime is a "fact of life"
and it is simpler for the public official to
learn to live with it than become involved in
a hopeless and even dangerous political struggle.
Many otherwise honest policemen can rationalize
ignoring organized crime because it provides
what the public wants, public pressures are to
deal with street crime, and all police forces
are understaffed anyhow. The same reasoning
easily applies to prosecutors' staffs. Politicians seeking elective office and in need of
money for their campaigns can in much the same
way justify accepting campaign contributions
from the criminal organization or the help of
campaign workers turned out by crime controlled
local unions. From the standpoint of organized
crime, accommodation has two advantages. First,
it provides many of the benefits that direct
bribery does at a usually lower money cost. Second,
it can set the stage for bribery. The legislator
who has accepted a campaign contribution from
organized crime is vulnerable to being accused
that he did so as a bribe, and thus he stands
to be defeated at the next election.[28] Since,
potentially, he has the name, he may as well
have the game and go the next step of actually
being on the pay-roll. The same pattern applies
to officials down to and including the policeman
on the beat.

Although corruption in either form is
the foundation of organized crime's pressure
on government, the shift into legitimate business
means that crime leaders can also act in their
capacity as businessmen to bring pressure on
government. Thus, modern organized crime has two
options it can follow simultaneously: pressure
by corruption and violence, and pressure through
standard group politics.

It should be noted, once again, that
the political geography of the American system
increases the vulnerability of the political
system to penetration by organized crime. City
councilmen, state legislators, and district attorneys are elected from relatively small districts, districts which by the expenditure of
enough money and effort by criminal organizations
can be controlled. This means that the elected
officials themselves will be controlled by organized crime. As we saw in Chapters II and V,
pressure groups that can concentrate their resources in small geographic areas improve their
strategic positions. The same generalization
applied to organized crime.

How Powerful?

Just as there is no full agreement as
to the extent of the power of corporations in
American politics, there is no agreement on the
power of organized crime. The criminologists
and organized crime opponents have a degree of
vested interest in raising shouts of fear such
as, "The iron-fisted rulers who control the Mafia
have locked a strangle hold on American politics."[29]
More skeptical analysts would argue that organized
crime has yet to gain control over many of the
most powerful institutions of American life,
such as the giant corporations, the AFL-CIO,
the massive federal bureaucracies, and the U.S.
Supreme Court to name only some.

On balance, it would appear that both
points are reasonably well taken. Despite the
infiltration of crime into business and labor
unions, most of these groups still seem to wield
power for their own ends. However, it would
be an error to overlook the potent presence of
organized crime especially at the state and local
levels of government. At least some cities do

169

seem to be virtually the political property of
organized crime. In other cities there is no
doubt that crime syndicates are in a position
to shape much of law enforcement, the administration of justice, and the award of government
contracts and business licenses and permits.
Few cities, and their adjacent areas, regardless
of size, would be safe in assuming there is no
exercise of the power of organized crime on their
political systems.

        This reality means that organized crime
is not simply a local power. State judges and
legislators are, in most instances, selected
out of local constituencies. The same is true
of U.S. Congressmen. If organized crime is able
to gain a powerful grip on local party officials,
to control some labor union locals, to amass
and use money in political campaigns, it is able
to influence and perhaps dominate the electoral
system in its area.

        Because of its secrecy, and because in-
filtration into legitimate business and labor
is now so common, it is difficult to make any
measured estimate. The observer can never be
sure whether he is seeing a "legitimate" pressure
group at work or one that is acting as a front
for organized crime. The foregoing discussion
does lead to two safe generalizations, however.
First, organized crime has the strategic position
to act as a powerful pressure group in American
politics. Second, it has the interest to do
so. It would be remarkable if it has chosen
to voluntarily restrain itself.

References for Chapter VII

[1]There are a number of useful general works on organized crime in America. Among them are: Robert F. Kennedy, The Enemy Within (New York: Harper and Brothers, 1960); Ralph Salerno and John S. M. Tompkins, The Civic Confederation: Cosa Nostra and Allied Operations in Organized Crime (Garden City, N.Y.: Doubleday, 1969); Donald R. Cressy, Theft of the Nation (New York: Harper and Row, 1969); Nicholas Gage, The Mafia Is Not An Equal Opportunity Employer (New York: McGraw-Hill, 1971). Richard D. Knudten, Crime in a Complex Society (Homewood, Ill.: Dorsey Press, 1970) places organized crime in a larger context. Peter Maas, The Valachi Papers (New York: G. P. Putnam, 1968) is one of the major sources on the structure and workings of organized crime. Ron Parambo, No Cause for Indictment: An Autopsy of Newark (New York: Holt, Rinehart, and Winston, 1971) is a specific case study of the impact of crime in that city, as is John A. Gardiner's The Politics of Corruption: Organized Crime in an American City (New York: Russell Sage, 1970) of Reading, Pennsylvania.

[2]Harold J. Vetter and Jack Wright, Jr., Introduction to Criminology (Springfield, Ill.: Charles C. Thomas, 1974), p. 390.

[3]Victor S. Navasky, Kennedy Justice (New York: Atheneum, 1970), points out that Hoover remained skeptical even after 1957 and did much to block any systematic investigation of organized crime (pp. 44-45).

[4]A major exception is John J. Harrigan's textbook on urban politics, Political Change in the Metropolis (Boston: Little, Brown, 1976).

[5]Cressy makes this point in strong terms.

171

[6] Knudten, p. 187.

[7] Cressy, Chapter I.

[8] Salerno and Tompkins, p. 377; Cressy, p. 52. There is no agreement as to the proper name for the organization. I follow Maas and Cressy here.

[9] The term "family" was given to the local chapters of the organization.

[10] U.S. Senate Committee on Commerce, Report on the Effects of Organized Crime on Interstate and Foreign Commerce (Washington, D.C.: U.S. Government Printing Office, 1972).

[11] President's Commission on Law Enforcement and the Administration of Justice, Task Force on Organized Crime, Organized Crime (Washington, D.C.: U.S. Government Printing Office, 1967), p. 8.

[12] Cressy, p. 112.

[13] Ibid., pp. 233-34.

[14] Salerno and Tompkins, p. 102.

[15] Ibid.

[16] Ibid., p. 198.

[17] Francis Ianni, Black Mafia (New York: Simon and Schuster, 1974).

[18] John Berthelson, "Mob Is Believed Draining California Social Programs," Washington Post article reprinted in the New Orleans Times-Picayune (March 7, 1977), Section 1, p. 3. Berthelson reports that Mexican-American organizations, originally formed in prison as self-protective associations, have moved into extortion

rackets directed at Los Angeles neighborhood health clinics. La Cosa Nostra is apparently withdrawing from the newer organizations' areas and allowing the two competing gangs (one of which is significantly named "Nuestra Familia") to fight it out between themselves.

[19]President's Commission, pp. 2-4.

[20]Vetter and Wright, p. 384. Ramsey Clark, former U.S. Attorney General, argues that estimates of the revenues of organized crime are substantially inflated, Crime in America (New York: Simon and Schuster, 1970), p. 73.

[21]Cressy, p. x; Vetter and Wright, p. 392.

[22]There was evidence of leadership crises in the Chicago area in 1975 and 1978.

[23]Francis Ianni and Elizabeth R. Ianni, A Family Business: Kinship and Social Control in Organized Crime (New York: Russell Sage, 1972).

[24]Gardiner has noted that public reaction to organized crime is largely one of indifference unless corruption becomes so blatant as to be impossible to ignore.

[25]Knidten, p. 193ff.

[26]Salerno and Tompkins, pp. 331-33.

[27]Cressy, pp. 252-53.

[28]Michael Dorman, Payoff (New York: David McKay, 1972), p. 3.

[29]Dorman, p. 1.

CHAPTER VIII

CASE STUDY: THE PUBLIC SERVANT

In 1976, two students of public administration wrote, "Public employees . . . collectively
constitute one of the most powerful special interest lobbies in the nation."[1] What they were
pointing to is a set of interests whose importance
has expanded rapidly in the last thirty years,
and a set of interests which can exert enormous
influence on governmental decision-making.[2]

The role of public servants--those people
who work for government--as a pressure group
evokes economic, social and ideological interests
and touches upon redistributive, regulatory,
and constitutent policies. As a member of
organized groups, the public servant has a special
form of access to policy-making. Although classic
group theory ignored the role of public employees,
we now know that they will diligently pressure
policy-makers in a variety of ways, and not simply
to "shape policy," but to shape policy in what
they see as their own interests.

Public servants as pressure groups further
raise painful issues.[3] Among these are: should
they be allowed to unionize? If allowed to unionize, should they be allowed to go out on strike?
How much of the tax dollar should go to wages,
salaries, and fringe benefits rather than direct
services to the public? To whom (or what) should
the public servant be loyal: "the public interest?" his organization? his supervisor? his
own professional judgment? Is he given the proper
recognition for the work, often dangerous or
tedious, that he performs? In what ways is he
entitled to be politically active?

175

That we have no clear or accepted answers to these questions indicates the extent to which the organized public servant poses a set of major policy problems. And, in the absence of answers, pressure groups enter in an attempt to provide them.

The term "public servants" includes the employees of federal, state, and local governments, with the addition of some important top administrative persons and elected officials especially at the local government level. As pressure groups, they appear in a number of guises: as members of public employee unions; as members of special associations of high level officials, such as the International City Management Association and the International Association of Chiefs of Police; and various organizations, usually organized on a statewide basis, of elected officials such as sheriffs, and city and county treasurers; and, finally, as members of various governmental agencies, especially those that have developed a high sense of professionalism and a sense of ideological commitment, such as the military departments at the national level and urban planning and social welfare departments at the local and state levels.

These groups behave much like other pressure groups, bringing their power to bear on other segments of the government to satisfy their own interests. They are, however, separated from other pressure groups because of the dual role they play: they are not just pressure groups but are part of the government itself. As part of the government, these groups feel the pressures applied by other interests and in their governmental role deal with those pressures as they can; at other times, however, they actually engage in competitive struggle with "outside" pressure groups and with the rest of government itself. This dualing gives public servant pressure groups certain advantages in their strategic position; it also imposes some

176

handicaps on them. It is clear, however, that the power of public servant groups has grown in the last few decades.

The Nature of the Public Servant Organization

The involvement of public servants in pressure group politics is the result of a shift away from party politics.[4] Until well into the twentieth century, almost all public servants held their positions by virtue of the patronage system or by direct election to office. Since the primary qualification for holding a patronage position was party loyalty, public servants performed two jobs. One was their nominal job, policeman, building inspector, health official. The more important, however, was the job of party worker. Most, if not all, public servants were expected to work for the electoral success of the party that put them in power, or, in one-party situations, for the faction in office. For the public servant this was not only what his political leaders expected, but the surest and only way he could guarantee his continued employment in the job and, perhaps, eventual promotion. As a system, patronage had the advantages of providing a base for the party organizations and of allowing the voters to know who was responsible for the conduct of government. If the police force were ineffective, it was the party's fault. If the state park program were corrupt, the responsibility was the party's.

With these political advantages went some distinct governmental disadvantages. Party loyalty is an inadequate substitute for technical and administrative skills. As governmental activities expanded, and the public's dependence on these activities increased, discontent with slipshod, indifferent state and local, as well as federal, administration increased especially

177

among the growing urban middle classes. Moreover, patronage politics was simply too well
adapted to corruption; in many places government
posts were literally bought and sold, often on
the theory that the purchaser would more than
recover his investment in bribes and kickbacks.

The Decline of Patronage

        The counterattack on the patronage system
came primarily through the civil service system,
adapted from Great Britain's revulsion against
patronage politics and formally acted into law
by the federal government in 1883. The principal
feature of civil service was that the prospective
employee had to prove his "merit" by competitive
examination before he could be hired, and, once
hired was protected from dismissal for purely
political reasons. Civil service substituted
job performance for party loyalty as the standard
for holding non-elective governmental positions.

        Not surprisingly, civil service grew
slowly at the federal level and even more so
at the state and local level. Although by the
1970s, most federal employees were under civil
service of some kind (the military and top policy-
making positions being the major exceptions),
the situation remained one in which the majority
of state and local employees remained outside
civil service requirements.[5] This means that
political criteria still rank as an important
factor. Two trends, however, have further eroded
the vitality of the patronage system. One is
simply that the jobs available to patronage dis-
pensers are often not that attractive. Frequently they are the more menial blue collar
jobs or lesser clerical posts. They are important to the functioning of the government but
party workers are not clamoring to be appointed
to such jobs. The result is that the appointing

authority must often take whomever he can get,
regardless of party loyalty.

Second, and more significant, the demand
for effective governmental performance continues.
Often a patronage dispenser can find a person
who combines both party loyalty and skills;
when he cannot, however, he frequently feels
he must opt for the skills. The risk of a dis-
satisfied public is a sufficient danger to warrant
dissatisfying an occasional loyal campaign
worker.[6]

These trends have converged in an increasing "professionalization" of government
employees.[7] As a consequence the employee is
more apt to think of his job as a life-long
career; one in which he will gain more and more
skill and rise progressively up the ladder of
the administrative hierarchy in his area of
specialization. He tends to have, in short,
a psychological vested interest in his job.
Further, he tends to become loyal to his "profession" rather than some political leader or
even the head of his agency. And, as a policeman
or a firefighter or a social worker, for example,
he is apt to think in terms of defending his
profession, his organization, and incidentally
himself, from "outside interference."[8]

The Professional Associations

What has occurred has been the development
of a set of shared attitudes, external to party
politics, and centered around the occupational
specialties of the various employees.[9] One result
has been the creation of a number of interest
groups, many of which immediately or eventually
became pressure groups. Table 7 lists a number
of these associations with the 1972 memberships
and the dates they were founded. As the table

179

TABLE 7

SELECTED PUBLIC SERVANTS ASSOCIATIONS, 1972

Name	1972 Membership	Date Founded
International Association of Fire Chiefs	8,000	1873
International Association of Chiefs of Police	8,000	1893
Public Personnel Association	4,363	1906
International City Management Association	4,800	1914
Fraternal Order of Police	80,000	1915
National Association of Housing and Redevelopment Officials	8,700	1933
American Society of Planning Officials	8,000	1934
International Association of Coroners and Medical Examiners	400	1938
National Police Officers Association	23,000	1955
National Association of County Administrators	290	1959
International Narcotic Enforcement Officers Association	4,500	1960
Afro-American Patrolmen's League	1,200	1968

SOURCE: Encyclopedia of National Associations, 1972.

180

shows, several came into being in the nineteenth
century and early twentieth century. The rapid
growth of these occurred as the concept of "professionalism" caught on, a concept they themselves
attempted to foster. Many were established in
the early stages of development of an occupational
specialty, as with the International City Management Association (the first city manager came
into being in 1907) and the International Association of Fire Chiefs (in 1873 few cities had
regular fire departments). In most cases, these
associations were committed to establishing rigorous standards of professional performance, educating their members in new developments in their
fields, and fostering a public image of ability
and dedication. Often this meant breaking with
"politics and politicians" and asserting the
independence of the public servant from "political"
considerations in the conduct of their governmental tasks.

At a more mundane level, the associations
concerned themselves with salary issues, conditions of work, the length of work-weeks, and
the need for higher levels of governmental expenditures on the programs that were of interest
to their members. However, most were and still
are "ideological" in their interests with an
increasing concern with economic interests.

Significantly, through their national
meetings and publications they provided a means
for occupational specialties within government
to interact as a group. Many encouraged the
development of state associations producing a
"national-chapters" type of organizational structure, thus providing a basis for pressuring
state legislatures for reform of laws and regulations affecting their professions and governmental duties.

Traditionally these associations were
not aggressive as pressure groups, seeing their

tasks as raising the quality of government by
improving the professional standards of their
members. In a sense, they chose to "work from
within." By informing, educating, and imbuing
their members with a sense of commitment to the
demands of their careers, the association's goals
would be achieved by the appreciation of a well-
served and grateful public. More recently they
have opted to pressure government, especially
since the end of World War II and the federal
government's expansion in the range of grants-
in-aid to state and local governments. Thus,
the National Association of Housing and Redevelop-
ment Officials has lobbied hard for increased
governmental support of public housing and slum
renewal; the International Association of Chiefs
of Police has been a vigorous supporter of the
federal Law Enforcement Assistance Administration,
a program to provide technical, financial, and
research assistance to state and local police
forces.

Public Employee Unions

        While the professional associations have
done much to generate a sense of professionalism
among public servants, and have worked to improve
their economic status, for a long time they made
little progress in satisfying the economic needs
of public employees. And, one of the severe
and chronic problems of public servants was the
gap between wages and salaries for public employees and equivalent benefits for the employees
of business. The size of the gap varied from
occupation to occupation, one level of government
to another, and region to region. Lower level
federal employees generally are now at par with
their counterparts in private enterprise (although
top-level employees could earn more outside
government). At the state and local level, the
differences are apt to be more extreme.[10] Often

also "fringe benefit" packages are less: the
public servant receives less medical insurance
coverage, fewer paid holidays, fewer paid sick
days, and retires on a smaller pension than his
fellow worker who is employed by a business
corporation.[11] If he is a policeman, a fireman,
or a social worker he may also be expected to
work longer hours and receive no overtime for
the effort expended.

Not surprisingly, the union movement
early on recognized an opportunity in the field
of public employment and began to fill the gap
left by the various professional associations.
Table 8 lists some of the larger public employee
unions, with their dates of creation and their
memberships. Despite the early dates of the
founding of many of these unions, "a fact well
known to union organizers [is] that prior to
the late fifties, most government employees were
indifferent and even highly resistant to unionization."[12] The 1960s saw dramatic changes occur,
however. From 1960 to 1968, the membership of
the International Association of Firefighters
grew by 40 percent; of the American Federation
of State, County, and Municipal Employees by
73 percent; of the American Federation of Teachers
by 196 percent; and of the American Federation
of Government Employees by 321 percent.[13]

There is no simple explanation for the
sudden willingness of government employees to
join unions. One possibility seems to be in
the union movement itself. The 1950s and 1960s
saw a "flattening" in the success of the major
unions in organizing and adding to their membership rosters. Public employees represented a
potential new source of growth and so organizers
stepped up their campaigns to reach especially
state and local employees. Further, the 1950s
and 1960s saw a rapid expansion in state and
local employment. Although difficult to document,
it appears that a substantial number of the

183

TABLE 8

SELECTED PUBLIC EMPLOYEE UNIONS, 1972

Name	1972 Membership	Date Founded
National Alliance of Postal and Federal Employees	40,000	1913
American Federation of Teachers	250,000	1916
National Federation of Federal Employees	80,000	1917
International Association of Firefighters	155,000	1918
American Federation of Government Employees	300,000	1932
American Federation of State, County, and Municipal Employees	510,000	1936
American Postal Workers Union	300,000	1971

SOURCE: Encyclopedia of National Associations, 1972

public employees to that time had begun their
careers during the Great Depression, a time when
any job was gratefully received. This attitude
had carried over and few were willing to risk
rocking the boat by joining a union. The new
generation, beginning work in the 1950s and 1960s,
however, were more anxious to share in the material
benefits of the society they were serving. To
them unionization was a rational way of pursuing
this interest.

Employee Associations

        Closely related to, but actually competi-
tive with, employee unions are what can be called
"employee associations" or "quasi-unions."[14] In
general, they came into being during the period
1920-1950, usually to pursue some specific cause,
such as the adoption of civil service or a pension plan, and continued on a statewide basis.
Most are affiliated with the Assembly of Governmental Employees, a national federation.   In
1969, the AGE claimed thirty-two affiliates with
a total membership of 618,000. The state employee
associations are often in turn federations for
local associations. Like the unions, the employee
associations are economic pressure groups and
while varying substantially in composition and
aggressiveness, they are "united in their opposition to national unions of public employees."[15]

        Although the three types of public employee
organizations have differed in nature, militancy,
and base, the recent tendency is for each to
become more like the unions in attitudes and
political tactics. This convergence is apparently
rooted in a common set of interests among public
employees: the desire for greater economic rewards, feelings of low status, and a sense that
aggressive pressure will be more profitable than
moderation or passiveness.[16]

Institutional Groups

An additional dimension of public servants as pressure groups is their role within the context of their specific governmental agencies. One effect of the increasing involvement of government in all aspects of the life of the nation has been the creation of administrative agencies which are devoted to the self-conscious pursuit of public policies and goals. Often, these agencies are composed of professionals who have a clear view in their minds of what the proper goals of government should be, what their relation to those goals are, and how they should be attained. What results can be called an "institutional pressure group," one which occurs within government itself.[17]

The most familiar, and longest standing, of these institutional pressure groups is of course the military. But at the national level, the uniformed services are not alone: public health officials, the FBI, the CIA, the Civil Rights Division of the Justice Department, and other highly cohesive and self-conscious groups appear. Similarly, at the local level, firemen, policemen, urban planners, social workers, and highway engineers among others have specifically shared attitudes.

These institutional pressure groups face the rest of government in a complicated fashion.[18] At one level, they may genuinely believe that they are entrusted with an important policy or program, and for them to fail to fight to see their programs generously funded and supported is to fail in their duty. At another level, there is self-interest. Programs which are expanding in money, personnel, and responsibilities mean promotions, salary increases, and more power and prestige.

186

Further, as will be discussed in greater detail in Chapter XII, administrative agencies do not work in a vacuum. They are linked to pressure groups outside of government and to legislative committees. Thus, there is a desire to "deliver" to those who have supported the agency, and often delivering means being able to shape policy in a way which is satisfactory to both institutional group and its supporters.[19]

What was once behind-the-scenes bureaucratic maneuvering often today takes on the character of true pressure group politics, with agencies, devoting as much time to public relations, lobbying, and searching for allies among other pressure groups as any corporation, civil rights, environmentalist, or union group does. And, these pressure group tactics may even reach into the electoral process, with policemen, teachers, firemen, and other public servants overtly supporting one candicate for public office over another, in an effort to see legislators or chief executives elected who are "sympathetic" to the group's interests.

Within government policy-making itself, there may be a steady and constant pressure upon decision-makers to follow the policy preferences of the institutional group. Since administrators often have a monopoly of information and expertise in a given policy area, executives or legislators can be forced into the position that to go against the group's will is to risk making a fundamental error--and to risk reading in the newspaper some morning that they failed to follow the advice of their knowledgeable "professionals."

The existence and growth of professional associations, unions, and employee associations have helped to sharpen employee awareness, giving their members a stronger sense of identification

with a common set of values and deliberately
fostering the values. Moreover, these organizations provide an alternative vehicle for action:
the public servant who feels his interests are
not being met by the rest of the government is
not confronted with a "shut up or get out" choice.
If pressure by and from within his agency fails,
then he can turn to his association or union
to press his interests. A policeman, for example,
concerned with "permissiveness" toward criminals
can, with his fellow policemen in his department,
press for harsher penalties to be written into
state criminal codes; he can work to the same
end through his local chapter of the Fraternal
Order of the Police; and he also may pursue the
same interest through the local chapter of the
International Conference of Police Associations.
There is, of course, a risk that multiple memberships may lead to cross-pressuring; in general,
however, this rarely occurs.

What has emerged, then, in the past two
decades is the appearance of the public servant
as a political force, structured by rapidly growing pressure groups and sets of basic interests
pursued through those groups. It seems probable
that the pattern will continue and accelerate.

Public Servants, Government, and Power

One of the most important political resources public servants bring to bear on the
political system is their numbers. One 1970
estimate of total membership in all unions and
employee associations arrived at a figure of
2,008,000 or roughly 20 percent of all state
and local employees for that year.[20] The Tax
Foundation (p. 9) arrived at higher figures,
placing the total of such membership for state
and local governments at 2,668,000, representing
26 percent of all such employees. They also

estimated that 1,411,000 federal employees belonged to unions or associations, representing
52 percent of total federal civilian employees.[21]
There are no reliable more recent estimates,
but it seems safe to assume that both the absolute
figures and the percentages have continued to
increase. Using 1970 as the base year, however,
it can be said that at that time well over
4,000,000 government employees belonged to unions
and employee associations and, thus, about one-
third of all employees were members of organized
pressure groups dedicated to pursuing their interests.

This membership is not evenly distributed
throughout the nation or by form of government,
however, In general, the highest levels of
organization appear in the Northeast and on the
Pacific Coast and in the large cities (cities
with populations of 50,000 or more). The Midwest
and especially the Far West and Southern regions
lag behind the rest of the country in public
employee organization and counties and state
governments trail behind cities and the federal
government.

Organization

Organizationally, public servant pressure
groups vary enormously. The larger unions, such
as the American Federation of State, County,
and Municipal Employees (AFSCME), the American
Postal Workers Union, and the American Federation
of Teachers are affiliates of the national AFL-
CIO. Each in turn is a federation of locals.
The AFSCME had, in 1972, 1900 locals. The Postal
Workers Union had 6000. In general, public employee unions stress organization maintenance
and an elected, but powerful leadership, following the practice of other types of unions. Both
the professional and employee associations also
have local chapters and elect officers and boards

of directors, but the full-time executive director
and his staff usually hold the reins of leadership. Relatively little attention has been given
to the internal dynamics of public servant organizations, but it appears that the iron law of
oligarchy is at work, and with it the familiar
distribution of members among an activist cadre,
an active membership, and a mass membership.

Money

        Even less is known about the money re-
sources of the various groups. All charge membership dues. In 1969, the dues for local members
in the AFSCME were around four dollars a month
per person, most of which was passed on to state
and national AFL-CIO treasuries.[22] This meant
that this one union alone was generating more
than $2,000,000 a month, to go into hiring staff,
establishing a strike fund, and providing for
public relations and organizing work.[23] The
employee associations generally levy lower dues
on their members, arguing that whatever affiliation they have with a national organization is
far less costly to the members than for the unions.
For the employee unions, then, there are larger
sums of money but financial control tends to
shift to the national level, and with it leadership control. For the employee associations,
there is less money in aggregate, but the local
leadership is apt to have greater control over
what is taken in. The greater part of all the
dues levied by the professional associations
go to the national organizations and leadership
is largely concentrated at the national or state
levels (the major exception is the National Education Association, with a history and pattern
of strong local control).

        Public servants working from the context
of their governmental agencies as pressure groups
must largely depend on informal organization

190

and leadership.[24] Their advantage, of course, is that they already are brought together in a situation where they see each other on a daily basis and where they have a steady flow of information at their finger tips. In a sense, they are "pre-organized" by their very presence as government employees. Up to a point, then, they have as assets the resources of their agency. The limits they often confront, however, appear in the form of an agency director who is a political appointee and the possibility of factions and jealousies among the agency's employees. It is relatively rare for the basic interest to include all employees of an agency and, thus, within the context of the agency there is no clearly defined formal pressure group organization with its own resources and directed goals.

Leadership Skills

Leadership skills seem to vary widely among public servant pressure groups. In general, the public employee unions seem to be the most aggressively led. At least some of the employee associations have long had at best indifferent leadership: executive directors content to produce a monthly newsletter and arrange an annual meeting. The competition from the union movement has acted as a spur to many associations, however, and thus state and local associations in many areas are giving more attention to organization maintenance, interest clarification, and speaking out on behalf of their members. Professional associations have tended to go through a similar pattern. Content once to be the moderate, quiet spokesmen for a "middle class" style, many, including the American Nurse's Association and the National Education Association are giving more effort to assertive and direct leadership.

191

One advantage of public servant pressure
groups over other types of groups is that they
can draw on people who are already intimately
familiar with the workings of government. They
are accordingly spared one of the more onerous
tasks of pressure group leaders: simply finding
out how to get around in the intricacies of
modern governmental systems.

Status and Image

A major problem confronting public servant
pressure groups is that of status and image.
On one hand, large segments of the public have
at best mixed feelings about public employees
in general and organized public employees in
specific. The image of "the bureaucrat" is a
common one: a time-serving, secure paper-shuffler
who has never had to meet a payroll or compete
in the "real world" of business. When the image
of people clamoring for higher pay, shorter hours,
or basic changes in public policy is tied to
that of the bureaucrat, the public reaction is
often hostile. Further, the union movement itself was long suspicious of public employees,
regarding them as not true workingmen. Although
the success of unionization of public employees
has helped dampen that original distaste (public
employees in 1970 were about 11 percent of all
union members), vestiges still remain. Ironically, the joining of public employees with
the union movement has further damaged the employees' image.

Even with these disabilities, however,
the picture is not entirely gloomy from the
public servant's standpoint. There is some evidence that the status of the public employee
has risen in recent years, in part because of
the growing number of people who find work in
state and local government especially[25] and in
part because of the very image of professionalism

192

that professional associations have worked so
hard to foster. Further, with the union movement
now accepting public employees as valid members
of the work world, other union members grant
them more respect. In addition, the unionized
public employee has available the impressive
public relations machinery of organized labor.

Competition

        The competitive situation of public ser-
vant pressure groups is one of the more complex
patterns of American politics. As already noted,
employee associations came into being deliberately
to challenge employee unions. While the latter
have grown rapidly, so have the associations.
The National Education Association, as a professional association, has attempted with some success to compete with the AFT. In almost every
state rivalries are intense and the maneuvering
often has the effect of limiting the political
effectiveness of any one group. The opponents
of employee organizations have, in some cases,
contributed to these rivalries. Both businessmen, the top management of state and local governments, and many elected politicians regard
employee unions with alarm.[26] They believe,
correctly, that a militant public union movement
will raise the costs of government with resulting
tax increases. Many quietly encourage the development of local associations as a counter
to nationally affiliated unions on the often
justified hypothesis that a purely local organization will have neither the resources nor the
inclination to be militant in pressing its demands.

        Analogous conditions work on the public
servant within his agency. There, his group
must compete with the pressures of other administrative units, each of which feels it can make
a compelling case for its particular policy concerns.

193

Top management and elected leaders can play these
demands off against each other, following a divide
and conquer strategy. Thus, for example, civilian
Secretaries of Defense and Presidents have been
able to play army, air force, and navy off against
each other, in effect diluting the total pressure
by exploiting interservice rivalries.

It seems safe to judge that historical
circumstances have tended to shift gradually
in favor of public servant pressure groups. Civil
service, professional standards, and the public's
desire for effective performance continue to
spread, and with this spread come increased opportunities for the organized public servant to
free himself of party political control, establish his own responsive organizations, and pressure government to meet his interests. If nothing
else, the extension of governmental activities
into wider and wider areas of concern mean that
public servant organizations can expect their
political resources to have a greater impact.

How Powerful?

The strategic position of public servant
pressure groups is a mixed one. Even with the
liabilities already discussed, however, it is
clear that, as two observers said of the city
employee, "it is not surprising to find he is
one of the most important pressures on city
government. Collectively, city employees are
often the most important."[27]

The power of the public servant stems
from three sources. First, it is the public
servant in the agencies of government through
which the activities of government must be carried out. Although he is a "servant," he has
a mind of his own, and with that mind his own
expertise, skills, and political abilities. If
he and those who share his interest strongly

194

disagree with a policy, it can be undermined to the point of ruin by delays, sabotage, and indifference. It can be extraordinarily difficult to force a number of people to do something they would prefer not to. Further, if public servants believe a policy is misguided or poorly conceived or fails to serve their interests they can leak their views to the media, which are often hungry to find a good news story that points up the ineptness of elected politicians. In consequence, legislators, chief executives, and politically appointed agency directors are forced to regard their employees with some respectful fear.

A second source of power lies in the electoral strength of organized public employees. Especially at the local level of government, where voter turn-out is usually much lower than that of national elections, organized and dis-satisfied employees can exert a powerful leverage on election results. The city councilman or mayor who fails to give an attentive ear to the demands of his employees can expect that they will campaign vigorously against him. The result may well be defeat at the polls for the politi-cian and little hope of continuing his political career.

The third source of power is the one that has gained the most attention and concern: the strike.[28] Even today probably few Americans are aware of their dependence on public employees in almost every aspect of their lives, ranging from the removal of the twenty-two pounds of trash and garbage each family generates every day to the movement of traffic and people, oppor-tunities for recreation, medical attention, and personal safety. It is literally true that a strike by some group of public employees can bring a city to a halt. At the lesser extremes, a strike can delay a child's education, inflict enormous cost and inconvenience on the entire public, and lead merchants and other businessmen to the brink of bankruptcy.

195

Because of the dangers implicit in public
employee strikes, the federal government specifically prohibits them, as did thirty-two states
as of 1971. In addition, another nine states
prohibited strikes by employees in sensitive
positions (such as policemen and firemen). Despite the laws against strikes, however, public
employees have found a workable substitute in
"job actions," that is, slow-downs or large numbers
of employees calling in sick (a practice known
as the "blue flu" among policemen). Job actions
are usually not as catastrophic as a full-fledged
strike, but the effects are generally serious
enough to badly damage the community affected.

Moreover, as New York City discovered
during the 1960s, employees may go out on strike
in disregard of the law.[29] And, as that city
proved, despite fines and even jail penalties
against group leaders, the strike is a powerful
enough weapon for the employees to win their
goals.

For a number of reasons, public employees,
like their counterparts in industry, often prefer
not to resort to the strike. Strikes always
cost the employees substantial sums of money
in lost pay during the period of the walk-out;
the outcome is always an unknown; and usually
public sympathy turns against the strikers in
a protracted struggle, especially one that involves major sacrifices for the public.[30] As
a threat, however, it is a powerful one, meaning
that public employee pressure groups have a strong
bargaining position in dealing with elected
leaders.

Moreover, if past trends in the growth
of public employee groups continue, these groups
will have greater money, membership, and public
relations resources to draw on in case they feel
they must resort to a work stoppage. Public
servant pressure groups will become even more
politically powerful in the future, with major
consequences for governmental policy-making.

196

References for Chapter VIII

[1]Charles E. Lutrin and Allen K. Settle,
American Public Administration: Cases and Concepts (Palo Alto, Cal.: Mayfield, 1976), pp.
15-16.

[2]There are several useful guides to public
employee relations. George E. Berkley, The Craft
of Public Administration (Boston: Allyn and
Bacon, 1975), pp. 160-71 is a very valuable brief
summary. U.S. Advisory Commission on Intergovern-
mental Relations, Labor-Management Policies for
State and Local Government (Washington, D.C.:
U.S. Government Printing Office, 1969) has one
of the best compendiums of basic data and issues.
Legal complexities can be explored in Kurt L.
Hanslowe, The Emerging Law of Labor Relations
in Public Employment (Ithaca, N.Y.: Cornell
University Press, 1967). See also Felix Nigro,
Management-Employee Relations in the Public Service
(Chicago: Public Personnel Association, 1969)
for a good general survey.

[3]Many of these issues are discussed in
Richard Murphy and Morris Suckman, eds., Crisis
in Public Employee Relations in the Seventies
(Washington, D.C.: Bureau of National Affairs,
1970).

[4]Frederick C. Mosher, Democracy and the
Public Service (New York: Oxford University
Press, 1968) is the best history and analysis
of changing patterns in the public service.

[5]Charles R. Adrian, State and Local
Governments, 3d ed. (New York: McGraw-Hill,
1972), p. 317. See also Raymond Wolfinger, "Why
Political Machines Have Not Withered Away and
Other Rivisionist Thoughts," Journal of Politics
34 (May 1972): 365-98, and Martin Tolchin and
Susan Tolchin, To the Victor: Political Patronage

from the Clubhouse to the White House (New York: Vintage, 1972).

[6]The U.S. Supreme Court in 1976 in the case Elrod v. Burns delivered what may turn out to be the final crippling blow to patronage. In a 5-3 decision, involving the sheriff's office of Cook County (Chicago), Illinois, the Court held that the dismissal of persons because of their party affiliation was a violation of the First Amendment freedoms of speech and association. Such dismissals may take place for "policy-making" positions but no others. Whether the Elrod decision will apply to patronage that occurs when one faction of a party replaces another, and how easily the decision can be enforced remain to be seen. Without question, however, the consequences will be far-reaching.

[7]See Mark Abrahamson, The Professional in the Organization (New York: Alfred A. Knopf, 1961) for a discussion of the implications of "professionalism."

[8]Theodore Lowi, "Machine Politics--Old and New," in Bureaucratic Power in National Politics, ed. Francis E. Rourke (Boston: Little, Brown, 1972), pp. 278-82.

[9]The following discussion generally follows Jack Stieber, Employee Unionism: Structure, Growth, and Policy (Washington, D.C.: The Brookings Institution, 1973). See also, S. J. Makielski, Jr., State and Local Employee Relations (Charlottesville, Va.: The University of Virginia Institute of Government, 1971).

[10]A valuable source of information on the pay scales of local employees is the International City Management Association, Municipal Year Book (Washington, D.C.: International City Management Association, published annually).

[11] It must be noted, however, that in certain cities, such as New York and San Francisco, municipal employee pension plans threaten to "bankrupt" the cities within the next two decades or so.

[12] Tax Foundation, Unions and Public Employment (New York: Tax Foundation, 1974), p. 7.

[13] Ibid., p. 13.

[14] See Stieber, pp. 8-9.

[15] Ibid.

[16] Status concerns, that is, basic "social interests" are an important factor in many public servant groups. See, for example, Francis Fox Piven, "Militant Civil Servants in New York City," in Rourke, pp. 408-19; Arthur Niederhoffer, Behind the Shield (Garden City, N.Y.: Doubleday, 1967); and J. Joseph Loewenberg, "The Post Office Strike of 1970," in Collective Bargaining in Government: Readings and Cases, eds. J. Joseph Loewenberg and Michael H. Moskow (Englewood Cliffs, N.J.: Prentice-Hall, 1972), pp. 192-202.

[17] The term "institutional interest group" is from Gabriel Almond and G. Bingham Powell, Comparative Politics: A Developmental Approach (Boston: Little, Brown, 1966), p. 75.

[18] For detailed discussion of this point, see Lowi; Piven; James Clotfelter, The Military in American Politics (New York: Harper and Row, 1973); Harmon Ziegler, The Political Life of American Teachers (Englewood Cliffs, N.J.: Prentice-Hall, 1967); Richard H. Merelman, "Public Education and Social Structure: Three Modes of Adjustment," Journal of Politics 35 (November 1973): 798-829.

[19]John Kenneth Galbraith, _Economics and the Public Purpose_ (Boston: Houghton Mifflin, 1973), Chapter 16, points up the convergence of interests of public servants and outside supporters, especially the corporations.

[20]Stieber, p. 13

[21]Tax Foundation, p. 9. James L. Perry and Charles H. Levine, "An Intergovernmental Analysis of Power, Conflict, and Settlements in Public Sector Bargaining," _American Political Science Review_ 70 (December 1976): 1185-1201, arrive at figures close to the Tax Foundation estimate, i.e., 2.3 million union employees, and 1.7 million in other associations.

[22]Stieber, p. 45.

[23]The Congressional Quarterly lists spending for lobbying efforts of three groups as: the American Postal Workers, $393,399; National Education Association, $162,755; and the National Association of Letter Carriers, $160,597. Congressional Quarterly, _The Washington Lobby_, 2d ed. (Washington, D.C.: Congressional Quarterly, 1974), p. 38. It will be recalled that these were reported expenses limited to "direct contact" with Congressmen.

[24]See the discussion by Howard McCurdy, _Public Administration: A Synthesis_ (Menlo Park, Cal.: Cummings, 1977), Chapters 3 and 4.

[25]In 1952, approximately five million persons worked for state and local governments; in 1976 the number was around eleven million.

[26]Jesse Simons, "The American City and Its Public Employee Unions," in _Collective Bargaining in the Public Service_, ed. Gerald G. Simons (Milwaukee: Industrial Relations Research Association, 1966), p. 79.

[27]Edward C. Banfield and James Q. Wilson, City Politics (Cambridge, Mass.: Harvard-MIT Press, 1963), p. 210, emphasis in the original. See also David T. Stanley, Mamaging Local Government Under Union Pressure (Washington, D.C.: The Brookings Institution, 1972).

[28]David Ziskind, One Thousand Strikes of Government Employees (New York: Arno, 1940, 1971); Robert Walsh, Sorry--No Government Today: Unions vs. City Hall (Boston: Beacon Hill, 1969); Robert A. Liston, The Limits of Defiance: Strikes, Rights, and Government (New York: Franklin Watts, 1971).

[29]Raymond D. Horton, Municipal Labor Relations in New York City: Lessons of the Lindsay-Wagner Years (New York: Praeger, 1973).

[30]The number of public employee strikes has shown a steady rise, however, from 38 in 1962 to 412 in 1970. Ira Sharkansky, Public Administration: Policy-Making in Government Agencies, 3d ed. (Chicago: Rand McNally, 1973), p. 153.

PART II

ARENAS AND TARGETS

CHAPTER IX

PUBLIC OPINION AND ELECTIONS

The structure of American politics and
government presents pressure groups with a variety
of choices in attempting to influence public
policy. Elections, the three branches of government, and the three levels of government mean
that groups can concentrate their efforts in
any or all of these arenas, or institutional
settings in which basic decisions are made.

Within each arena there are usually a
number of different targets on which efforts
can be focussed. Some groups will tend to spe-
cialize, putting most of their attention into,
for example, the executive branch and within
that arena, on one administrative agency as its
target. Thus the American Association for the
Advancement of Science concerns itself especially
with the National Science Foundation, and the
Public Personnel Association devotes most of
its attention to the work of the U.S. Civil Service Commission. Others will span a wide variety
of arenas and include a number of targets. The
AFL-CIO becomes actively involved in the electoral process; it lobbies Congress and various
congressional committees; it exerts pressure
on several administrative agencies, and does
not confine itself to the federal government
but works at the state and local levels as well.

To a degree, a group's strategic position
affects where it spends its resources. Those
which are relatively wealthy in organizational
assets, money, skills, and membership can attempt
more than those less well endowed.[1] But a group's
choice of arenas and targets is also a leadership
decision, a matter of determining where a group's
interests lie and at what point in the governmental

system they can be most effectively satisfied.
To use a somewhat fanciful example, for organized
crime to try to corrupt the U.S. Supreme Court
would be, if successful, a master stroke, but,
realistically, the leaders of the Cosa Nostra
are wiser to concentrate their attention on local
prosecuting attorneys.

Access Points

        Two general points about the structure
of the American system must be recalled. One
is that it is a system of "multiple access points
and multiple veto points." That is, there are
a number of places where any particular pressure
group can gain access. Among the 535 members
of the U.S. Congress, for example, the odds are
favorable that there is at least one legislator
who will give time and attention to almost every
interest conceivable, ranging from the Ku Klux
Klan to the International Workers of the World.
If rebuffed in Congress, then among the 800-
plus administrative agencies there may be an
open ear. And, if turned away there, the group
will perhaps find it possible to make a "federal
case" out of its interest and pursue the issue
through the courts. The same pattern of multiple
access points occurs at the state, and to a lesser
extent, at the local level. Some pressure groups,
in fact, work two or more levels of government
simultaneously, seeking the access point that
will give them the most favorable results. Both
civil rights and environmentalist groups have
found this to be a profitable strategy.

Veto Points

        Counterbalancing the multiple access
points are, however, the multiple veto points;
that is, in the American system of checks and

206

balances, often only one person or a small number
of people are institutionally placed so they
can prevent government from acting. The most
obvious example is the veto power of the President. It takes only a simple majority (50 percent plus one) to pass a bill in Congress. If
the President vetoes it, however, it requires
a two-thirds majority to overrule his veto in
each house. This means that the President and
no more than thirty-four Senators can block the
will of sixty-six Senators and, conceivably,
the entire membership of the House of Representatives.[2]

Multiple veto points appear less dramatically but as significantly elsewhere in the
governmental system. Legislative committee chairmen both in Congress and in state legislatures
can often strangle action. The courts can
adjudge an administrative or legislative act
illegal, or, often as effective, issue a writ
of injunction (an order that no action be taken)
while a question is waiting resolution by the
courts, frequently a process involving years.
Frequently a few administrators can, by dragging
their feet, nullify a policy that legislature
has passed, chief executive has signed into law,
and courts have approved.

The significance of multiple veto points
is they give an advantage to pressure groups
which are fighting defensive battles, that is,
trying to prevent a policy from being changed
or a new policy being adopted. This means the
pressure group which can gain access to a veto
point and maintain its access is in a position
to block all the very best efforts of its rivals
or opponents. In short, access to a committee
chairman, a top administrator, a chief executive,
or the courts can often be enough to stifle governmental action indefinitely.[3]

A second major characteristic of the
American political system is that few if any

decisions made by government are really permanent ones. Court decisions are reversed by a later court of different composition; legislative acts are amended at the next session; administrative rulings are "reinterpreted." This "non-finality of decisions"[4] means pressure groups must be willing to, and adapted to, carry on protracted struggle, not for just a period of months but even years and decades. It is this protracted nature of political struggle that places such a high premium on organization, that is, directed human effort over time.

With these preliminary considerations in mind, it is useful to examine the major arenas and targets of pressure group politics, the strategic goals that groups seek in each and the tactics that they bring to bear in the struggle. The most important of these arenas are public opinion and elections, legislatures, the executive branch, and the court systems. Although not touched on in detail here, pressure groups can also be found at work in arenas such as state constitutional conventions, and special task forces or study commissions set up to arrive at an "independent" appraisal of some important public problem.[5] In brief, it is safe to say that in America, where there is politics there is pressure group politics.

Public Opinion

Although the authors of the U.S. Constitution and most state constitutions went to some effort to insure that those who govern are protected from the mass public's volatile moods, public opinion in the sense of the deeply held values and preferences of the adult population is considered to be the final source of authority and legitimacy in a democratic society.[6] At any given time it is unlikely that governments are doing precisely what "the people" want. Politicians, however, confronted with the necessity of facing public opinion periodically during elections would prefer to please that public rather than anger it.

One of the difficulties with public opinion, however, is knowing just what it might be in any practical sense of the word. Today pollsters accurately chart public feelings toward any number of issues, but generally these samplings reflect answers to questions that the pollsters believe are important, and the answers themselves frequently provide no real guidance.[7] If Americans, for example, rate "inflation" as "the most serious problem," the political leader still has no explicit direction for action. Does he dare cut back on popular programs on the justification this will reduce inflation? Should he advocate wage and price controls, knowing that many of "the public" are going to be quite unhappy to find it is their wages and salaries that are frozen? Further, opinions fluctuate. In a system of government that places a high value on the "will of the people" one of the least known quantities is that will.[8]

Propaganda

Pressure groups have responded to this confusion by attempting to take advantage of it (as have, also, political parties). The goal of a pressure group is to shape or influence public opinion to give the group the highest status and image possible and to turn public opinion into actions favorable to the group. Typically, pressure groups rely on one or both of two strategies in seeking this goal: propaganda aimed at the public as its target, and propaganda aimed at "opinion leaders" as its target.

209

In the language of the craft of espionage,
propaganda comes in two forms: black propaganda
or white propaganda. Black propaganda, or "dis-
information," is simply lying. It may be outright falsehoods, attributing incorrect but
believable statements to one's opponents, or
"planting" false information where one's rivals
and opponents will believe it. During the most
hectic days of the civil rights movement, for
example, "evidence" was constantly being turned
up that Dr. Martin Luther King was in the pay
of "the communists." Occasionally this evidence,
entirely fictitious, made its way into the hands
of nationally syndicated columnists where it
was apt to be given greater credence by the
public than had it issued directly out of a
local sheriff's office or the F.B.I.[9]

White propaganda on the other hand includes the telling of the entire truth, partial
truths, advertising, and public relations; that
is, it is the effort to influence public opinion
by presenting the most favorable position possible
without the resort to lying.[10] A corporation
might run an advertisement saying "Corporation
X CARES! Yes, we care about the environment.
In the last year Corporation X spent $1,000,000
in pollution control to guarantee you healthier
air and purer water," etc. In fact, Corporation
X may have spent the money because it was under
orders from the state pollution control board
to conform to minimum standards or close down.
In this case, the corporation is not precisely
lying, it is only (understandably) failing to
tell the whole truth and trying to reap some
benefits from what is to it an uncomfortable
situation.[11]

In general, pressure groups tend to rely
on white propaganda in trying to mold public
opinion. There are times and settings when black
propaganda will be terribly effective: in a
tense situation, when the victim of the propaganda

210

is a low status group, and when the source of
the lie is a highly credible one. During the
McCarthy era of the 1950s it was often sufficient
only to accuse a group of "communist infiltration"
to destroy its effectiveness. In the "post-
Watergate era" of the 1970s charges of corruption
became common.

As useful as black propaganda can be
for those employing it, it has its dangers. If
exposed, a group will gain a reputation for un-
scrupulousness and as a player of dirty tricks.
It can, as a consequence, lose much of its public
image and status, many of its invisible members,
and even some of its mass or active members.
Political leaders will be reluctant to deal with
the group and it thus loses access. The short-
term gains of black propaganda are generally
outweighed by the long-term costs.

White propaganda is an entirely different
matter. It is commonly expected that a group
should make its "best case," and while honesty
has its rewards, the public relations expert
would argue that honesty should be leavened with
careful attention to image. Without lying, then,
it is assumed that a pressure group should argue
its position with all the skill its leadership
possesses and its budget allows.

The purpose of white propaganda is to
persuade the public that a pressure group has
"right" on its side, and to actually enlist public
support: through letters to governmental decision-
makers and to the editor, through donations of
money, and perhaps where membership criteria
do not stand in the way, even the recruitment
of new members of the group. The first, and
necessary, step in this process is to gain the
attention of the public which, at a time when
the newspaper and magazine reader and the television watcher is bombarded with "messages,"
is difficult to achieve. A dramatic situation

211

or event helps. Thus demonstrations, protest
meetings, and mass marches are effective because
they become news which also allows a group to
express its point of view. Strikes serve the
same purpose.[12] When doctors in California
threaten to go on strike because of the rising
cost of malpractice insurance, as occurred in
1975, they immediately focus attention on their
interest and generate a high level of public
concern.

Public Relations

Other groups rely on more traditional
modes of attempting to reach the public. Corporations, especially, are not in a position to
use the highly dramatic techniques and so will
use advertising in the media, encourage their
public information officers to maintain contacts
with civic clubs, women's groups, and schools,
and produce appealing annual reports directed
to the mass of their shareholders. Participating
in worthy civic projects is also a heavily used
public relations technique. No one has ever
been able to determine how effective these propaganda efforts are, or whether they are effective
at all. Media specialists often argue that "the
public" is infinitely manipulable. Most evidence
indicates the contrary. Relatively few people
read magazines and newspapers with any great
regularity and attention, and those who do are
apt to have already formed opinions. Although
today television reaches virtually every American
from cradle to grave, most who watch now tend
to "screen out" advertisements and give their
attention only to material they are interested
in.[13]

These are, at least, the short-run impacts.
The long term effects of intensive advertising
campaigns are less sure. It may be (although

212

it is not proven) that a message repeated long
enough and skillfully enough will reach some
members of the public and modify their attitudes. As a tactic, however, it is expensive,
sufficiently so to put it beyond the reach of
virtually all pressure groups except the most
wealthy.

Opinion Leaders

        Attempting to reach the public directly,
then, is an uncertain and difficult proposition.
It is generally conceded that a more effective
means of shaping public opinion is to reach
those people and institutions that are thought
of as "opinion leaders." The theory is that
relatively few of us are attentive to public
issues unless our attention is called to those
issues by someone. Further, even fewer of us
are able to form an opinion on most issues without the guidance of someone we respect, whose
knowledge and attitudes we defer to. This someone may be a clergyman, a newspaper columnist
or television commentator, a teacher, a parent,
a friend, or a supervisor at work. Communications theory has demonstrated that most opinions
are formed in a two-step process.[14] The opinion-
leader comes to a judgment and he in turn influences his circle of acquaintances or his
audience. Thus, if a propaganda effort can reach
any large number of opinion leaders, it can be
assumed they will of their own volition take
up the task of influencing the rest of the public.

        Contemporary pressure group propaganda
techniques are today largely engrossed in this
task. Business groups such as the Committee
for Economic Development and the American Enterprise Institute regularly issue reports that
are carefully researched and documented and are
directed to members of the media and the teaching

professions, among others. The AFL-CIO follows
a similar practice. "Canned" editorials are
produced and sent to newspapers. Often a harried
editor will publish the editorial with few changes
as a time-saving device. For less enterprising
newspaper reporters, the well-written press re-
lease is a god-send. He can submit it to his
editor intact, and the pressure group will see
its very words published as they were written.
The press conference works as effectively for
television, especially local stations which lack
the manpower to probe beyond the prepared statements of the group leaders holding the conference.

On occasion, a journalist (whether
television or newspaper) can become the virtual
captive of a pressure group. In covering some
specialized area, he is dependent on the pressure group leaders for "inside" information,
cooperation, and help in preparing his stories.
Since his performance at his job depends on continued good relations with the group, he will
rarely produce copy unfavorable to the group.

The skilled public relations staff of
a pressure group devotes much of its time to
building good contacts with opinion leaders.
If successful, the efforts pay off in an assur-
ance that the information transmitted by the
opinion leaders will, at minimum, be neutral
to the group's interest. Under the best circumstances, the opinion leaders will in effect become
spokesmen for the group. Skill, an understanding
of the needs of the opinion leaders, credible
yet persuasive information, and often low-key
entertaining at meals and parties can do much
to move an opinion leader in the direction a
pressure group wants.15

A pressure group whose leadership is
skilled and sufficiently well financed can certainly have some impact on public opinion. It

214

cannot reverse unfavorable historical circumstances, but one group can do much to build a
high status and image and communicate to its
own members, its invisible membership, and a
sizable portion of the public that its interests
are valid and deserve recognition in the political process. Any group that achieves this much
can be satisfied that its propaganda efforts
have been a success and it is in a favorable
position to apply pressure on other targets in
the political system.

Elections

One of the pay-offs of a successful
propaganda program is the leverage it gives a
pressure group in the process of electing officials to public office.[16] And, as useful as
it is for the public to think well of a group's
interest, for the group it is far more important
how the elected official feels, since he is the
one who makes the most basic governmental decisions.

Money

The people of the United States are called
upon to elect an enormous number of officials,
nearly 500,000. Since many of these officials
are considered to be "minor," voter turn-out
is often small. Elections for school board members, state commissioner of agriculture, state
insurance commissioner, county supervisor, and
most judicial posts will bring out as few as
ten or fifteen percent of the eligible voters.
This means that the mass-membership, well-organized
pressure group stands a chance to exert a large
amount of power on who wins those offices. Further, the huge numbers of federal, state, and
local elections require large sums of money:

215

for workers, office space, postage, advertising, telephones, travel expenses, and entertainments such as rallies, barbecues and coffee klatches. With elections increasingly dependent on public opinion surveys, computer analysis of the results of the surveys, and the experts to do both, another major cost item has been added to a hopeful candidate's budget.[17]

In addition, the principal means by which the parties select their nominees for political office today is through the primary election, which means an office-seeker must expect to pay for at least two elections, and perhaps three if state law requires winning a clear majority in the primary election which means he must fight his closest opponent in a "run-off" primary. The consequent hunger for money that the electoral system creates is another major opportunity for pressure groups.

The purpose of a pressure group's money contribution is simply to insure that the person ultimately elected to office will be in debt to the group for its donation. Thus contributions are often heaviest by groups who expect to benefit directly from their contributions. The group is, in effect, specifically "targeting" its contribution to influence the policy process (see Table 9).

Political party activists want their particular nominee to win. Pressure groups only need to assure themselves that whoever wins he will be sympathetic to the group. Thus, many pressure groups contribute to both parties, especially if the parties are reasonably well matched, usually giving the bulk of their contribution to the party which seems most likely to win.[18] The one major exception to this rule is in those areas where one or both of the parties have become almost literal extensions of a major pressure group. Michigan is often cited as an example where the Democratic Party is an extension

216

TABLE 9

TARGETED CONTRIBUTIONS TO THE
1972 NIXON CAMPAIGN

Group	Amount	Comments
ITT	$100,000-400,000	Facing an anti-trust suit
Trucking Industry	600,000-700,000	Worried about status before the Inter-state Commerce Commission
Seafarers' Union	100,000	Faced Justice Department prosecution
American Milk Producers	600,000	Sought favor-able price supports
Northrop Corpo-ration	150,000	Major defense contractor
Litton Indus-tries, Inc.	226,187	Major defense contractor

SOURCE: William J. Crotty, <u>Political Reform and the American Experiment</u> (New York: Thomas Y. Crowell, 1977), pp. 144-47.

217

of the United Autoworkers Union and the Republican
Party is, similarly, an extension of the auto-
mobile manufacturers.[19] The party struggle is
really more a struggle between two sets of pressure groups than the "classic" party struggle.

Relation to the Parties

        In examining national elections, at one
time it was common practice for scholars to try
to draw a clear distinction between "parties"
and "pressure groups."[20] Often this separation
exists more in theory than in practice. The
advantages to a pressure group of capturing the
machinery of one of the political parties (or
both) is too great for groups ever to have remained aloof from national electoral politics.
During the nineteenth and early twentieth centuries, the great corporations played a significant role in party decisions. Gradually the
power of the unions increased to a point where
they too had to be counted as a major factor
in selecting nominees, writing platforms, and
formulating appeals to voters. In recent years,
George Meany as former President of the national
AFL-CIO was as much a "leader" of the Democratic
Party as any U.S. Senator, governor, or mayor.

        As the capability of the parties to at-
tract the strong allegiance of the voters has
declined, the tendency has been for pressure
groups to try to fill the gap. As a result,
nominees for high office must seek the approval
not only of their party leadership but of powerful pressure groups as well, to gain the votes,
the money, the public relations machinery, and
"the legitimacy" that a nominee needs for a
successful bid for office. In many parts of
the country, party leaders find themselves competing with pressure group leaders for control
of the party. Minority groups, environmentalists,

218

and public servants organizations have joined
the corporations and older labor unions as con-
tenders for control, frequently opposed by the
"professional politicians" who have attempted
to preserve their and their party's role as
interest aggregator rather than interest articulator.[21]

Nominations

Within the electoral arena, pressure
groups have two targets: the process of selecting
nominees and the general election. The greater
advantage goes to pressure groups in the nominee
selection stage. Here, a number of people are
contending for the right to be the official
nominee of their party. As a rule, the formal
party organization remains neutral in this process, giving none of the candidates financial
or organizational aid. The rule is broken, but
only occasionally, and so pressure groups are
in a position to act instead of the party organizations, donating money and campaign assistance
to preferred candidates. Since the candidates
themselves do not have the skills and finances
available from the party that they need, they
are apt to be appreciative of any help a pressure
group offers. The ideal scenario for the pressure group is to see the nominees of both parties
in debt to or sympathetic towards the group's
interest. If this is the case, for all practical
purposes the group can sit back and let the
general election take whatever course it may.

Because of the importance of the pre-
primary maneuvering and the results of the primary,
and because of the relative vulnerability of
the candidates to group influence, pressure group
activity is apt to be most intense at this stage
of the election process. Much of what transpires
may be invisible to the general public, however.
Meetings are held between group leaders and the

219

candidates or their representatives. The candidates' attitudes are probed: does he understand the importance of the group? Does he
understand its interests? What does he intend
to do to meet its needs? Is he trustworthy?

Skilled group leaders examine each candidate's background carefully and in depth to
determine if his actions have matched his words
and if there are any dangerous signs in his past
performance. Each will be evaluated as to his
chances of victory and whether he is worth investing time, money, and effort in. When one
or more suitable candidates are found, the group
leadership can then funnel money, manpower, and
expert advice to the candidate. If it is a high
status group or one considered to have "clout"
among a certain bloc of voters it may even give
a public endorsement, although this usually
occurs only if a group feels reasonably assured
its chosen man will be a winner. The group itself must muster its own membership, assign them
political tasks, perhaps levy special donations,
and use its public relations apparatus to reach
opinion leaders.

Elections

If all goes perfectly, both parties will
nominate someone the pressure group can "live
with."[22] If, however, the group is unsuccessful
with one or both, so that it becomes actively
involved in the general election, usually its
efforts become more observable to the public.
It may have to openly endorse one nominee, a
sure indication that the other nominee is un-
friendly to the group's interests. If not, then
it is, as already mentioned, probably contributing to both in the hope of gaining access no
matter who wins. But, often, its position is
weaker. The group must now compete with other
pressure groups; it must compete with party

leaders who often prefer that their nominee not
be too closely identified with any one interest
for fear of alienating someone else, and the
nominee itself, having won the primary, is apt
to feel more independent, more confident in
his own appeal and skill. Nonetheless, experienced group leaders know that judiciously placed
contributions, sensible and valid advice, and
simply being helpful in whatever ways possible
build a firm foundation for future relationships
with the person once elected to office. He will,
after all, have to stand for office again.

In some situations, pressure groups
actually offer their own candidates. This is
a practice that has now become quite common for
minority groups. Business associations, and
corporations, have long encouraged young executives to "become active" in politics. Labor
unions frequently do the same. And, there is
some evidence organized crime has fielded its
own candidates at least in some cities. Public
servants are virtually the only pressure groups
which are usually denied this opportunity, since
today in most states government employees are
forbidden to seek office while still on the public
payroll. In "nonpartisan" settings, that is,
those communities which forbid by law persons
running for office on a party label, often the
candidates must depend on a pressure group base
to even get started.

Benefits

What benefits do pressure groups gain
from active participation in the electoral process? As one interviewee said of a man recently
elected to an important post, "We elected him.
He knows it. When we talk, he listens." That
is, a pressure group may almost literally "own"
a legislator, a judge, or an executive. When
this is the case, the group is assured of access

221

to the policy-making process. Not only will
favorable governmental decisions be made, but
that precious commodity, information, will be
readily available to the group. And, by its
access to one important person, it will auto-
matically have access to others, including top
administrators as well as other elected officials.

More often a group cannot expect to have
full possession of a top decision-maker. Rather,
having helped him win his position, it has the
right to demand and receive his special attention.
Particularly for groups which must work in an
intensely competitive situation, this is a worthwhile, even a vital, advantage. They are not
necessarily assured the governmental decision-
maker will always act on their behalf, but they
do know he will try to; that their business will
be placed high on the list of things for the
official to do; that, in short, they have "access"
to his time and effort while there are other
groups and individuals whose requests will go
ignored or forgotten. As expensive, difficult,
and demanding as participation in the electoral
process is, access is a sufficiently large re-
ward to make it worthwhile.

Power, Public Opinion, and Elections

How powerful are pressure groups in shaping
public opinion and in influencing the outcomes
of the electoral process? As already discussed,
it seems likely that group leaders _believe_ they
have more impact on public opinion than they
do.

In some instances, circumstance, group
goals, and group efforts all come together to
produce a major impact on public opinion. This
clearly occurred during the civil rights movement
and the Anti-War movement of the late 1960s.

222

The errors of governmental decision-makers, the
drama of the issues involved, the groups' tactics
in appealing to the public, the focus of the
media on the events so created all merged in
a way to compel the attention of a large part
of the public and, probably although not certainly,
changed the attitudes of sizable segments of
the public. In each case, organized pressure
groups played a vital role, a necessary role,
but it is not demonstrable the groups can be
given the full credit for causing a change in
public opinion. In a somewhat similar fashion,
Common Cause helped to focus attention on the
need for basic political reforms, but the pressure group itself was aided enormously by the
Watergate scandals (Common Cause's membership
went from 100,000 in 1972 to approximately
300,000 in 1975). As always, historical circumstances directly affect a pressure group's effectiveness in politics.

        Aside from these dramatic and ambiguous
examples, it is difficult to safely assert either
the effectiveness or ineffectiveness of pressure
group efforts in molding public opinion. Clearly
group leaders believe propaganda is important;
clearly they believe it has some effect. Whether
they are right or not is another matter. Of
all the possibilities, it seems most probable
that pressure group propaganda does help bring
certain issues to the attention of opinion
leaders who, in turn, help to focus public
attention on some (but not all) of these issues.
It is doubtful, however, that any one pressure
group or set of pressure groups can determine
what issues will be given attention or whether
public reaction will be favorable or unfavorable.
There are simply too many examples of major
pressure group attempts that at most enjoyed
a brief vogue and then passed into oblivion or
never even became "issues."

        The role of pressure groups in electoral
politics is another matter. Here group resources

223

can be brought to bear on relatively tangible
targets with measurable results. And here, whatever skills acquired in influencing public opinion and whatever successes gained offer pressure
groups concrete benefits. Further, it does seem
safe to say that although pressure group influence
has always been a factor in party politics, with
the disarray of the party system characteristic
of recent decades, pressure group power has
steadily increased.

One contributing factor to this growth
in group power has been the decline in the ability
of the parties to attract loyal adherents. As
already noted, the number of self-designated
"independents" has increased steadily over the
last two decades. Another measure, however,
is the increase in the number of split-ticket
voters; that is, people who will vote Democratic
for one office but Republican for another.[23]
Realistically put, this means that voters are
getting the "cues" for their voting behavior
from some other source than the party label.
Pressure groups are one--not the only--source
of these cues. Although groups must continue
to compete with the parties and with "image"
politics in influencing voter choices, pressure
groups have advantages over each. In relationship
to the parties, pressure groups do offer strong
stands on issues rather than ambiguous straddles;
in relationship to the candidates for office
who try to depend entirely on "charisma," some
pressure groups have the organizational vehicle
to engage in mass election politics and the money
to buy an "image" as well.

It should not be accepted that pressure
groups today have a stranglehold on the electoral
process. In some situations, this is the case.
Especially in many less populated communities,
one or two groups may totally own the party machinery and dictate who can and will run for
office. In larger areas, this is less likely.

224

The competitive situation is usually too intense
for only one or a few groups to hope to control
elections. The very competitiveness preserves
a role for the party politician as an interest-
neutral person who can act as mediator and interest aggregator.

Nonetheless, pressure group money,
numbers, organization, and skill when brought
to bear on the electoral process do affect the
choice and chances of candidates for office and
the eventual outcome of election results. And,
it must be kept in mind that the groups that
are richest in these resources have the best
opportunities to influence the electoral process.[24]

References for Chapter IX

[1]It will be recalled that the political
geography of interests is an important part of
a group's strategic base.

[2]During the 94th Congress, with Republican Gerald Ford as President, an "overwhelmingly"
Democratic Congress was unable to override presidential vetos time and again.

[3]This appears to be especially true in
city councils. Many operate by an informal rule
of unanimity, that is, unless all members of the
council agree, no action is taken. Betty H.
Zisk, Local Interest Politics: A One-Way Street
(Indianapolis: Bobbs-Merrill, 1973). The same
pattern apparently works for at least some administrative decision-making bodies. Irving L.
Janis, Victims of Groupthink (Boston: Houghton
Mifflin, 1972). Informal rules such as these
only strengthen the veto power of a pressure
group which can gain access to one decision-maker.

[4]S. J. Makielski, Jr., Beleaguered
Minorities: Cultural Politics in America (San
Francisco: W. H. Freeman, 1973), p. 117.

[5]See, for example, Ian D. Burman, Lobbying at the Illinois Constitutional Convention
(Urbana: University of Illinois Press, 1973).

[6]For an interesting examination of these
deeply held values, see Donald J. Devine, The
Political Culture of the United States (Boston:
Little, Brown, 1972). There are a number of
excellent works on public opinion. An older
but still valuable book is V. O. Key, Jr., Public
Opinion and American Democracy (New York: Alfred
A. Knopf, 1961). Two comprehensive texts are:
Alan D. Munroe, Public Opinion in America (New
York: Dodd, Mead, 1975), and Robert S. Erikson
and Norman R. Luttberg, American Public Opinion:
Its Origins, Content, and Impact (New York:
John Wiley, 1973).

[7]Key, in commenting on determining what public attitudes may be on various issues says, "American political disputation at times has the character of a debate over what the facts are . . . because once the facts are known, the decision is made" (p. 275).

[8]This point was partly demonstrated in the 1970 elections for Congress. Richard M. Scammon and Ben J. Wattenberg, The Real Majority (New York: Coward-McCann, 1970) argued early in that the real concern of Americans was the "social issue," that is, a hostility toward blacks and youths, a fear of "Crime in the streets," and a distaste for the permissive society. A number of Republicans campaigned intensely on the social issue and went down to defeat. There is, today, little talk of the social issue.

[9]David Wise, The Politics of Lying (New York: Random House, 1973) cites innumerable incidents of governmentally sponsored black propaganda.

[10]Although laymen generally consider "propaganda" to be a dirty word, social scientists regard it as a neutral term, one which refers to the effort to influence public opinion in political ways.

[11]John Kenneth Galbraith, Economics and the Public Purpose (Boston: Houghton Mifflin, 1973), p. 154 discusses corporate advertising.

[12]For a broad discussion on the efforts to manipulate public opinion, see Daniel J. Boorstin, The Image: A Guide to Pseudo Events in America (New York: Atheneum, 1972). A classic statement of the craft of public relations is Stanley Kelley, Professional Public Relations and Political Power (Baltimore: Johns Hopkins University Press, 1956).

[13]Munroe, pp. 117-39 discusses the effectiveness of manipulative efforts and the degree to which the public is attentive to these efforts.

[14]Frank R. Feigert and M. Margaret Conway, Parties and Politics in America (Boston: Allyn and Bacon, 1976), p. 358. The two-step flow was identified by Elihu Katz and Paul F. Lazarsfeld, Personal Influence (Glencoe, Ill.: The Free Press, 1955).

[15]Bribery, direct or indirect, plays an undetermined role in the process as well. Some journalists, who are frequently poorly paid, hope to become public relations people. By pleasing a powerful pressure group, this ambition may be fulfilled. Consultantships to academics can serve the same purpose.

[16]There are a number of useful texts on elections in America. Feigert and Conway is comprehensive. James L. Sundquist, Dynamics of the Party System (Washington, D.C.: The Brookings Institution, 1973) places presidential elections in an historical context as does Walter Dean Burnham, Critical Elections and the Mainsprings of American Politics (New York: W. W. Norton, 1970) with somewhat different conclusions. For those interested in the nuts-and-bolts aspects of elections, Edward Schwartzman, Campaign Craftsmanship (New York: Universe Books, 1973), Chester G. Atkins, Getting Elected (Boston: Houghton Mifflin, 1973), and James M. Perry, The New Politics: The Expanding Technology of Political Manipulation (New York: Clarkson N. Potter, 1965) all are valuable.

[17]The Citizens' Research Foundation has estimated the costs of elections in Presidential election years increased from $175 million in 1960 to $425 million in 1972. Of the latter

sum, $138 million was spent on the presidential
contest; $98 million for the Congress; and $190
million for those state and local elections held
that year. Alexander Heard, Financing Politics:
Money, Elections, and Political Reform (Washington, D.C.: The Congressional Quarterly, 1976),
pp. 16-17.

[18]Heard, pp. 85-87.

[19]L. Harmon Ziegler and Hendrik van Dalen,
"Interest Groups in the States," in Politics
in the American States, eds. Herbert Jacob and
Kenneth Vines, 2d ed. (Boston: Little, Brown,
1971), pp. 122-61.

[20]See for example V. O. Key, Jr., Parties, Politics, and Pressure Groups, 5th ed.
(New York: Thomas Y. Crowell, 1964).

[21]This thesis is elaborated in Everett
Carll Ladd, Jr. and Charles D. Hadley, Trans
formations of the American Party System (New
York: W. W. Norton, 1975), pp. 313-28.

[22]In one-party settings, the prenomina-
tion maneuvering takes on added importance, of
course, since the primary or run-off primary
is for all practical purposes the deciding
election.

[23]Walter de Vries and V. Lance Torrance,
The Ticket-Splitter: A New Force in American
Politics (Grand Rapids, Mich.: William B.
Erdmans, 1972).

[24]It is appropriate to note that there
is a lively discussion as to how significant
money is as a factor in electoral politics. See
Heard, Chapter 3; and Stanton A. Glantz, Alan
I. Abramowitz, and Michael P. Burkart, "Election
Outcomes: Whose Money Matters?", Journal of
Politics 38 (November 1976): 1033-1038.

CHAPTER X

LEGISLATURES

In 1972, three young scholars working
with Ralph Nader published a book in which the
title of the first chapter was "Who Owns Congress?"[1] Their conclusion was: "the special
interests," especially corporations.

Whether or not one accepts the generalization that the corporations "own" Congress,
it is true that legislatures, national, state,
and local are the natural habitat of pressure
groups. James Madison recognized as much when
he commented, "The regulation of these various
and interfering interests forms the principal
task of modern legislation and involves the
spirit of party and faction in the necessary
and ordinary operations of government."[2]

Legislatures are vulnerable to pressure
group influence because, first, the sheer number
of politicians in them, whether Congress or
state assembly, means the odds are good that
any pressure group can gain access to one or
more law-makers. Second, the frequency of elections for legislatures means that pressure
groups which invest in political campaigns have
numerous opportunities to find ways of making
a legislator grateful for its help.[3]

There is a third reason legislatures
are important to pressure groups: the legal
powers and processes of these bodies. In the
Anglo-Saxon tradition, the legislative branch
of government is assumed to be the "first branch."
It is the body which must pass all laws, approve
all expenditures of public money, supervise the
actions of the executive, and investigate administrative and even private behavior.[4] Although

231

legislatures vary greatly in how well they carry
out these tasks, or in whether they carry them
out at all, the existence of the legal authority
means that Congress or state or local legislature
is an important point of access to the governmental policy-making process for pressure groups.
The processes of legislatures also encourage
pressure groups to seek access. A small foot-
hold can have large effects.

Pressure Groups and the World
of the Legislator

Legislative action is necessarily collective action. Nothing occurs without the
consent of a majority "present and voting,"
whether it is the entire chamber or a committee
or subcommittee. This means each legislator
must, in some way, gain the agreement of a
number of other people before his pet bill can
be passed. The result is what is variously called
"wheeling and dealing," "logrolling," or "back-
scratching." Whatever the name, the essence
of the process is the same: I'll vote for your
bill if you vote for mine. A network of mutual
agreements is thus built up around every legislative action, based on the difficulties involved
in getting a large number of people to act together.[5] From the standpoint of the pressure
group, then, only one legislator who is in debt
to the group means in legislative terms a large
number of potential votes. For the experienced
legislator, this is sufficiently ordinary enough
business that he feels no great fears about his
"integrity." He is simply keeping the legislative machinery in motion.

Process and Pressure

In following the log-rolling pattern,
the legislator is encouraged in his behavior

by the sheer volume of business he faces. A
state legislator in a thirty or sixty day session
may be expected to vote on as many as 500 different bills, ranging from an appropriation to
help cattle farmers whose herds have been struck
down by hoof-and-mouth disease, to standards
of licensing for cosmetologists. A U.S. Congressman faces an even heavier and more bewildering work-load, since he is responsible for the
affairs of not just one state but the entire
nation and its relations with foreign countries.
In a single year, Congress faces a workload of
around 30,000 bills, of which 1,000 will be
passed into law.[6]

    With the heavy load he carries, even
the most conscientious legislator must turn for
advice and help to someone other than himself
and his often overworked staff. That is, unless
the legislator is especially knowledgeable in
a given policy, or unless he feels the issues
touch him personally, he will seek a voting "cue"
from someone else. In general, he will turn
to a colleague whom he trusts and considers an
expert in the policy area.[7] Often this "expert"
is a person who sits on the committee responsible
for studying and reporting out bills on the particular subject.[8]

    In turn, while committee members gain
a high level of expertise over time in their
subject areas, they also are often overworked
and under-staffed.[9] They necessarily gain their
information from someone who has the information.
This may be a pressure group. As the U.S. Congress discovered during the "energy crisis,"
it was necessary to go to the major oil companies
to determine the status of petroleum and natural
gas supplies for the nation. Even much of the
information passed on by administrative agencies
comes in its original form from pressure groups
whose staffs have done the research and analysis
and have the needed data on hand.

Moreover, committees function by log-
rolling just as the larger legislative body does.
The pressure group, then, need gain access only
to one or two committee members to almost guarantee that it will be successful if not all the
time then most of the time.

Underlying the advantages that go to
pressure groups because of the informational
and vote-gathering needs of legislators is the
political power a pressure group can exert on
public opinion and the electoral process. Few
legislators can be sure what the "public" wants
him to do, especially on the more detailed and
complex questions that face him.[10] Do "the
people" of his district really favor more flood
control projects? Do they genuinely want stricter
water pollution control standards for industry?
Should a new study be made of organized crime?
How much money should be appropriated for legal
assistance to the poor? He cannot be sure that
the people of his district or state even know
about these issues or if they do whether they
care about them. Yet, he has two good reasons
for wanting to act correctly on issues like
these: so that he can effectively represent
his constituents and so that he can be re-elected.

Information and Pressure

Once more, the lack of information the
legislator suffers from is an advantage to the
pressure group.[11] With its skill in propaganda,
it can insure that letters to the legislator
are written and that other people write letters
to the editor which will be clipped and shown
to the legislator by his staff. A delegation
of "concerned citizens" will make a trip to the
capitol to express the "will of the people" to
the legislator in his office. He will receive
phone calls from opinion leaders and persons

234

of great prestige in his district. For lack
of any other sure guidance, he must accept that
this is the nearest approximation to public
opinion he is going to get, especially if one
side or the other of the issue is supported by
a well-documented research report.

Even the most skeptical legislator who
knows full well that most such outpourings of
public sentiment are contrived by a well-organized
pressure group must take into account that the
pressure group is well-organized and intends
to fight for its interests. If there is no
countervailing pressure, then the legislator
must assume that the pressure group represents
a potent political force which if ignored is
going to punish him at the next election. For
all practical purposes, it does represent organized public opinion.

Some legislators have tried to counter-
balance the influence of pressure groups as the
principal agencies of public opinion by conducting their own public opinion polls.[12] As a
source of information and a corrective, the polls
are only partly successful. Most of the public
has views on the "great issues," but only rarely
are these the objects of the most intense concern of pressure groups. Further, on more explicit questions, it is apt to be group members
who are best informed and they are thus the people
who will answer the survey questions with a firm
answer instead of a "Don't Know." The legislator
reading the poll results which show that 80 percent are uninformed on a specific issue but 20
percent care very strongly that he vote a particular way is often not gaining real insight
into voting behavior. Instead he is seeing the
fruits of a successful pressure group effort
to keep its members informed.

Where the legislator is in the position
of knowing that most of his campaign funds,

"volunteer" election workers, and major organizational base is a pressure group, of course
his situation is simpler. He knows he would
not have been elected without the group's support
and knows he will not be re-elected without that
support. His holding office is living proof
of the power of the group in his district and
among its voters. He would be both ungrateful
and foolish indeed to ignore the group's interests, and more often than not he does not even
need to be told by the group's leaders what they
want him to do.

In the world of the legislator, then,
the pressure group is one source of "cues" as
to how he should vote; of information both on
policy questions and how his constituency feels
about those questions; of campaign contributions
and electoral support (or potential opposition):
and often of persistent and steady reminders--
pressure--as to what the group wants him to do.
He can choose to ignore these factors, but unless he is very naive, he knows he is doing so
at a risk to his political future and even his
ability to function effectively while in office.

The Search for Access

Much of the preceding discussion would
seem to be an ideal set of circumstances to many
pressure group leaders. These are the wistful
groups whose preferred candidate for office has
been defeated; who contributed money to the
legislator who won but only as one contributor
among a number of rivals and competitors; whose
money resources are too limited for important
campaign contributions; who are recently formed
and have had no chance to participate in the
electoral process; and who for a number of other
reasons have little or no direct claim on the
ear of legislators, or who may need to reach

236

legislators with whom they have previously had
little or no contact. In other words, they must
establish a relationship with legislators who
already hold office.

The Lobbyist

Many pressure groups faced with this
chore turn to the services of a professional
lobbyist, that is, an expert in making contacts
with legislators based, often, on his own prior
legislative service, or having served as a legislative staff person or, in some cases, simply
long exposure to and acquaintance with the legislative system.13 Some lobbyists are the full-
time employees of a pressure group. Many
corporations and labor organizations, for example, hire their own lobbyists. Other lobbyists
offer their services as consultants, serving
on a one-time basis for some special issue a
group is concerned with or on a retainer basis,
in effect holding a contract with the pressure
group to keep its leadership informed and look
after the group's interest in the national or
state capital. One state lobbyist described
his activities to the author as follows:

> I have two things to offer. One is my
> knowledge, my personal familiarity with
> the needs, problems, ambitions, and weak-
> nesses of the legislators. I know who
> needs to be flattered and who has to be
> given hard, solid evidence. I know who
> is dreaming of being governor or senator
> and who wants to stay right where he is.
> Second is my personal contacts. In fifteen
> years you make a lot of friends if you try
> to. As long as I don't ask them to do some-
> thing that will hurt them or violate their
> principles, they'll do it for me. And I
> return the favor by helping them.14

237

The knowledgeable lobbyist, then, is
as important to the pressure group as any other
highly placed staff or leadership position. The
lobbyist uses all the techniques available to
a pressure group: providing information, encouraging the group he represents to write letters
and send delegations, testifying before hearings
to make the group's viewpoint a part of the record, and above all, relying on his own personal
charm and friendships. The advantage a full-
time lobbyist provides the pressure group is
that he knows which legislators need to receive
the brunt of the group's attention. His experience tells him which are the key committees and
the key members on those committees; which legislators might be sympathetic to or susceptible
to the group's pressures, and when an issue is
coming up for decision. He is able thus to help
the group use its resources in the most efficient
fashion rather than scatter its efforts in fruit-
less and wasted attempts to influence the wrong
people at the wrong times. Table 10 gives some
idea of the number of registered lobbyists in
selected states.[15]

Not all lobbyists are equally skillful.
Legislators agree (and lobbyists appear to agree
with them) that persuasion is the most effective
lobbying technique.[16] Someone who understands
the needs and problems of legislators, who has
done his "homework" and presents a carefully
thought-through and researched case, and who
approaches the legislator courteously and hon-
estly can expect to be well received. Others
who resort to overt threats or who have an arro-
gant manner tend to raise the tempers, and
resistance, of the legislators with whom they
deal.

The Influence Peddlers

Some lobbyists are influence peddlers,
that is men who can or claim they can buy the

238

TABLE 10

NUMBER OF REGISTERED LOBBYISTS IN
SELECTED LEGISLATURES, 1973

Legislature	Number of Lobbyists
U.S. Congress	1,120
Florida	1,394
Minnesota	1,254
Texas	1,052
California	552
New York	136
Delaware	63
Wyoming	17
Mississippi	13

SOURCE: Malcolm E. Jewell and Samuel C.
Patterson, The Legislative Process in the United
States, 3d ed. (New York: Random House, 1977),
p. 281.

votes of legislators for a hefty fee. They are
the functional equivalent of La Cosa Nostra's
corrupters, except they work free-lance. It
is not clear how common nor how successful the
influence peddler is. Some observers feel he
is the norm,[17] others, such as the lobbyist
quoted above, are skeptical. He commented,

> I'm not that familiar with how they do
> things in Washington, but around my state,
> fellows like that are pretty much avoided
> like the plague. Once a legislator accepts
> a pay-off from a fellow like that that
> legislator can never again call his soul
> his own.

He continued reflectively, however, "But it does
happen. It does happen."

Although direct bribery may not be as
common as many believe, much the same effect
can be achieved by forms of indirect bribery.
The legislator can be booked for speaking en-
gagements to the pressure group's membership
at a handsome fee. The law firm of which he
is a partner can have several new and wealthy
clients. The late Everett Dirksen, Republican
leader in the U.S. Senate, for example, was
partner in a law firm in a small Illinois town,
a law firm that boasted some of the largest and
most wealthy national corporations among its
clients.[18] The legislator and his family can
be provided with expenses-paid vacations, generous gifts for Christmas and birthdays, and a
giddy round of parties and entertainments where
they rub elbows with world famous entertainers,
socialites, artists, and statesmen.[19] Depending
on the legislator, he may be able to resist these
blandishments. Many appear to feel that it is
all part of the "political game," however, and
accept that in return for all these benefits
the least they can do is help out their "friend,"
the pressure group lobbyist.

240

As with the task of the corrupter, the
lobbyist does not need to gain access to every
legislator. Because of the importance of log-
rolling and of leadership positions within legislatures, good access to only a few legislators
is all he needs to satisfy the group he represents. There is a scale of value among legislators. One of the leadership, such as speaker
or floor leader, is more valuable than a rank
and file member; a committee chairman more valuable than a committee member; a veteran expert
more valuable than a freshman; an energetic
legislator more valuable than a lazy one; and
a member of the majority party in the chamber
more valuable than a member of the minority
party. The most sought after lobbyists are those
who count among their friends the "more valuable"
in each category. Such a lobbyist is to the
pressure group who pays his salary or fees worth
every cent of his high price.

Benefits

What precisely do pressure groups stand
to gain from access to the legislative process?

First, some groups seek the creation
of new policies and programs. Environmentalists
lobby for federal land use regulations. Minority
groups seek new social welfare programs. Consumer oriented groups press for the establishment
of consumer protection and advocacy agencies.
The goal here is to set into motion entirely
new governmental processes and commitments.

Second, and simultaneously, other groups
seek to block policy changes. In some cases,
these are the direct opponents of the groups
just mentioned. In other cases, groups seek
to block policy proposals generated out of administrative agencies. A large amount of the

241

lobbying of corporations is to prevent changes
in tax law, regulatory procedures, and safety
standards that businesses have accommodated themselves to and even found profitable. As three
critics put it, "It used to be that corporations
helped their candidates in return for an even
larger slice of the government's pie; nowadays
. . . their main concern is to guarantee against
shrinkage. . . ."[20] Groups whose members have
come to depend on state and federal contracts
for highway construction, space probes, military
research and development, flood control projects, and tax incentives apply pressure for
the continuation of these programs and resist
strenuously any reduction in the amounts of money
allocated to these programs.

Third, groups which favor changes attempt
to guarantee that any changes specificically
benefit them. The struggle is to see who gets
which slice of the pie and whose slice is largest.
Usually the struggles are complex and even esoteric, involving disputes over "formulas" and
the exact phrasing of a bill. How many dwelling
units in what period of time must a construction
firm produce in order to qualify for a state
grant for producers of low income housing? Should
these be "starts," "substantial completions,"
or "approved completions?" A choice of words
that to the uninitiated might seem to be a minor
matter can mean the loss or gain of thousands
or even millions of dollars to the groups affected by the proposed legislation. Questions
of this kind are usually resolved only after
intricate maneuvering, pressures, and negotiations.
Usually those groups with the best access are
the ones who triumph in these struggles.

Finally, access to the legislature leads
to access to other agencies of government. A
legislator's power is not limited to the legislature. Normally he also does a large amount
of "casework," that is, helping his constituents
in their dealings with administrative agencies.

Often casework is on behalf of confused individuals, disabled veterans whose checks have inexplicably stopped arriving, a small businessman whose loan application has never been acknowledged, a student seeking information for a term paper. Many times, however, casework is carried out for pressure groups. Since legislators must vote on the appropriations that finance an administrative agency, when a legislator calls or sends one of his staff to ask that further thought be given to a proposed regulation, or that a program benefiting some particular interest be hurried up, the administrator feels it is necessary to listen to and usually act on that request. In much the same way, the chief executive, whether governor or president, must be able to work with powerful legislators. In order to get his programs passed, he is often willing to make concessions to a legislator who speaks on behalf of some pressure group.

Although access to the legislative branch of government does not guarantee a pressure group that its interests will be satisfied, legislative access does grant a group a position of power. The rewards are great enough to warrant even the high costs of campaign expenditures, lobbyist's fees, and public relations efforts.

Legislatures and Pressure Group Power

How much influence do pressure groups wield in the legislative process? As is so often the case in the study of pressure groups, it is easier to find disagreement than a general agreement.

Pressure without Power

Three positions have emerged. One is that pressure groups and their lobbyists have

little power at all over legislators.[21] It is
argued that the legislator may be pressured,
but ultimately he will make up his own mind,
and if he is influenced at all it will be by
his calculation of his re-election chances, his
party allegiance, and other influential legislators.[22] In the final analysis, the most a
pressure group can do is to provide a public
rationale for a vote the legislator has already
decided to cast. The group, through its flood
of letters, "expert" testimony, and carefully
researched reports allows the legislator to say,
"I voted as I did because all the experts and
public opinion felt this was the right thing
to do." Rather than being an influence, the
pressure group is used by the legislator as a
public relations front.

It must be recognized that there are
some methodological problems with this interpretation of group influence. Almost invariably
the research is based on interviews with legislators. It would be expecting a great deal to
ask any lawmaker to voluntarily label himself
a "tool of the special interests." Moreover,
as one perceptive scholar has pointed out, contacts between legislator and pressure group
representative are not always seen as such by
the legislator.[23] The lawmaker may regard the
relationship as one of mutual help and
information-sharing between people trying to
solve a common problem.

The Pressure Group Dominant

The second viewpoint is the one represented by the quote at the beginning of this
chapter. The legislator is, in fact, owned by
pressure groups, so many observers argue. Based
as he is in a localized constituency, often without any effective party organization to support

244

him, always in need of money for his election campaigns and to support the lifestyle he feels is required of a high public official, he early on sells his soul to the most powerful pressure groups and becomes their hand maiden in the legislative process. The legislative process, then, is less a party struggle or a conflict between powerful politicians than it is an arena where pressure group interests are thrashed out with legislators acting only as pawns to be moved about by the invisible lobbyists.

This second viewpoint has long been a popular one and not merely among muckrakers and reformers.[24] As this chapter has discussed, there is good reason to accept this interpretation. Pressure groups are active, and influential, in the legislative candidate selection process, the election, and afterwards. They hire skilled professionals whose task is to bring subtle and not-so-subtle pressure to bear on legislators whose positions in the legislature can be of benefit to the group, and they can at least occasionally find legislators who are going to submit to those pressures. Before this assessment is accepted at face value, however, a number of other points must be considered. In the first instance, it must be remembered that as weakened as the political parties have become in recent years, they are still a potent force in American politics. Very few people can attain high office without allegiance to and the support of one of the major political parties. Legislators then are indeed apt to follow the party's position. Only infrequently can a pressure group ask a legislator to disobey his party leadership and have him do so. In those cases when it can, it is because it so completely controls his electoral base it would be political suicide for him to ignore the group's wishes. Among U.S. Congressmen, at least, for a pressure group to have that complete a grip on a legislator seems to be the exception rather than the rule.[25]

245

In the second instance, the legislative arena is a highly competitive one for pressure groups. Although there are power differences among groups, often two powerful sets of interests will collide over a particular issue. In the struggle for funds for urban mass transit systems, for example, powerful pressure groups were aligned on both sides of the question. In situations like this, groups tend to cancel each other out. Instead of log-rolling, division occurs. The elected politician has more freedom to seek a compromise based on his own efforts than to feel forced to follow the reasoning of any one group or set of interests.

In the third place, it must be remembered that pressure group leaders and their lobbyists are not always skilled.[26] They may miscalculate how much pressure legislators will accept before rebelling. The groups become too blatant in their lobbying campaigns and damage their image in the eyes of the press and the legislators. Often they may be fighting a cause for which there is simply too much public support for legislators to ignore, as with popular programs like medicare for the aged and the defeat of the Anti-Ballistics Missile. Historical circumstances as embodied in public opinion can overcome a pressure group no matter how good its access is.

A Policy Focus

The most contemporary position accepts that there is an important element of truth in both the previous positions. Stated briefly, the power of pressure groups will vary with the kind of policy issue faced by the legislature.[27] Depending upon whether the policy is distributive, redistributive, regulatory, or constituent, group power will be greater or less.

In distributive policy-making, group influence is apt to be significant. Here the legislature is distributing "divisible" benefits of usually narrowly focused economic interests, which often have a specific geographic base (just as the legislators do). The individual legislator's goal is to satisfy "the folks back home"; the group hopes to attain maximum benefits. As it happens, the pressure group's goal and the legislator's coincide. Moreover, each legislator has the same goal. A great deal of cheerful back-scratching can go on with mutually satisfactory results for everyone. This is the traditional pattern of pork barrel legislation, tax laws, and grants-in-aid. It must be noted, however that the process is not so much one of a pressure group exerting power over a legislator as it is one of establishing a working relationship in which legislator and pressure group understand their common interests.

Redistributive policies, however, are a more delicate and complex area. Here a broader range of interests are apt to be affected--not merely economic but social and ideological interests. Broad alliances of groups form in favor of or against the particular policy proposal and there is little log-rolling. Instead a basic division occurs within the legislature with ideological questions foremost. David Vogler hypothesizes that the conflicts are rarely resolved within the legislature itself but instead within the executive branch or outside government. Two additional factors probably need to be added. First, the strength of one side or the other in a redistributive struggle is sharply affected by the historical circumstances in which it takes place. Second, legislators would apparently prefer to see the conflict transferred to another arena, such as the courts or the executive branch. Thus, whether a pressure group has access or not to the legislature may become irrelevant: the decision is made elsewhere.

247

This appears to have been the case for such redistributive policies such as social security,
welfare, the Civil Rights Act of 1964, and the
War on Poverty (in all of which the executive
branch took the leading role) or desegregation
(in which the courts took the principal role).

Regulatory policies, in contrast, are
ones in which the legislature takes the crucial
role, at least initially. Because regulatory
policies touch a fairly broad range of economic,
social, and ideological interests, group activity
is intense. The legislature takes on the role
of broker in the group struggle. Competitive
pressure group activity helps to cancel out the
power of any single set of interests, and the
result of the struggle is usually a compromise,
one which may be more symbolic than concrete,
with an executive agency or the courts left to
fill in the details (see the next two chapters).
In regulatory decision-making, groups play an
important part in making sure the regulations
are "fair," that is, that some powerful and pressing interest is not left out of the compromise.
This has been the pattern of policies established
to regulate segments of the economy, to protect
the environment, and to allocate natural resources.

Finally, constituent policies involve
less concrete "benefits" than shifts of power
or the opening up of the political system to
some group or set of interests previously denied
access.28 Because there are redistributive aspects to constituent policies, legislators similarly prefer to see the decisions transferred
elsewhere. It is, for example, notoriously
difficult to get state or local legislatures
to reapportion their electoral bases to reflect
population shifts; the courts are usually required
to make the final decision. The groups involved
in constituent policies are usually ideologically
oriented. While their activities may support

248

or oppose a legislator's position, party considerations appear to be the dominant ones in the
mind of the legislator, especially if the proposed policy may threaten or improve his chances
of re-election.

Once again it appears that historical
circumstances play a crucial role: efforts to
"open up the system" enjoyed a broadly based
vogue in the years immediately after the Watergate and related scandals. Not only Congress
but state legislatures and city councils adopted
"sunshine laws," freedom of information acts,
and requirements that legislators make public
their financial records. Many of these policy
changes were forced on legislators as a protective
measure, one that they hoped would "restore
public confidence" in the institutions of government, and themselves.

Evaluation

It should be kept in mind that the patterns just described are more in the nature of
hypotheses than firmly proven conclusions. However, the policy focus on pressure group power
in the legislature does fit with our models of
the bases of group politics and of group power
(see Illustration One and Five). That is, it
seems reasonable to expect that pressure group
influence, or the influence of any one group,
is going to vary with interest base, power resources, and strategic position in interaction
with the type of policy under consideration in
the legislature. Knowing this much, we would
be safe in rejecting the flat conclusions that
groups have no power or that they have almost
absolute power over the legislative process.
In short, group influence will vary from time
to time and issue to issue. Legislators are
not the helpless captives of pressure groups,
but neither is the legislative process divorced
from the impact of group power.

249

References for Chapter X

[1]Mark J. Green, James M. Fallows, and
David R. Zwick, Who Runs Congress? (New York:
Bantam, 1972), p. 6.

[2]James Madison, "Federalist No. 10" in
The Modern Library Edition, The Federalist (New
York: Random House, n.d.), p. 56.

[3]In a comparative study of pressure group
activities in Canada and the United States, Robert
Presthus concluded that groups tend to concentrate on the bureacracy in Canada and on the
legislature in the United States. Robert Presthus,
Elites in the Policy Process (Cambridge and New
York: Cambridge University Press, 1974).

[4]Not surprisingly, there is an impressive
literature on legislatures. One of the most
valuable works is Malcolm E. Jewell and Samuel
C. Patterson, The Legislative Process in the
Unites States, 3d ed. (New York: Random House,
1977) because it compares Congress and state
legislatures and has a useful bibliography. On
Congress specifically, there is David J. Vogler,
The Politics of Congress, 2d ed. (Boston: Allyn
and Bacon, 1977), and Aage R. Clausen, How Con-
gressmen Decide: A Policy Focus (New York: St.
Martin's Press, 1973). See also Stephen K.
Bailey, Congress in the Seventies (New York:
St. Martin's Press, 1970), and Leroy N. Riesel-
bach, Congressional Politics (New York: McGraw
Hill, 1973). On state legislatures, a basic
source of data is the Council of State Govern-
ments, State Legislatures: Their Structure and
Procedures (Lexington, Kentucky: Council of
State Governments, 1974); Wilder Crane, Jr. and
Meredith M. Watts, Jr., State Legislative Systems
(Englewood Cliffs, N.J.: Prentice-Hall, 1968).
See also John C. Wahlke, Heinz Eulau, William

Buchanan, and Leroy C. Ferguson, The Legislative
System: Explorations in Legislative Behavior
(New York: John Wiley, 1962), and George Blair,
American Legislatures: Structure and Process
(New York: Random House, 1967). There is far
less material on local legislatures. Betty Zick,
Local Interest Politics: A One-Way Street
(Indianapolis: Bobbs-Merrill, 1973) concentrates
on city councils. Carl S. McCandless, Urban
Government and Politics (New York: McGraw-Hill,
1970), Chapter 8 is an excellent summary.

[5]Jewell and Patterson, p. 340.

[6]James T. Myers, The American Way (Lexington, Mass.: D. C. Heath, 1977), p. 326.
See James C. Kirby, Jr., Congress and the Public
Trust (New York: Atheneum, 1971), pp. 5-11,
for a good description of the workload of Congressmen.

[7]Donald R. Matthews and James A. Stimson,
Yeas and Nays: Normal Decision-Making in the
U.S. House of Representatives (New York: John
Wiley, 1975), p. 45. This hypothesis has been
verified by Helmut Norpoth, "Explaining Party
Cohesion in Congress: The Case of Shared Policy
Attitudes," American Political Science Review
70 (December 1976): 1156-1171. H. Owen Porter,
"Legislative Experts and Outsiders: The Two-
Step Flow of Communications," Journal of Politics
36 (August 1974): 703-30 has found the same pat-
tern to hold in state legislatures.

[8]John Kingdon, Congressmen's Voting Decisions (New York: Harper and Row, 1973), p.
101. Jewell and Patterson, p. 411.

[9]Jewell and Patterson, p. 412, note that
turn-over in committee memberships in state
legislatures is much higher than in Congress,
providing greater opportunities for pressure

group influence. For a good survey of committees, see Richard F. Fenno, Congressmen in Committees (Boston: Little, Brown, 1972).

[10]Jewell and Patterson, Chapter 13, discuss the relationship of legislator to his constituents.

[11]Robert W. Miller and Jimmy D. Johnson, Corporate Ambassadors to Washington (Washington, D.C.: American University Press, 1970) describe the methods which corporations use to try to communicate "public opinion" to legislators. See also Jewell and Patterson, ibid., and pp. 291-93.

[12]Jewell and Patterson, p. 310, note that Congressional polling has increased to the extent that in 1958 only about 25 percent of Congressmen relied on polls; by 1970, 74 percent did, despite many Congressmen placing only limited trust in the results.

[13]For good discussions of lobbying and lobbyists, see Lester W. Milbraith, The Washington Lobbyists (Chicago: Rand McNally, 1963) who concludes lobbyists have very little influence. Harmon Ziegler and Michael Baer, Lobbying: Interaction and Influence in American State Legislatures (Belmont, Cal.: Wadsworth, 1969) arrive at the conclusion that lobbyists have more influence than Milbraith believes, but less than "Classic" group theory ascribed to them. See also Miller and Johnson, and Zisk. Jewell and Patterson, Chapter 12, sum up the current state of knowledge about lobbying and lobbyists.

[14]Compare with Miller and Johnson on the corporate lobbyist, "[His goal] is to accumulate obligations from those he meets. He does this by various means, but the object is to accumulate them without permitting them to be repaid, thereby building a constantly increasing stockpile" (p. 57).

[15] It must be kept in mind that by no means do all lobbyists register. Further, the states of Hawaii, Idaho, Louisiana, Nevada, Utah, and West Virginia did not require any lobbyists to register. Apparently no local governments provide for lobby registration.

[16] Charles L. Clapp, The Congressman: His Work As He Sees It (New York: Doubleday, 1963), p. 198; Porter, p. 718.

[17] Robert N. Winter-Berger, Washington Pay-Off (New York: Dell, 1972).

[18] See Drew Pearson and Jack Anderson, The Case Against Congress (New York: Pocket Books, 1969) for some of the more blatant examples of Congressmen benefiting from their private business connections.

[19] In the spring of 1977, both the U.S. Senate and the House adopted codes of ethics to limit the nature and kind of outside income and gifts that members of Congress might receive. Senators, for example, limited themselves to $1,000 per year in speaking fees. Gifts from any one person were limited to a value of $100 each year. There are, however, numerous loopholes in the codes (e.g., a Senator may receive unlimited gifts from a relative who may well have received the gift from someone else).

[20] Green, Fallows, and Zwick, p. 22.

[21] Milbraith; see also the excellent discussion of this viewpoint by Ziegler and Baer, Chapter 1.

[22] Porter, p. 709.

[23] Vogler, p. 271.

[24] See, e.g., Michael Parenti, Democracy for the Few, 2d ed. (New York: St. Martin's Press, 1977).

[25] Clausen, p. 24.

[26] In the spring of 1977, for example, the AFL-CIO was sharply defeated on critical issues of picketing and economic stimulus. The press quoted Speaker of the House "Tip" O'Neil as saying that the labor forces had been unskillful and failed to do their homework.

[27] What follows is largely drawn from Vogler, pp. 265-97. See also David R. Mayhew, Congress: The Electoral Connection (New Haven: Yale University Press, 1974).

[28] Vogler does not discuss constituent policies.

CHAPTER XI

THE EXECUTIVE

Although the legislative branch is the natural "hunting ground" of pressure groups and their lobbyists, few major interests can afford to limit their attentions to Congress or state legislature. The passage of a law by a legislative body does not guarantee the printed words will become the reality of governmental action. It is the task of the executive branch to insure that "the laws be faithfully executed" in the words of the U.S. Constitution and most state constitutions. If the executive branch acts slowly, or selectively, or not at all, the law can be as effectively nullified as though it had never been passed.1 A pressure group that wants to see governmental action occur, then, must keep at least one eye cocked in the direction of the executive to be certain its program has not been shunted to one side. Those groups who hope to block action find the executive branch another potential source of veto points.

Two other facts of modern governmental life contribute to the importance of the executive branch as an arena for pressure group politics. One is simply that much, if not most, legislation is first drafted by administrators rather than legislators. As many as 90 percent of the public bills that come before Congress are first written in the executive branch. While Congressmen "mark up" these bills (as rewriting them is called) in committee, the basic thrust, much of the fundamental language, and priorities are usually set by that crucial first draft. The same pattern holds for state legislatures, occasionally more so, since many state legislatures meet for very brief periods and thus have little time for the tedious work of preparing bills in proper form.

255

The other fact that contributes to the importance of the executive has been the steady shift of power delegated to administrators by legislatures. As detailed as modern legislation is, there are still too many contingencies, too many areas of the uncertain for lawmakers to even attempt to prescribe what actions the executive branch must take. Is a school district really making a good faith effort to racially integrate or is it engaged in delaying tactics? Is a contractor qualified to build the new city hall? Is a certain radio station following the terms of its federal license? Does a group of financiers have sufficient capital to start a new bank and is the community in which they want to locate it capable of supporting another bank? Is a product being fairly advertised? The list of issues which must be decided by administrators is today almost endless. In effect, much regulatory and redistributive policy-making is transferred by the legislature to the executive branch.

These administrative decisions are not arbitrary. They are based on rules and guidelines, but the rules and guidelines are prepared by the administrative agencies that apply them.[2] They become, in effect, "quasi-laws," and the knowledgeable lobbyist hopes to have as much access to this lawmaking process as he does to legislative deliberations. Often, he does.

The Nature of the Executive Branch

As an arena for pressure group politics, the executive branch can be thought of as consisting of three sets of targets. These are the chief executive, the executive administrative agencies, and the independent regulatory agencies. Each represents a different set of opportunities and problems for pressure groups, calling for different strategies in gaining access and wielding power.

The Presidency

The "model" of the modern chief executive
is the President, that is, the single person who
sits at the head of the executive branch and
shapes it to his will.[3] In reality, even the
President cannot be thought of as a single person.
The drain on his time and energies is too great
for him to attempt to do the job alone. Every
modern President has been forced to depend on
his staff agencies to provide him with information, help him make decisions, and carry out
the routine duties of the office.[4] The most
important of these staff agencies have tended
to be the Office of Management and Budget, concerned with supervising the actions of the executive administrative agencies and with setting
priorities, and the National Security Council,
concerned with advising the President about and
coordinating for him defense and foreign policy.[5]

Further, Presidents at least since Woodrow
Wilson have depended heavily on a few personal
advisers, who, wherever they might be located
in the executive branch, have been a source of
advice and guidance.[6] Roosevelt's "Brain Trust,"
Kennedy's "Irish Mafia," and Nixon's trio of
Haldeman, Ehrlichman, and Mitchell are the most
notable examples. In a practical sense, then,
the modern Presidency is not a one-man institution. Although the President chooses--and may
fire--his advisers at will, he is as dependent
on them for help as they are on him for their
jobs. This means that to gain access to the
Presidency does not require gaining access to
the President himself but to one of those people
on whom he relies.[7]

The Governors

The situation for the governors of the
states is even more complex.[8] In virtually all

the fifty states, the executive power is divided
among a number of elected officials, each elected
statewide and separate from the governor. As
a consequence, the governor has no meaningful
political control over these officials. And
often these positions are of great interest to
pressure groups. An elected superintendent of
education, commissioner of agriculture, or commissioner of insurance inevitably is a primary
target of group pressures in his policy area.
Moreover, such officials are rivals to the
governor in dealing with legislators, local
governments, and pressure groups.

Although many governors have large formal
powers, such as control of the budget, the item
veto, and extensive appointment powers, the mere
existence of a "plural executive" of several
elected top officials fragments the executive
function. And fragmentation means pressure group
opportunities, to such a degree it has been argued
pressure groups have fostered the fragmentation
and fight vigorously to maintain it.[9]

Local Executives

At the local level of government, the
executive role is one of weakness.[10] Approximately half the nation's cities elect "weak"
mayors, that is, executives with few or no budget
powers, no veto, and little or no appointment
power.[11] Even the "strong mayors" often must
compete with other elected officials. Only a
handful of counties rely on a strong central
executive. Besieged as they are by insoluble
financial problems, tense race relations, and
limited resources, many local executives find
the major decisions affecting their jurisdictions
are made at state and national levels of government. Pressure groups themselves consequently
shift their focus of attention to these arenas

as a reflection of the relative powerlessness
of the local executive.12

Group Benefits

Whether President, governor, or mayor,
chief executives are targets of group pressure.
As with legislators, the search for access begins
during the electoral process. The need for money
and manpower is proportionally greater for those
seeking their jurisdiction's highest office and
pressure groups attempt to exploit the opportunity
to gain future access with the same tactics they
use for legislators.

If "their" man is elected, pressure groups
can expect to gain greater benefits from access
to the chief executive than from access to any
single legislator, simply because executive power
is so much greater than an individual legislator's.
The chief executive makes critical appointments
to administrative agencies, gives these agencies
policy and even detailed direction, prepares
the budget in which specific dollar figures are
attached to programs, and uses his political
power to expedite or block legislative action.
Further, his broad policy commitments can importantly influence pressure group interests.
A presidential commitment to a strong national
defense posture means contracts and profits to
those businesses which provide military arms
and supplies; a commitment to a detente in the
Cold War between the superpowers can mean increased trade opportunities for TNEs. Emphasis
on domestic concerns may mean enlarged opportunities for blacks and other minorities.

Governors and mayors make similar, if
not as sweeping, kinds of decisions: between,
for example, attracting new industry or strengthening the educational system or investing in
streets and highways. In each case, some groups
stand to benefit more than others.

259

Unsurprisingly, then, much pressure group effort is devoted to propaganda appeals to convince the chief executive that the health, or safety, or prosperity of the nation (or state, or community) depends on his adopting policy commitments favorable to the group's interest. These appeals may be face-to-face or expressed through media campaigns. Their goal in each case, however, is to remind the chief executive of his debt to the group in helping him get elected while couching the appeal in terms of a larger concern.

For good reasons, then, the chief executive and his staff are apt to be primary targets of group pressures. But these same reasons mean that a pressure group will face stiff competition from other groups and political party leaders in attempting to win the undivided attention of President, governor, or mayor.

The Bureaucracy

As a result it can often be as profitable and less demanding to focus on one or more of the executive administrative agencies as a target for group pressure.

These are the agencies of government charged with the actual conduct and carrying-out of public policy.[13] Frequently grouped together as "departments" (such as Housing and Urban Development at the national level, or Natural Resources at the state level), the most important units tend to be "bureaus," the major subdivisions of a department (such as the Federal Bureau of Investigation as a subdivision of the U.S. Department of Justice). This is where policy is carried out, where the actual decisions of what is to be done, whether it can be done and how fast, are made. It is also the place where

the greatest amount of information is collected
as to real conditions in the policy area, the
information so essential to executive and legislative action.

The Appointment Process

Pressure groups go to great effort to
try to secure the appointment as director of
a bureau someone who is sympathetic to the group's
interests. Pharmaceutical and food processing
firms hope to convince the President that the
head of the Food and Drug Administration should
be someone who understands "the problems" of
their industries. Trucking interests will pressure the governor to appoint someone committed
to extensive road-building to the state bureau
of highway construction. The local medical association usually pays keen attention to prospective
appointments to the local health department.

In making these appointments, chief executives often--and traditionally--consult with
affected pressure groups, even asking for names
of suitable candidates.[14] In part, this consultation process is a practical necessity: it is
impossible for even the most knowledgeable chief
executive to know who is qualified to head a
particular agency. The President, for example,
must appoint about 800 bureau chiefs whose functions range from mine supervision to coordinating
federally sponsored educational programs. He
can, of course, leave much of the screening to
the department head, but if a mistake is made,
it is the President who is blamed and must bear
the brunt of pressure group and media criticism.
Governors and mayors face similar pressures,
although usually the number of major director-
ships they have to fill are less numerous.

Because the appointment process is an
easy way for the chief executive to pay off his

261

campaign debts, more often than not pressure group recommendations are the determining force in who heads an administrative bureau. And, once the new director is in office, group leaders and lobbyists rest assured of good access to the bureau's operations.

The Administrative Process

Group pressure is by no means limited to the appointment process in influencing the performance of executive administrative agencies, however. As with the legislative process, the group leaders and lobbyists will attempt to build and maintain continuing relations with not only the agency director but lesser members of the agency as well. They do so with the familiar techniques: providing information and assistance, helping with the preparation of bills to be sent to the legislature, speaking up for the agency during appropriations hearings, and conducting favorable propaganda for the agency in the media. The skilled lobbyist will also build a network of personal friendships among members of the career staff of the agency, which not only assures that the group he represents will get a hearing, but also that he will receive advance information on any proposed policy or program changes.[15]

As already mentioned in Chapter X, group access to the legislative process also leads to access to the administrative process. Every public administrator knows that, sooner or later, his agency's operations will be reviewed in appropriations hearings, and, if something has gone wrong, in a full-scale legislative investigation. The prudent administrator then has himself an interest in remaining on good terms with pressure groups which influence powerful legislators.

The pay-off for pressure groups which gain access to the administrative bureaus is a rich one. Modern government is so complex, the range of responsibilities of even a small agency usually so great, that programs can be lost in the bureaucratic maze, either by inattention or intention. Those groups anxious to see some particular program carried out must in effect "sponsor" it through the executive stage. If they are vigorous enough, they can see their program take priority over others lacking the same political backing. If, on the contrary, the group's goals are to see a program blocked, the sympathetic help of a skilled administrator will guarantee that little action is taken and that only over a long period of time.

The Independent Regulatory Commissions

The third set of targets in the executive branch are the independent regulatory commissions.[16] At both national and state levels, these agencies are created to regulate some important sphere of the economy. The first national regulatory commission was the Interstate Commerce Commission, established to control railroad rate setting and later expanded to the trucking industry. Today, the use of the air waves (the Federal Communications Commission), and the stock market (the Securities and Exchange Commission) among others are regulated at the national level. Table 11 shows the U.S. regulatory commissions. At the state level, similar bodies exist to regulate insurance companies and public utilities especially.

Independent regulatory commissions gain their reputation for independence because their memberships are composed of persons appointed to serve long periods of time (six to eight years) thus limiting the chief executive's control over

263

TABLE 11

U. S. INDEPENDENT REGULATORY COMMISSIONS: 1977

Commission	Date Created
Civil Aeronautics Board	1938
Commodity Futures Trading Commission	1974
Consumer Product Safety Commission	1972
Federal Communications Commission	1934
Federal Energy Commission	1977
Federal Maritime Commission	1961
Federal Trade Commission	1914
Interstate Commerce Commission	1887
Nuclear Regulatory Commission	1974
Securities and Exchange Commission	1934

SOURCE: U.S. Government Manual (Washington, D.C.: General Services Administration, 1977), pp. 462-604.

their actions and because, rather than reporting
directly to President or governor, they report
to the legislature. Typically, they function
to set rules for the conduct of the businesses
they oversee, establish rate schedules that the
firms may charge, establish what are "fair" profit margins, or determine what are fair modes
of operation of the businesses. The goal is
to insure that a competitive climate is maintained, or, in the case of public utilities which
are a "natural" monopoly, that the rates charged
the public for telephone, electricity, and natural
gas service are not exploitive.

As might be expected, the activities
of the regulatory commissions are of intense
interest to the businesses and their trade associations that are regulated. More recently,
consumer groups also have become concerned with
how well they achieve their goals.

Since at least the 1950s, it has been
argued that for all practical purposes, the regulatory agencies are the "property" of the pressure
groups speaking for the regulated industries.
The Interstate Commerce Commission, for example,
early after its creation in 1887 began to hand
down decisions favorable to the railroads. The
pattern set then has continued for state and
federal agencies.

Three major reasons account for the successful conquest of regulatory commissions by
pressure groups. First is the nature of their
work. Without exception, it is technical, complex, and obscure, involving an understanding
of the more esoteric levels of accounting, business management, and markets. Few except those
actually involved in the businesses can fully
understand the information required to make decisions. Most regulatory agencies are under-
staffed and thus their staffs depend on data
provided by industry. Because they are

"independent," neither chief executive nor legislature is anxious to appropriate money for larger
staffs for agencies about which the general public
has little awareness.

Second, the very complexity of their
activities poses an appointment problem for the
chief executive. If he appoints someone as commissioner who has no knowledge of the regulated
business, that person will be hopelessly ineffective. If he appoints someone from the industry,
that commissioner is probably going to be highly
sympathetic to the regulated industry. Frequently,
the latter route is chosen as the simplest and
most politically useful. The result is that
with a few important exceptions independent regulatory commissions are led by members of pressure
groups.[17]

Third, the working methods of the commissions favor well-organized and skillful pressure
groups. The process of determining what are
"fair" rules requires elaborate research, moun-
tains of data, and numerous hearings.[18] Each
allows the pressure group to have a voice in
the decision, often with little or no opposition,
or if there is opposition, one rarely as well
informed as the industry groups. The large span
of time that such decisions take favor the industry groups as well. Group organization means
that a steady, long-term pressure can be applied,
and this is pressure directed at people already
predisposed to favor the group's interests.

Regulation occurs certainly, but it is
usually regulation of a kind to protect already
well-established and politically skilled interests. As has been pointed out, even those commissioners who begin their careers with reformist
zeal over time are wearied to the point that
it is easier to merely act as a negotiator among
firms within the same regulated industry, expressing as an administrative ruling decisions
these firms have made between themselves or with
the staff of the commission.[19]

For the economic pressure groups involved,
the capture of the regulatory agencies is a highly
desirable goal. While not free of government
red tape, they do know that the regulatory process will do them no great harm and that often
it operates to prevent new competitors from gaining a significant place in their markets. The
independent regulatory commissions stand as a
vivid example of the power of pressure group
politics.

Group Power and the Executive

To what extent is the executive branch
of government subject to control by pressure
group influence? During the nineteenth and early
twentieth centuries, pressure groups largely
were forced to work through the political parties
to gain access to the executive process. The
sources of patronage were too great and the parties too well organized (and their loyal workers
too hungry for government jobs) for much group
influence to be brought directly to bear without
the party leaders acting as intermediaries.

In more recent decades, however, the
disorganization of the political parties has
led to a closer relationship between pressure
group and administrator.

Party Competition

The political party is by no means dead,
however, and in the appointment process especially
party leaders retain a lively and powerful interest. Chief executives continue to need the
services of party activists to gain and hold
their offices and thus will listen to party leaders
as well as pressure group leaders.

In making appointments to cabinet level positions, bureaus, and regulatory commissions, however, the claims of pressure groups and political parties are not mutually exclusive. Party leaders have long accepted that certain administrative agencies are designed specifically to speak for and placate sets of interests. The departments of Agriculture, Labor, and Commerce for example were created with just this purpose in mind. Further, both party leaders and pressure groups accept that a man can be a loyal Democrat or Republican and at the same time sympathetic to group interests. It continues to be true, then, that pressure groups and parties must to some degree share in the selection of administrative officials, but it appears that this tacit agreement does little to diminish group influence.[20]

Bureaucratic Competition

A much more serious obstacle to pressure group power is the nature of the bureaucratic agencies themselves. As discussed in Chapter VIII, public administrators have their own group interests and are, consequently, reluctant to surrender their goals to those of an "outside" pressure group.

Several basic trends reinforce this pattern. One is that federal administrators, at least, are highly educated, tend to come from middle- or upper middle-income backgrounds and thus, it may be inferred, are not anxious to be merely the servants of some special interest group.[21] Additionally, it has been determined that because of their similar social backgrounds, administrators often share a common perspective on public policy and the role of the bureaucracy in carrying out that policy.[22]

Second, the impact of "professionalism" has already been discussed. It is worth noting

again, however, that with professionalism goes
a technical skill and a commitment to organizational and professional goals that are not quickly
subverted to pressure group interests.

Third, "the men who rise to the top in
the federal service are themselves excellent
politicians."[23] The same can be safely said
of those who rise to the top in state or local
bureaucracies. That is, public administrators
bring their own political skills, and detailed
knowledge of government, to any test of strength
with other pressure groups.

Joined together, these trends produce
an impressive power base for bureaucratic agencies. And, one effect of this power base is
that group "access" may in reality mean that
the administrative agency controls the pressure
group rather than the reverse. In some instances,
this may be through a process of cooptation,
that is, bringing the pressure group into administrative decision-making as a way of guaranteeing
group support for the agency's activities. Cooptation was consciously pursued by the Tennessee
Valley Authority, the U.S. Department of Agriculture, and more recently, some War on Poverty
agencies.[24]

In other instances, cooptation may in
fact be no more than direct bureaucratic control
of a pressure group. The group, being dependent
on the administrator for the satisfaction of
its interests, almost literally takes orders
from him. A powerful administrator, one who
is thoroughly entrenched in his position and
political base, can dispense favors to groups
which support him and harm those foolish enough
to oppose him or to refuse to obey his commands.[25]

The more general pattern, however, would
appear to be the one that has been referred to
as "the triple alliances."[26] Pressure group,
bureaucratic agency, and legislative committee

269

or sub-committee over a period of time work out
a mutually satisfactory relationship by which
the interests of all are fulfilled, creating
what may be a virtually unbeatable power combination. By sharing information, providing
each other with political support, and resisting
incursions from either rival pressure groups,
administrative agencies, or even chief executives,
the triple alliances are able to dominate policy-
making in their areas of concern.[27]

An important point to be noted, however,
is that the "outside" pressure group is not the
controlling influence. It is only one member
of a partnership, and it must be assumed that
in most cases the group will be forced to make
its demands conform to the goals of other members
of the partnership.

An important advantage of a triple alliance for a participating group is that the
coalition serves to exclude other potentially
competitive pressure groups. Thus "late-comers"
may find there is no way of gaining access to
an already tightly meshed arrangement, one that
is so comfortable to all concerned they are indifferent to the goals of other and newer groups.

Evaluation

As with the legislative process, then,
pressure group power is neither uniformly distributed across the executive branch nor is it
by any means a dominating influence.

Although chief executives will listen
to pressure groups--indeed, often feel they must
listen to them--the relationship is not a one-
way street. As Joseph Califano has pointed out,
when presidents help a pressure group, they expect to be helped in turn, and not simply with

270

campaign contributions and votes but with active lobbying efforts on behalf of programs that the chief executive wants passed in the legislature.[28] Thus, "access" to a chief executive can create future obligations as well as confer benefits.

Moreover, as the Senate investigation of the Watergate scandals revealed, the power of the presidency has grown to a point that "requests" for campaign money may be closer to executive extortion than to a group's search for access. At least some corporations apparently felt they needed to pay for "protection" against a vengeful exercise of executive power.

Group influence over the independent regulatory commissions seems to be more firmly established. The appointment process to these bodies and the nature of the work they do appears to create a relationship between pressure group and regulatory policy that generally works to the benefit of the groups who have gained access, which usually means powerful economic groups.

In dealing with other administrative agencies, group influence may indeed be significant, but the power of the public servant as an institutional pressure group cannot be ignored. In many cases, perhaps most, the best that a group can hope for is to be a working partner in a triple alliance, which nonetheless probably serves to satisfy the group's interests.

Unfortunately there is insufficient research to draw upon to analyze the group role in executive policy-making from the standpoint of a policy focus. It is possible, however, to hypothesize that group influence is greatest in regulatory policy-making by the executive branch. Power must be shared with others-- legislators, administrators, party leaders, the chief executive--in distributive, redistributive,

271

and constituent policies. And, it is necessary
to repeat, in some circumstances a group may
actually be used as a tool of the executive.

It must be kept in mind also that a
politics built on alliances or mutual interest
satisfaction requires that those who participate
bring something of value to the partnership.
A pressure group hoping to join forces with legislators and administrators, or to establish a
relationship with the chief executive, must have
the resources to make the coalition worthwhile
to the other parties. Thus, those groups with
substantial resources and a crucial strategic
position have an advantage over groups which
are less well endowed.

References for Chapter XI

[1]For an excellent general discussion, see Ira Sharkansky, Public Administration: Policy-Making in Government Agencies, 3d ed. (Chicago: Rand McNally, 1975).

[2]Ernest Gellhorn, Administrative Law and Process (St. Paul, Minn.: West, 1975). Although a bit technical, this work is an extremely useful discussion of the policy-making processes of administrative agencies, especially through the use of "rule-making."

[3]There are a number of good works on the modern presidency. A selection of essays may be found in Aaron Wildavsky, ed., The Presidency (Boston: Little, Brown, 1969). Richard E. Neustadt, Presidential Power: The Politics of Leadership (New York: John Wiley, 1960) is an outstanding analysis of how and why presidents make the decisions they do. Emmet John Hughes, The Living Presidency: The Resources and Dilemmas of the American Presidential Office (New York: Coward, McCann, and Geoghegan, 1973) places the development of the presidency in historical perspective as does Arthur M. Schlesinger, Jr., The Imperial Presidency (Boston: Houghton Mifflin, 1973). Hughes's work is slightly less flavored by the trauma of Watergate than Schlesinger's.

[4]Thomas E. Cronin, ed., The Presidential Advisory System (New York: Harper and Row, 1969) contains a good set of essays on the sources and nature of advice to the President.

[5]Former President Richard M. Nixon (1969-1974) departed from this pattern, creating new advisory agencies and shuffling activities and functions among a few top advisers. See Richard P. Nathan, The Plot that Failed: Nixon and the

Administrative Presidency (New York: John Wiley,
1975), pp. 45-49.

[6]Patrick Anderson, The President's Men
(Garden City, N.Y.:   Doubleday, 1968).

[7]Ibid., pp. 98-102 and 159-67 describes
how influence seekers reached presidential advisers during the Truman and Eisenhower presi-
dencies.

[8]Joseph E. Kallenbach, The American Chief
Executive: The Presidency and the Governorship
(New York: Harper and Row, 1966).   The classic
study, although somewhat dated, is Coleman B.
Ransone, The Office of Governor in the United
States (University, Ala.:   University of Alabama
Press, 1956).   See also Thad L. Beyle and Oliver
J. Williams, eds., The American Governor in Be-
havioral Perspective (New York: Harper and
Row, 1972).

[9]Grant McConnell, Private Power and American Democracy (New York: Alfred A. Knopf, 1966),
Chapter 6.

[10]Much less systematic attention has been
given to local chief executives, in part because
of the bewildering variety of offices and powers.
Leonard I. Ruchelman, ed., Big City Mayors: The
Crisis in Urban Politics (Bloomington: Indiana
University Press, 1969) is a good collection
of essays.   David Rogers, The Management of Big
Cities: Interest Groups and Social Change Strategies (Beverly Hills, Cal.:   Russell Sage, 1971)
addresses specifically the problems of mayors
facing group pressure.

[11]Many cites today use the "council-
manager" plan in which the city council appoints
a chief administrative officer.   The city manager
usually has full budget and appointment powers
but does not possess the veto.   See the symposium,

"The American City Manager: An Administrator in a Complex and Evolving Situation," *Public Administration Review* 31 (January/February 1971): 6-42.

[12] Richard M. Merelman, "Public Education and Social Structure: Three Modes of Adjustment," *Journal of Politics* 35 (November 1973): 798-829 discusses the "shift up" of policy-making, largely as a result of pressure group influence.

[13] See Sharkansky; Carl E. Lutrin and Allen K. Settle, *American Public Administration: Concepts and Cases* (Palo Alto, Cal.: Mayfield, 1976); George E. Berkley, *The Craft of Public Administration* (Boston: Allyn and Bacon, 1975); and Howard McCurdy, *Public Administration: A Synthesis* (Menlo Park, Cal.: Cummings, 1977) among other valuable discussions of the role of the bureaucracy in policy-making.

[14] Harold Seidman, *Politics, Position, and Power: The Dynamics of Federal Organization* (New York: Oxford University Press, 1971), pp. 102-7. Joseph A. Califano, *A Presidential Nation* (New York: W. W. Norton, 1975), p. 138. Theodore Lowi, *At the Pleasure of the Mayor* (New York: The Free Press, 1964).

[15] Robert N. Miller and Jimmy D. Johnson, *Corporate Ambassadors to Washington* (Washington, D.C.: American University Press, 1970), pp. 91-95 note that in the average work-week of corporate lobbyists, 7.4 hours go to contacts with Congressmen, 7.1 hours to contacts with executive agencies.

[16] The "classic" study of federal independent regulatory commissions is Marver Bernstein, *Regulating Business by Independent Commission* (Princeton, N.J.: Princeton University Press, 1955). More up-to-date is Louis M. Kohlmeier, *The Regulators: Watchdog Agencies and the Public*

Interest (New York: Harper and Row, 1969).
William M. Cary, Politics and the Regulatory
Agencies (New York: McGraw Hill, 1967) is interesting as an "insider's" view of the process.
John A. Larson, ed., The Regulated Businessman
(New York: Holt, Rinehart, and Winston, 1966)
has compiled a number of articles which reflect
the businessman's perspective. There are few
systematic studies of the regulatory process
at the state level. One of the best summaries
is Daniel R. Grant and H. C. Nixon, State and
Local Government in America, 3d ed. (Boston:
Allyn and Bacon), Chapter 20. Local governments
do not usually regulate business by independent
commission.

[17]Morton Mintz and Jerry S. Cohen, Power,
Inc.:   Public and Private Rulers and How to Make
Them Accountable (New York: Viking, 1976) note
that in the period 1970-1975 of forty-five people
appointed to federal regulatory agencies, twenty-
one came directly from the industries they were
intended to regulate (pp. 20-21).

[18]Gellhorn implies as much, Chapter 1.

[19]Bernstein; Cary. See also Ralph Nader,
Mark Green, and Joel Seligman, Taming the Giant
Corporation (New York: W. W. Norton, 1976).

[20]Theodore Lowi, The End of Liberalism:
Ideology, Policy, and the Crisis of Public Au-
thority (New York: W. W. Norton, 1969), p. 90.
See also Lowi, At the Pleasure of the Mayor.

[21]W. Lloyd Warner, et al., The American
Federal Executive (New Haven, Conn.:   Yale University Press, 1964). Kenneth John Meier, "Representative Bureaucracy: An Empirical Analysis,"
American Political Science Reveiw 69 (June 1975):
526-42.

[22]Joel D. Aberach and Bert A. Rockman,
"Clashing Beliefs Within the Executive Branch:

The Nixon Administration Bureaucracy," American Political Science Review 70 (June 1976): 456-68.

[23]Nathan, p. 54.

[24]Philip Selznick, TVA and the Grass Roots (Berkeley: University of California Press, 1949); McConnell, pp. 75-77.

[25]Robert A. Caro, The Power Broker: Robert Moses and the Fall of New York (New York: Alfred A. Knopf, 1974). Herbert Kaufman, "Robert Moses: Charismatic Bureaucrat," Political Science Quarterly 90 (Fall 1975): 521-38 expresses some skepticism as to whether Moses was as powerful as Caro urges.

[26]Nathan, p. 41.

[27]This is a pattern that Lowi identifies at the local level of government, "Machine Politics--Old and New," in Bureaucratic Power in National Politics, ed. Francis E. Rourke (Boston: Little, Brown, 1972), pp. 278-82.

[28]Califano, p. 141.

CHAPTER XII

THE JUDICIARY

Although it may be unfair to say that
"it's a rich man's justice and a poor man's law,"
often the difference between justice delayed
(and therefore denied) and justice promptly and
effectively administered is the power of the
contending suitors. And often, probably more
often than most American realize, that power
is a function of the involvement of pressure
groups in the judicial process.[1]

Underlying many of our court decisions,
and thus much of American law, has been the work
of pressure groups. The NAACP, for example,
successfully contested the "white primary" and
the poll tax as applied in southern states. The
result was the guarantee of the right to vote
for not only black Americans but many poor whites
as well. The Jehovah's Witnesses shaped American
Constitutional law by insisting on the Supreme
Court's dealing with fundamental issues of the
Bill of Rights. The American Civil Liberties
Union has struggled to maintain freedom of expression and political beliefs in a long series
of state and federal cases.

Less dramatic than these cases and other
constitutional issues such as "one man, one vote,"
criminal law, and abortion, pressure groups also
play a fundamental role in the shaping of administrative and civil law, ranging from anti-trust
issues to land use control at the local level
of government. Over two decades ago, Jack
Peltason was able to say "A judicial decision
is but one phase in the never-ending group conflict, a single facet of the political process."[2]
This flat generalization is today as valid as
when it was made, as increasingly environmentalist

groups, civil rights and other minority organizations, homeowner's groups, taxpayer's associations, and consumer's organizations as well as
the more familiar panoply of business and other
economic interest groups turn to the courts as
one means of gaining access to public policy-
making and to either advance or block some action
in which the groups have an interest.

Two barriers exist to a full understanding
of the role of pressure groups in the judicial
process. The first is the nature of the American
system of law. American legal thinking clings
to the stated faith that legal proceedings are
a contest between an individual and the "the
people" (in criminal proceedings) or between
two individuals (as in civil proceedings).[3] This
means that journalistic--and legal--accounts
of cases often overlook the collision between
competing pressure groups and see the process
not as a power struggle but as a "rational" contest over points of law. The general public,
and even the trained observer, is often accordingly denied comprehension of the participants
and their interests in the judicial process.

The second barrier to ready understanding
is the deference granted to the law and to
judges.[4] Most Americans would apparently prefer
to believe that the court system is somehow
"above politics," that we are governed by laws
not the men--and the organizations influencing
them--who make and interpret those laws. This
widespread deference is in no small measure a
factor that influences pressure group behavior.
As a result, group pressures are apt to be less
overt when brought to bear on the judicial system,
and thus less easily seen by the casual observer.

Legal Access to the Courts

Another barrier to our understanding
of the role of the courts in pressure politics
is that of all the arenas, technical skill is
the most important in gaining access to the court
system. There are few specific legal hurdles
a group must jump to apply pressure in the electoral system, or upon public opinion, or to make
contact with a legislator, a chief executive,
or an administrative agency. Expecially for
the federal courts, however, the situation is
very different. Although it may sometimes seem
that Americans believe they can sue almost anyone
over any issue, the process of gaining a court
hearing is not so simple. Four major criteria
have to be satisfied before a court is willing
to even listen to a case, much less render a
decision. The criteria are the doctrines of
standing, ripeness, mootness, and political questions.[5]

Standing

Bill Jones, a retired bachelor, has been
reading in the newspapers and seeing on television controversy after controversy about school
busing. He becomes increasingly annoyed and
distressed. He feels that the basic rights of
the children involved, both black and white,
are being violated by their being "forced" to
attend some particular school, often far removed
from their homes. He feels the issue needs to
be resolved, because it affects all Americans
in some way. Busing has apparently contributed
to the "white flight" to the suburbs, thus adding
to the problems of the cities; enormous sums
of public money are spent on buses and fuel at
a time when energy sources are in short supply;
the educational process is disrupted; and there

281

are occasional riots or near riots which require
a police presence, again leading to heavy public
expenditures.

There is no doubt Bill Jones has a grievance; it could be said he has a "legitimate"
grievance, but does he have a legal one? Were
he ever to persuade a lawyer to take his complaint
to court in an effort to prevent school boards
from busing children, he would find that despite
all his arguments, his case would be thrown out.
The judges would tell him, perhaps sympathetically,
that he lacked "standing to sue."

The major element of standing is that
the person, or group, bringing suit must have
a "substantial interest" in the case. And "substantial interest" means, first, that the person
must be directly affected by the action (or non-
action) being complained about; and, second,
the effects must be significant and immediate,
not remote, minor, or abstract. As outraged
as someone might be at witnessing a friend being
unnecessarily brutalized by a policeman, the
friend must sue the policeman, not the witness,
for he has not been directly affected in a substantial way.

One result of the doctrine of standing
is to limit the range of cases that pressure
groups can bring into court. Further, the effect
has been to give an advantage to economic rather
than social or ideological groups. Corporations,
for example, can usually more easily demonstrate
standing when a regulatory policy affects the
firm's profits than can environmentalist groups
show they have standing to ask a court to prevent
some project from damaging an esthetically pleasing part of the natural environment.

Many groups are able to achieve a kind
of "quasi-standing" through the filing of amicus
curiae (friend of the court) briefs. The amicus

282

curiae brief is an argument made by a person,
or a group, who does not have standing in the
strict sense of the word but does convince the
court that the outcome of the case is a matter
of concern to the group. Thus it is possible
for a pressure group to present its arguments
and hope they will influence the judges' thinking. In general, the courts are more relaxed
about allowing amicus cruiae briefs to be filed
than they are about the question of standing.

Ripeness

It is a long-standing aphorism among
lawyers that "hard cases make bad law." One
way the courts avoid dealing with "hard cases"
is to rule that the issues are not yet "ripe,"
that is, the legal questions being raised have
not crystallized to a degree that allows a judicial remedy. Often the courts will apply the
doctrine of ripeness on the basis that while
an aggrieved party may well fear some action
will damage him, events have not proceeded far
enough to show this to be the circumstances.
In effect the courts say, "Come back to us when
and if you can show real harm has occurred or
will occur." As with the doctrine of standing,
it is usually easier for economic groups to
satisfy the doctrine of ripeness than ideological
or social groups, because economic effects can
generally be demonstrated with facts and figures
and appear relatively quickly.

Mootness

In some cases, a party to a suit may
clearly have standing, an issue may indeed be
ripe, but the courts will refuse to rule on it
because circumstances have changed so that a
legal case no longer exists. One of the most

283

hotly contested cases of the early 1970s, for
example, was the De Funis Case.[6] In brief,
De Funis, a white applicant to law school, felt
he had been subjected to "reverse discrimination"
when a number of black students with lower scores
were admitted to the law school and he was not.
He was permitted to attend classes on a proba-
tionary status while the case was being resolved
by the courts. Seventy-one different pressure
groups filed amicus curiae briefs, more than
in any other case in twenty years. The case
took nearly three years to reach the U.S. Supreme
Court. By the time it had, De Funis was ready
to graduate. The court pointed out that no issue
existed, since once De Funis received his degree,
his admission to law school was obviously irrelevant. That is, the case was now moot.

The significance of treating cases as
contests between individuals must again be noted.
In the De Funis Case, the issue--"reverse discrimination"--remained a real one, but the circumstances of the individual involved in the
case changed, meaning "the controversy" no longer
existed from a legal viewpoint. Thus for a pressure group to build a case around an individual
is to risk seeing their work go for naught:
death, a move to a new home in a different jurisdiction, graduation, a change in jobs are all
natural circumstances in the pattern of human
lives that can leave a case hanging in the limbo
of mootness. Again it would seem that economic
organizations, especially the corporation with
its legal standing as a person, have an advantage
over social or ideological groups which frequently must build their cases around the harm
done to some specific human being.

Political Questions

On occasion, the courts will refuse to
decide a case because they feel it violates the

constitutional principle of the separation of
powers: to resolve the issue would intrude the
judgment of the judicial branch into the performance of executive or legislative functions.
In legal language, the question is a "political"
one, properly resolved by those branches of
government which are supposed to represent the
will of the people. Although the doctrine is
not that frequently invoked, individuals or groups
angered by a legislative or executive action or
non-action must recognize that the courts may
refuse to take the case.

The federal courts will also occasionally
apply a fifth doctrine, that of "adequate state
grounds."[7] When a case is appealed to the federal
courts after having been decided in the state
courts, the national judiciary may refuse to
hear the case even though federal issues are
involved, because there was a sufficient basis
in state law for the decision to have been rendered. For a long period, the U.S. courts refused to hear most criminal law cases on just
that ground, although the pattern began to change
in the early 1960s.[8]

Effects

The overall effect of these doctrines
is to create a number of technical barriers to
group access to the court system. As has been
proven by a large number of pressure groups,
these barriers can be overcome, but their very
existence places a premium on legal skill, the
money to hire that skill and to pursue a case
over a long period of time, and an organizational
base to gain the money and to carry on a protracted struggle.

As an hypothesis--not yet proven--it
could be argued that gaining legal access to

285

the courts is easier for economic groups than
for social or ideological interests. During
the late 1970s, for example, there was a bitter
debate among students of the judicial process
over whether the U.S. Supreme Court was applying
the doctrines of standing, adequate state grounds,
and ripeness to limit the access of environmental,
civil rights, civil liberties, and consumer groups
to the court system.[9] Others felt that the Court
was being too "permissive," hearing cases that
should have been rejected.[10]

It must, moreover, be kept in mind that
the doctrines are interpreted by the courts themselves, which is to say the men and women who
are sitting as judges. Who these men and women
are and how they apply the doctrines becomes
then not just a question of law but of politics.

Structure of the Judicial System

Perhaps the outstanding feature of the
American judicial system is that it is a _federal_
one. That is, there are national courts with
their own specific jurisdictions, state courts
with theirs, and even local courts with theirs.[11]

Most criminal proceedings, for example,
are matters of state concern as are civil matters
such as divorce, property disputes, and claims
for damages inflicted by one individual or another. Civil rights cases, controversies having
to do with the U.S. Constitution, anti-trust
proceedings, and price-fixing cases among others
are matters handled by the national courts. Local
courts are often responsible for judging minor
crimes (misdemeanors) and small claims by one
person against another.

There are, however, areas of overlap.
Many cases formerly treated as "state" may be
appealed to the federal courts as involving a

286

constitutional issue. Defense attorneys, for
example, will attempt to find grounds for an
appeal based on a constitutional issue (such
as the defendant was not properly warned of his
rights or there was too long a lapse of time
between arrest and arraignment before a judge).
In other cases, both federal and state laws may
apply to the same situation: a person arrested
for peddling narcotics has broken both state
and federal laws; someone may have attempted
to evade both federal and state income tax laws;
a firm may violate both federal and state laws
in selling its stock under false pretenses.

　　　　This complexity contributes to both the
length, and cost, of legal proceedings. A case
may begin in the lowest level of state courts,
wend its way to the appeal court, then to the
state supreme court. From there it may go, perhaps, to the U.S. Supreme Court. At each step
it can take months before a hearing is set and
arguments heard. Thus, a hard fought controversy
can well take two or three years before it is
resolved, if not longer. Moreover, in the early
1980s, fifty dollars an hour was a common rate
of compensation for attorneys (many demanded
and received more) which means that the legal
costs of lengthy proceedings easily could run
to tens of thousands of dollars.

　　　　The complexity of the judicial system
is not limited to jurisdictional questions, however. In many jurisdictions, there is more than
one judge who might hear a case, and as experienced trial lawyers know, judges vary greatly
in their diligence, skill, grasp of the law,
and personal value systems.[12] One judge might
be more prone to commit a "reversible error"
than another, that is, make mistakes or comport
himself in a way that on appeal his decision
would be overturned by a higher court. Consequently, the skilled attorney studies the values,
quirks, and failings of judges and will attempt

287

to maneuver his client's case into the judge's
court which is most apt to lead to favorable
results.

Judicial Selection

        And it must be kept in mind that above
all else judges are politicians. Basically three
systems are used for the selection of judges
in the United States.[13] These are: appointment
by the chief executive with the consent of one
or both houses of the legislature (used for federal
judges and by twelve states); direct election
by the voters (used by thirty-three states);
and the so-called "Missouri Plan" or "merit selection" in which the governor makes an appointment
from a list of nominees that an "independent"
commission submits to him. Once the judge has
served a number of years, the voters are given
a chance to vote "yes" or "no" as to whether
he will be continued in office.[14] Virtually none
are rejected by the voters.[14] This system is
used by nine states.[15]

        However chosen, though, it is rare for
a judge to be selected simply because he has
proven himself to be a knowledgeable and skilled
attorney. He must more importantly have brought
himself to the attention of political leaders
through his contributions of money or time, his
loyalty, and his possession of the "right connections" in influential political circles.[16]
This is by no means surprising, because a judge-
ship is the highest attainment of an attorney.
With nearly half of all legislators lawyers,
the competition for judicial posts is a lively
one, promising as it does great status in the
community, often generous salaries, and a sur-
cease from constantly running for office, as
even elected judges usually hold office for six
to eight year terms and generally have little
difficulty in being re-elected.

288

The political base of the judge means,
however, that for a period of his life he has
followed the same practices other politicians
have. He has run for office, sought party and
pressure group support, made alliances, formed
political friendships, and built up a set of
values and habits that are adapted to the rough-
and-tumble world of practical politics.[17] This
does not mean that once a man sits upon the bench
he will make all or even any of his decisions
purely on the basis of his political values and
commitments. It does mean, however, that he
has through his own experience found that labor
organizations are "cooperative" or "hostile,"
for example; or that environmentalist groups
are a threat to the free enterprise system or
sincere proponents of preserving that which is
vital to the health and beauty of the nation.
He is, in short, a political activist whose values
include a degree of loyalty to party and certain
interests, and whose ambitions may include rising
to even higher judicial positions.[18] Where the
law is clear, he must follow the law; where it
is vague and ambiguous, as it so often is, he
is open to persuasion and to follow his own bent.

As with other office seekers, consequently,
pressure groups attempt to influence the process
of selecting judges. The appointment of federal
judges, and especially U.S. Supreme Court judges,
generates the most public attention. Because
of the relative "finality" of federal court decisions, pressure groups show an active interest
in who is appointed to these posts. Civil rights
groups, for example, carefully scrutinize the
records and attitudes of nominees to the U.S.
Supreme Court. Labor unions are quick to check
the backgrounds of potential justices who will
decide major economic issues, as are business
groups.

The American Bar Association has long
stood in a special relationship to the federal

289

appointment process.[19] Its Committee on the
Federal Judiciary rates prospective nominees
as submitted to it by the U.S. Attorney General.
The President is then free to ignore their ratings,
but ever since President Truman's administration,
presidents have followed fairly closely the ABA's
recommendations.

Because the U.S. Senate must "advise
and consent" to the President's nominations,
pressure groups have access to the appointment
process through Congress. The hearings held
by the Senate Judiciary Committee provide a public
forum to praise or attack a nominee, and access
to senators allows for quieter lobbying if a
group feels it necessary.

Although there are fewer data available
on the selection process of state judges, it
would appear pressure groups are even more active
if less visibly so than at the national level.[20]
While in most states it is considered bad form
for judicial candidates to campaign openly for
office, whether appointed or elected, a degree
of energetic politicking goes on, either through
party leaders or through pressure groups. As
with other appointments, governors and legislators are pressured to conform to group demands,
although often the rhetoric is softened in deference to the judicial system. Where judges are
elected, the role of pressure group support is
much the same as it is for other elective offices.
In Louisiana, for example, where politics of
all kinds are viewed in a skeptical if not cynical
light, pressure groups openly endorse judicial
candidates, and the candidates themselves solicit
(and perhaps pay for) group support.[21] What
is true of Louisiana is probably true of other
states, although the tactics may be more discreet.

Pressure Group Strategies

Once they are sitting on the bench, judges would appear to be far more insulated from pressure group influence than any other officials. They are closely hedged about by canons of ethics, by the deference given their status, and by the hazards attached to any sign of using their office "politically." Pressure groups as a consequence must resort to highly specialized strategies in attempting to influence judicial decision-making.

The NAACP and Segregation

An excellent, if not necessarily typical, example of pressure group strategy is that followed by the NAACP in attempting to force the U.S. Supreme Court to dismantle the structure of racial segregation in public schools.[22]

In 1896, in the case of Plessy vs. Ferguson, the Court laid down the doctrine that "separate but equal" facilities for black and white did not violate the Constitution.[23] In later decisions, the Plessy doctrine was repeated and reinforced. It appeared by 1930 that segregation was to be a legally sanctioned and permanent fixture of American life. One of the grimmest features of the doctrine was that in virtually no instance were facilities "equal" however separate they might be. Black schoolchildren walked miles to school while white children rode buses. Schools for blacks were freezing cold in winter and were always fire hazards. Black "colleges" taught less than the average white high school.

Although during the 1930s the NAACP was devoting most of its resources to fighting voting discrimination, it gradually geared up to combat

291

the "separate but equal" doctrine in schools.
The political problem it faced was a staggering
one: how to persuade the U.S. Supreme Court
to reverse itself, to get the Court to admit
that Plessy vs. Ferguson was a misreading of
the Constitution.

The strategy hammered out by the leadership of the NAACP was based on a clear understanding of the problem and the possibilities.

First, it was decided to attack school
discrimination from "the top down." The Plessy
doctrine was most vulnerable in the area of
higher education. Many Southern states had simply
failed to provide law schools, medical schools,
or engineering schools for blacks. Thus, they
had not established separate facilities, to say
nothing of equal ones.

Second, by working from the top down,
a series of precedents (already decided cases)
would be built up which could then be drawn upon
to launch the final attack on Plessy. Moreover,
the Court would be forced to deal with the reality
that the "separate but equal" doctrine was merely
a legal device to enforce inequality.

Third, the NAACP would systematically
collect data demonstrating the dreadful effects
of separation with inequality: blacks taxed
to pay for schools while their own children went
illiterate; black teachers paid starvation wages;
black science "laboratories" without lab equip-
ment; "libraries" without books; school buildings
without rest-rooms; playgrounds that were simply
giant mud puddles.

Fourth, the organization would support
only "good" cases. Instead of frittering its
resources away in trying to combat the tens of
thousands of instances of discrimination occurring every year, it would bide its time until
the clearest, most vivid, and best established
cases could be contested.

292

Finally, the organization would do every-
thing possible to maintain itself by recruiting
good legal talent, preserving an image of moderation and respectability, and thereby placing
itself in a position to attract high status allies
in its struggle.

The strategy was successful, culminating
in Brown vs. Board in which the Court overturned
the "separate but equal doctrine."24

Several points about the NAACP's strategy
need to be noted. Twenty years passed between
the formulation of the strategy and the Brown
decision. In that interval, generations of students had passed through the schools, and leaders
of the NAACP had come and gone. That is, only
an organization could have pursued such a long-
term program. Similarly, only an organization
with a widespread geographic base was in a position to sift and select from all the potential
cases and controversies which would be used to
build the series of precedents and good cases
that finally led to victory. And, only an organization could cultivate the legal skills, pay
the costs, and engage in the alliance-building
necessary to win the cases.

If the end of legal segregation had been
left to individual effort, it is quite possible
that Plessy vs. Ferguson would still be the ruling
doctrine. In short, a group could do what an
individual could not.

Perhaps unnecessary to say, relatively
few pressure groups undertake such long-term
strategies (relatively few are in the position
the NAACP was in). But the broad outlines of
the strategy are followed time and again: selecting cases carefully, seeking to build up
a backlog of useful precedents, drawing on the
best talent and research the group can afford,
and attempting to bring in high status allies
as amici curiae.

Pressure group leaders knowledgeable about the judicial process also know that judges are sensitive to the tides of public opinion.[25] To the extent possible, then, the propaganda devices available to groups will be used to shape the "climate of opinion" in which the case is resolved. Part of this climate of opinion are the law reviews which carry articles analyzing issues both before the courts and likely to arise. Groups will encourage the submission of articles by attorneys who are sympathetic to the group's goals.[26]

Benefits

The benefits to be derived from successfully influencing the judicial system are great enough to make careful planning and high costs worth the effort. Potentially, a group and its allies may truly "revolutionize" public policy, as with the <u>Brown</u> decision. In other, less dramatic instances, the group may see significant policy made to its advantage.

As noted in Chapter XII, many regulatory and constituent decisions are transferred to the court systems by legislatures. It is before judges that the specific details of economic regulation, environmental protection, the scope of consumer protection measures, the applicability of zoning laws, and a vast array of other policy issues are settled. The real and final form of a policy may be shaped in the judicial branch, and if a group wins there it will have achieved what it may have lost in the legislative or executive arenas.

The courts are valuable also as a veto point in the political system. When a governmental action promises to harm group interests, a court can often be persuaded to issue an injunction, that is, a court command that the

governmental agency not carry out the policy
until the issues have been resolved in a formal
legal suit. Environmental and historic preservation groups, for example, have often found
the injunction useful to stop construction or
demolition projects. While an injunction is
usually only a delaying tactic, it allows the
group breathing space to pressure the legislature
and to mount a propaganda campaign. Often also
the delay is sufficiently long to cause the
project to be abandoned as too expensive in terms
of the controversy it arouses.[27] The injunction
has also been used by government as a means of
forcing, or attempting to force, striking public
employees to return to their jobs.

Other Targets

        Although the discussion thus far has
focussed primarily on the courts, it must be
remembered that the legal departments of federal,
state, and local governments are an integral
part of the judicial system as well. The role
of these governmental agencies has always been
ambiguous. The U.S. Justice Department, for
example, has long been and continues to be a
rich source of patronage for the President, with
ninety-four U.S. Attorneys (one for each district
court) and the same number of U.S. marshals.[28]
The Attorney General initially screens potential
nominees for federal judgeships and, as importantly for pressure group interests, makes many
of the crucial policy decisions as to what kinds
of cases the federal government will pursue and
how vigorously. Is organized crime to be a major
target of the administration? Or civil rights
cases? Or anti-trust proceedings? Or labor
union malpractices?

        It has never been clear whether the Just-
ice Department should pursue all wrong-doers

295

without fear or favor or, in effect act as a
political extension of the incumbent President.
During the post-Watergate national soul-searching,
much was made of the "political uses" of the
Justice Department, but its practices during
the Nixon Administration were perhaps only somewhat more flagrant than under previous administrations.[29]

As the Senate investigation revealed,
pressure groups such as ITT directly approached
the Justice Department in an effort to prevent
or moderate proceedings the Department was bringing against these groups. Similarly, civil
rights organizations pressured the department
during the Kennedy and Johnson administrations
to be more diligent in pursuing desegregation
cases.

In forty-four of the fifty states, the
State Attorney General is popularly elected and
thus is virtually independent of the governor.
Often in fact he is a political rival of the
governor, hoping to use his post as a stepping-
stone to the governor's mansion. He has, however,
less control over state district prosecutors
than the U.S. Attorney General has over U.S.
Attorneys. In all but four states (Connecticut,
Delaware, Rhode Island, and New Jersey) the district attorney is elected by the voters of his
local jurisdiction.[30] Thus the state attorney
general can determine what actions his department
chooses or does not choose to bring to court
under state law, but the local district attorneys
are free to make their own decisions regarding
the same state laws.

Because both state attorney general and
district attorneys are elected officials, pressure groups become involved in the electoral
process as they do with other elective officials.
Moreover, with the attorney general's office
a promising start toward higher office, at least

296

some state attorney generals are reluctant to
anger powerful pressure groups in their states.
The same is often true for district attorneys,
while others hope, through the way they administer
their office during their tenure, to build a
set of clients for a rich private practice once
they give up office.

As was pointed out in the discussion
of organized crime, the importance of justice
departments whether national or state, to pressure groups lies in whether and how vigorously
these agencies choose to act on information that
might be harmful to the pressure group or its
competitors.   District attorneys can ignore
or actively investigate shady practices between
contractors, consultants and local governments.
State attorney generals may prosecute savings-
and-loan or insurance scandals to the full extent
of the law or "plea bargain" so that the officers
of the guilty firms receive no more than light
fines when finally convicted. A case may be
assigned to the most skilled trial attorneys
in the office or be badly put together, or proceedings may be dragged out over such a long
period of time that crucial evidence, such as
the recollections of witnesses, grows stale and
invalid.

If the government is defeated at the
lowest level of courts, it is the department
of justice which makes the decision to appeal
the case or not, thereby deciding whether to
increase the pressure group's costs and uncer-
tainties or not. In brief, the opportunities
to favor or disadvantage group interests in the
judicial process are extensive.

The Judiciary and Pressure Group Power

How much influence do pressure groups
exert over the judicial process? Some political

297

scientists have acknowledged group activity but
are reluctant to assert that pressure groups can
or do have the same power as they do in the legislative or executive arenas.[31] As one has argued,
it is a mistake to "confuse group activity with
group influence."[32]

Others place the judicial process squarely
within the context of pressure group politics.[33]
While admitting that group influence is more
covert and group leaders and lobbyists are careful to defer to the rhetoric of "an independent
and non-political" judiciary, they see pressure
group influence as nonetheless present and powerful at every stage of the process from the selection of judges and administrators of justice,
through the selection of cases and judicial
decision-making.

These analysts argue that what makes
group influence appear less is that in the judicial arena, influence is exerted more subtly
and more expertly. Except for the designation
of U.S. Supreme Court justices, little public
or media attention is directed toward the politics
of the judiciary, legal proceedings are complicated, obscure and difficult for the lay person
to follow, and judges, lawyers, and pressure
groups have a vested interest in maintaining
a generalized silence about the realities of
group power.

Limits to Group Power

With expert opinion divided it is extremely difficult to make a valid assessment
of the degree of pressure group influence in
the judicial process. While there have been
enormous quantities of research into the impact
of judicial decisions on other aspects of the
political process and into whether judges follow
an "activist" or limited view of their role,

298

relatively little has been done to explore the
more complex areas of judicial politics. As
a first step, we can note the limits to group
influence.

First, there are significant limits on
the potential role of pressure groups in the
judicial process. One of these is the status
and deference paid to the judicial process. There
are and have been corrupt judges,[34] there are
and have been judges who decide cases on self-
interested and highly political grounds. Many
politicians who are elevated to judicial posts,
however, do attempt to insulate themselves from
the crasser pressures of everyday politics, and
take very seriously their role as guardians of
the American system of justice. This attitude
is to some degree, at least, shared by lawyers,
lobbyists, and pressure group leaders. While
all might be willing to admit that a major judicial decision is "political" in the sense it
is governmental and affects the operation of
the political system, decisions based on pure
pressure politics need not be the rule of judicial behavior.

Second, pressure groups must accept the
limits which the law imposes when they enter
the judicial arena. Although, as noted, often
the law is vague or ambiguous, in most cases
there is a body of precedents, statutory law,
rules of evidence and argument, and procedures
which place outside boundaries on a judge's discretion. Few judges, however independent-minded,
relish being reversed on appeal, so there is
a strong tendency for judicial decision-making
to follow already established paths. The consequence is that no matter how sympathetic a
judge may be to a group's position, he might
rule against it because the law dictates that
he do so. It is true that courts will reverse
themselves, the most notable example being Brown
vs. Board. These reversals of policy are,

299

however, rare enough that a pressure group would be imprudent to count on them.

Third, pressure groups must compete with the political parties in the judicial selection process. Of all the positions available to the party faithful, none are more desirable than judgeships. Party leaders, from chief executives on down, protect their prerogatives in controlling the selection process more jealously than for any other governmental positions. In the election of state judges, pressure groups can involve themselves as in any other election, but again they must compete with the parties, and it is not altogether certain that contributions to judicial campaigns produce the same degree of access as they do for the election of legislators and executives.

All these limits are important ones. Together they do not create an "independent judiciary" in the sense that many of the public would like to believe, but they do serve to provide a barrier, for better or worse, to much of the direct hurly-burly of pressure group politics. The corridors outside a courtroom are never crowded with lobbyists button-holing judges on their way to pass judgment in contrast to the scenes typical of legislative corridors.

Group Potential

At the same time, however, we must be sensitive to the role pressure groups do play in judicial policy-making. Courts decide only those cases that are brought to them. Because of the cost and the time-lapse involved in the judicial process, pressure groups are major generators of legal proceedings. They have the money and the organization to pursue a case to final decision, an option individuals often do not

300

possess because of limited resources. Thus, most cases involving civil rights, civil liberties, equal opportunity, environmental issues, consumer interests, and major economic and ideological issues are pressure group initiated or supported. This means, in turn, pressure groups play a fundamental role in setting the judicial agenda, the policy issues which the courts have the opportunity to decide. To this extent, a highly important one, pressure group politics creates and defines the scope of the judicial process in American political affairs.

Some cases that involve group interests are initiated by governmental agencies. Often, however, these too are the result of either direct or indirect group pressures. Pressure group access to administrative agencies and to departments of justice does affect the actions these bodies take and thereby helps to set the judicial agenda. At the extreme, where La Cosa Nostra has infiltrated the judicial process no cases are brought against organized crime.[35] In less extreme situations, where a particular pressure group is dominant, it is rare to see actions brought against this group's interest or if brought, vigorously pursued. The geographic base of pressure groups and of the judicial system interact. Judges, whether federal or state, are usually long-time residents of the area or community where they sit on the bench. If one interest has been dominant in the area, the judge (who is a successful politician) may be little more than a product of and a spokesman for that interest.

Administrative agencies also can and do act as pressure groups in the judicial process, attempting to influence judicial appointments and bringing suit against non-governmental pressure groups. This is one reason why groups seek to influence the appointment of top administrators. Accordingly, some economic groups also consistently oppose the creation of consumer protection agencies, fearing that these bodies will, like environmental protection agencies, become anti-business pressure groups in the judicial process.

As already mentioned, pressure groups attempt to influence judicial decision-making through the amicus curiae brief. It is not clear how effective these briefs are in swaying a judge's thought processes. Probably a well-argued, carefully written, and thoroughly researched brief can tip the balance in a case where the issues are evenly balanced. No doubt a good brief can also bolster a side that would otherwise be weakly or ineptly handled. In some cases, the appearance of a high status pressure group in support of one side of a case may in a subtle way convince a judge of the merits of that position. While the results are difficult to measure, the ever-present possibility that an amicus curiae brief could make a difference is sufficient to ensure continued group participation in cases in which the groups are not direct parties.

Group propaganda aimed at public and judicial opinion may have long-run consequences. It is commonly held among observers of the judicial process that courts will incorporate into their opinions "an idea whose time has come." To support this line of argument, dramatic changes in civil rights, women's rights, the rights of the poor, economic policy, and land use and environmental decisions can be cited. It is, however, impossible to prove that courts were responding to shifts in public opinion (much less attributing those shifts to pressure group propaganda) rather than to changes in the make up of the judges sitting on the courts (which can be at least partly attributed to pressure group efforts). As discussed in Chapter VIII, the data do not yet support any hard conclusions

that pressure group propaganda campaigns significantly modify public attitudes. The possibility must be admitted to exist, however. And
group propaganda may serve to sharpen a judge's
consciousness of some economic or social problem
that he was previously unaware of, as it does
with the less highly placed citizen. Group propaganda, then, may change a judge's perspective
on the issues that come before him. No doubt
the civil rights, women's, environmentalist, and
consumer movements have all affected some judges
in this fashion.

     Further, although it is common to talk
of the "insulation" of the judiciary, this has
reference to federal judges more than state judges.
The former, with life tenure, high salaries, and
high prestige are indeed almost as insulated
as they choose to be. It is not certain the
same is true of the state judiciary. Simply,
too little is known about the day-to-day political
contacts of these men and women to assume that
all are free of direct pressure group politicking.

     On balance, then, we can say that pressure
group influence is at work in the judicial arena,
affecting the selection of those engaged in the
administration of justice and playing a large
role in setting the agenda of the courts. Further, group influence may shape judicial decision-
making through the amicus curiae brief and
through propaganda campaigns. At the present
stage of research, it is difficult to say more.

     As with other arenas of pressure group
politics, the advantage tends to go to those
with large political resources at their command.
Money, which can hire skilled legal counsel and
influence judicial elections, votes, organization, skilled leaders, high status are, as always,
assets. The power differential between the best
endowed and the not-so-well off is not as great
in the judicial arena as in others, however.

A small group, with modest resources, can gain
access to the judicial process and if fortunate
enough to find a sympathetic court can fundamentally influence public policy.[36]

References for Chapter XII

[1]An excellent general work on the federal
judicial system is Henry J. Abraham, The Judiciary: The Supreme Court in the Judicial Process, 4th ed. (Boston: Allyn and Bacon, 1977).
Herbert Jacob, Justice in America: Courts, Lawyers, and the Judicial Process, 2d ed. (Boston:
Little, Brown, 1965) examines both federal and
state judicial systems. Archibald Cox, The Role
of the Supreme Court in American Government (New
York: Oxford University Press, 1976 and Robert
G. McCloskey, The Modern Supreme Court, rev.
ed. (Cambridge, Mass1: Harvard University Press,
1972) are good studies of the Supreme Court.
Jack W. Peltason, Federal Courts in the Political
Process (Garden City, N.Y.: Doubleday, 1955)
is a study of the courts from a pressure group
perspective. For those interested in a general
introduction to the law, Robert T. Kimbrough,
Summary of American Law (San Francisco: Bancroft-
Whitney, 1974) is reasonably readable and ac-
cessible to the non-lawyer.

   On state judicial systems specifically,
see Daniel R. Grant and H. C. Nixon, State and
Local Government in America, 3d ed. (Boston:
Allyn and Bacon, 1975), Chapter 15 and their
excellent bibliography. Clement Vose, "Interest
Groups, Judicial Review, and Local Government,"
Western Political Quarterly 19 (March 1966):
85-100 is a good study of the effect of courts
and pressure groups at the local level of government.

[2]Peltason, p. 64.

[3]It will be recalled that corporations
are legally "persons."

[4]Respect for the judiciary has declined
as has respect for other governmental institutions, although not as dramatically. See the
Harris Poll as reported in James MacGregor Burns,
J. W. Peltason, and Thomas E. Cronin, Government
by the People, 9th ed. (Englewood Cliffs, N.J.:
Prentice-Hall, 1975), p. 5.

[5]For a detailed examination of standing,
see Karen Orren, "Standing to Sue: Interest
Group Conflict in the Federal Courts," American
Political Science Review 70 (September 1976):
723-41. Wallace Mendelson, "Mr. Justice Douglas
and Government by the Judiciary," Journal of
Politics 38 (November 1976): 918-37 discusses
all four doctrines in detail. Both articles
provide citations to relevant court decisions.

[6]De Funis vs. Odegaard, 416 U.S. 312
(1974). See Ralph A. Rossum, "Ameliorative Racial
Preference and the Fourteenth Amendment: Some
Constitutional Problems," Journal of Politics
38 (May 1976): 346-66 for a full discussion of
the background and implications of "reverse discrimination."

[7]Mendelson, p. 333.

[8]Ibid.

[9]Leonard W. Levy, Against the Law: The
Nixon Court and Criminal Justice (New York: Harper
and Row, 1974); Aryeh Neier, national executive
director of the American Civil Liberties Union,
argued this point in an address in New Orleans,
February 16, 1977.

[10]Mendelson; Robert J. Harris, "Judicial
Review: Vagaries and Varieties," Journal of
Politics 38 (August 1976): 173-208.

[11]Abraham, pp. 3-32, has an excellent
description of the complexities and significance
of jurisdiction in America.

[12]Donald D. Jackson, Judges (New York: Atheneum, 1974) is a fascinating, in-depth look at local, state, and federal judges based on interviews and direct observation.

[13]Jacob, pp. 98-99. Harold W. Chase, Federal Judges: The Appointing Process (Minneapolis: University of Minnesota Press, 1972) discusses political selection at the state level as well.

[14]Jackson, Chapter 1.

[15]These figures are for 1970. The count adds up to more than fifty states because some states use different systems for different levels of courts.

[16]Chase, p. 197.

[17]Ibid., p. 195.

[18]Stuart Nagel, "Political Party Affiliation and Judges' Decisions," American Political Science Review 55 (December 1961): 843-50; S. Sidney Ulmer, "Social Background As an Indicator to the Votes of Supreme Court Justices in Criminal Cases," American Journal of Political Science 17 (August 1973): 622-30.

[19]Chase, Chapter 4. Joel Grossman, Lawyers and Judges (New York: John Wiley, 1965). Victor S. Navasky, Kennedy Justice (New York: Atheneum, 1977), Chapter 5. Richard Harris, Decision (New York: E. P. Dutton, 1971) has a fine study of pressure group opposition to President Nixon's Supreme Court nominees.

[20]Grossman; Chase, especially Chapter 6.

[21]I would like to acknowledge the useful information provided by Dr. Edward F. Renwick, Director, Institute of Politics, Loyola University, New Orleans on this point. See Grant and Nixon, pp. 364-66.

^{22}What follows is based largely on Richard Kluger, Simple Justice (New York: Alfred A. Knopf, 1976), a magnificent study. Randall W. Bland, Private Pressure on Public Law: The Legal Career of Justice Thurgood Marshall (Port Washington, New York: Kennikat, 1973) is also a very useful work.

^{23}163 U.S. 537.

^{24}Brown vs. Board of Education of Topeka, 347 U.S. 483 (1954). Brown vs. Board was actually four cases, from Kansas, South Carolina, Virginia, and Delaware which had been "consolidated" into one case. See Kluger, pp. 779-82 for the text of the decision.

^{25}Richard J. Richardson and Kenneth N. Vines, The Politics of Federal Courts (Boston: Little, Brown, 1970), p. 106.

^{26}Peltason, p. 52.

^{27}Orren, p. 725.

^{28}Jacob, p. 27.

^{29}Navasky makes this point quite forcefully.

^{30}Jacob, p. 85.

^{31}For example, David B. Truman, The Governmental Process (New York: Alfred A. Knopf, 1951; rev. ed., 1971).

^{32}Jacob, p. 135.

^{33}For example, Peltason; Wallace S. Sayre and Herbert Kaufman, Governing New York City (New York: Russell Sage, 1960).

^{34}Joseph Borkin, The Corrupt Judge (New York: Potter, 1962).

[35]Ron Parambo, No Cause for Indictment: An Autopsy of Newark (New York: Holt, Rinehart, and Winston, 1971).

[36]This is the conclusion of Kenneth Dolbeare, Trial Courts in Urban Politics (New York: John Wiley, 1967), and Austin Sarat and Joel B. Grossman, "Courts and Conflict Resolution: Problems in the Mobilization of Adjudication," American Political Science Review 69 (December 1975): 1200-217.

PART III

PRESSURE AND DEMOCRACY

CHAPTER XIII

PRESSURE GROUPS AND DEMOCRACY

While it can be safely said that pressure groups are an important phenomenon in American political life, two fundamental questions remain to be answered. The first is analytical: how significant is the role of the pressure group in American politics? The second is normative (that is, a value question): Is pressure group activity "good" or "bad" for the American system of government?

The analytical question of group signfi-cance defies easy answers. On the one hand this is so because it is a question of power: to what degree do pressure groups modify the way the political system operates? On the other hand, the question is difficult because it is one of function: what is the relationship of pressure groups to the other elements of the political system and the way they behave? The preceding chapters have suggested some possible answers to these analytical questions, but we must now turn to a broader perspective.

Pressure Group Power

The astute reader has by now noticed that in the discussion of group power in the concluding sections of each of the preceding chapters, any generalizations have been sharply qualified by phrases such as "it seems that," or "it is not clear that," or similar language. Qualifiers such as these are necessary because, despite the long-standing concern by political science with the concept of power and influence, there is no consistently reliable or useful

313

means of measuring power.[1] That is, when we say "John Smith is a powerful man" we may mean (A) he occupies a place in the political and social system that ought to allow him to have his way on matters he considers important (a statement of potential); or (B) we may have observed John Smith's behavior and in numerous instances he has gotten his way (a statement of direct observation); or (C) events may consistently turn out to favor John Smith's desires and we believe he played a part in causing those events (a statement of inference); or (D) others may assert that John Smith is powerful and we accept them as credible observers (a statement of reputation or indirect observation).

Under ideal scientific circumstances we would accept only statements of direct observation as verifying the broader thesis of Smith's power, and we would accept these only after we had observed a large number of instances. In a great deal of political research, however, the analyst is barred from direct observation. Pressure group leaders and other political leaders do not take kindly to having an outsider watch their every move as they pursue their activities. Thus many conclusions about pressure group power (and the power of other political actors) depend on statements of potential, inference, and reputation or indirect observation.

By examining the resources of pressure groups (or other political actors) we can make some estimates of their potential. By examining the results of political activities (the output of the political system) we can infer that groups have shaped those outputs, largely by asking the traditional lawyer's question cui bono? Who benefits? Finally, we depend heavily on the recollections, memoirs, studies, and speculations of others. The essential point to keep before us, however, is that these methods are less than ideal and give us only partial answers.

314

Nor is the problem of observation the only one. When the psychologist, for example, uses a standardized test to measure "intelligence," he accepts that the test may well be flawed, that it is at best only a partial measurement, yet he has a ready means of making comparisons. No such standardized scale exists for "power." When we say "The NAACP is more powerful than the Audubon Society" it is not clear what we mean in any precise sense, because we have combined the ambiguity of what we mean by "power" as an observed phenomenon with the ambiguity of what we mean by "more powerful," that is, an unmeasurable quantity.

The Pluralist Position

These methodological remarks are necessary because pressure group theory has been rent by two opposing schools of thought concerning the power of groups in American society. The first is most commonly known as pluralism, which emphasizes the competitive situation of groups and thereby the limits placed on group power. The pluralist position was most clearly stated by David B. Truman, and has been amplified and defended in studies of national politics and a number of local communities.[2]

Put concisely, the pluralists have attempted to show that while pressure groups are a powerful force in American political life, none are able to dominate policy-making for any length of time. Because of the multiplicity of groups, their activities largely cancel each other out, producing a pattern of countervailing power. Moreover, as political resources are generally available to anyone, it is possible, although perhaps difficult, for new interests to organize and become active pressure groups. The emergence of new interests is further encouraged by the multiple points of access in

315

the American system. As a consequence, while
there may be some inequalities in the distribution of power among interests in the United States,
these imbalances are not controlling; power
potential does not guarantee any one group or
set of groups domination. In fact, domination
is prevented because no group can gain and maintain a commanding strategic position.

The Elite Position

        Pluralists have arrived at their position
largely by a combination of limited direct observations in the form of case studies of policy
being made, inference, and indirect observation.
Their principal theoretical opponents, often
referred to as elitists,[3] have arrived at their
position by chiefly statements of potential and
inference. Although elite theorists have occasionally differed as to who precisely rules
America, some arguing it is a self-conscious
upper class,[4] or a combination of top political,
military, corporate, and media leaders,[5] or the
leaders of the major corporations[6] all agree
that in effect there is a single, unified pressure
group which most of, if not all, the time establishes governmental priorities, dominates
decision-making, and benefits from the way the
political system operates. To support their
contention, it can be noted, for example, that
virtually all major leadership positions in "the
political economy," are drawn from "the wealthier
families of the economy."[7]

        Further, the distribution of wealth in
American society has changed very little since
the 1920s, and what changes have taken place
have favored the wealthy.[8] The structure of
American taxation policy favors the rich rather
than the middle- or lower-classes. Although
blacks and other minorities, as well as environmentalists and consumer protection advocates

316

have won some victories, elitists would argue
that these successes are minor, affecting at
most the peripheral areas of public decision-
making. Thus, in terms of "inputs" to the system
(the recruitment of leaders) and "outputs" (public
policy decisions), those who possess the greatest
resources show the greatest success. It may
be inferred, then, that this is the group which
dominates the decision-making process.

The debate between pluralists and elitists
has now been in full flood since the early 1950s
and for the methodological reasons outlined above
will probably continue unresolved. While the
battle is often heated--and sometimes confused--
it has had the advantage of focusing attention
on two major issues: first the degree to which
pressure group influece is a significant force
in American politics, a point on which both
pluralists and elitists agree; and second, the
role of strategic position in shaping that influence. A third point of some importance has
emerged as well, that is, the role of leaders
and leadership in both pluralist and elitist
view of the political system. Today, even the
most committed pluralists accept that group
leaders respond to their group members only within
limited ranges and play the major role in establishing the direction and structure of the group
(see Chapter IV).

In summary, then, it can be said that,
first, there is general agreement that in modern
America pressure groups exercise substantial
(although unmeasurable) power in public policy-
making. Second, this power varies among groups,
the differences being largely a result of the
strategic position of the various groups. Third,
group leadership plays a critical role in the
politically effective use of a group's other
resources and thus the power differentials among
groups. Fourth, group power has increasingly
encroached on the power of the political parties
in all arenas of politics, perhaps overshadowing

317

the role of party leaders in many instances.
And, finally, the overall conformation of political
power in America can be understood only by taking
into account pressure groups, whether one chooses
to call oneself "pluralist" or "elitist."[9]

The Political Function of Pressure Groups

The debate between pluralists and elitists
extends to include differing analyses of the
functions performed by pressure groups in American politics. As with the discussion of the
power of groups, the argument is partly empirical,
that is, a question of fact, but in this case
it also raises the normative issues of group
politics. And it is this latter issue which
cuts to the heart of the role of pressure groups
in a democratic order.

A politically democratic society should
fulfill certain conditions for its citizens.[10]
Many of these are protections, such as freedom
from suppression of dissent, freedom of religious
beliefs, and so forth, commonly referred to as
civil liberties. Others are conditions of participation, usually subsumed under the term "civil
rights." These include the right to select one's
rulers and periodically, if need be, reject those
who have been unsatisfactory or continue them
if they have effectively represented the citizen's
interest. Civil rights also include the opportunity to participate diectly in government,
either by seeking and holding public office or
expressing directly to office-holders one's wishes
and needs. Included within these rights is the
assumption of a rough equality or parity of political effectiveness among citizens when they
choose to exercise their opportunities.[11]

Both pluralists and elitists agree on
these fundamental premises. The area of disagreement occurs in the respective answers to

318

the questions: do pressure groups serve to help
or hamper in meeting these democratic conditions?
Stated in social science terminology, the question is: Are pressure group politics functional
or dysfunctional to a democratic system?

The Pluralist Assumptions

Pluralists adopt the position that pressure groups are an important, indeed necessary,
part of the modern political society. As briefly
discussed in Chapter II, the pressure group plays
a complementary role to the party. The political
party is the principal means by which the citizen
as voter selects his governmental leaders and
attains public office himself. Further, the
party, by aggregating voters into an active
collectivity, gives those who are elected the
legitimacy (consent of the governed) and power
to govern effectively. Pressure groups fulfill
the crucial function of aggregating citizens
in a different set of collectivities, those which
express to public officials how the power they
hold should be used, that is, what interests
must be satisfied if the elected official hopes
to continue in public office. As both pressure
group and party affiliation are voluntary, the
citizen is free to shift his allegiances as his
aspirations and interests shift. The important
point is that the two--political party and pressure group--are complementary. Without one or
the other, democratic representation would be
difficult, if not impossible, to achieve.

From the pluralist standpoint, then,
pressure group politics is functional to the
system. Groups permit the diversity of interests
which necessarily exist in a populous, indus-
trialized society to find expression. Party
politics impel political leaders to move toward
the center of mass opinion. The Abolitionists,

319

in the 1830s a small and reviled pressure group,
brought about a major change in the conscience
of the society. The suffragettes managed to
achieve the enfranchisement of half of the adult
population. Various peace groups, from the 1950s
to the 1970s, served as a reminder that war is
a dangerous option in a thermonuclear age. In
each case, the political parties sought to avoid
the issues raised by the pressure groups. In
each case, one or both parties came to adopt
the position the groups advocated.

The pluralist must, of course, accept
two conditions for his model of a democratic
society to operate. One is that the distribution
of power resources must be equal enough that
any interest can find expression. This, as a
condition, does not require parity: some interests inevitably will attract more followers than
others; some will appeal to the rich and thus
benefit from hefty donations and membership dues
while others, appealing to the less well off,
must always struggle to find sufficient funds.
But, as long as the opportunity persists, then
there will be the necessary competition which
insures one group will act as a check on another.
Through minimal limits on pressure group activity
added to the multiple points of access built
into the American system, it is hoped this condition can be met.

The second condition which the pluralist
must accept is the potential consequences of
pressure group activities. Like the laissez-
faire economist, the pluralist stakes his faith
in "the invisible hand of self-interest" working
through competition to produce an effect that
is, on balance, beneficial to the society as
a whole. The citizenry may have to tolerate
occasional aberrations and even damage, such
as the Prohibition Era and the various "red scares"
fuelled by radical right-wing pressure groups.
The steady, if often low-level, pattern of corruption in politics may be another consequence.

320

The pluralist feels, however, that as long as
the system remains competitive, self-correction
will take place, that is, the process is an
"equilibrating" one in which wild swings in any
one direction will be countered by the emergence
of organizations to bring a swing in the oppo-
site direction.

Elitists Assumptions

It is these two basic conditions of pluralist theory which most trouble elitists. They
accept that the first condition is, as the pluralists argue, a necessary condition of a democratic society. They do not accept, however,
as the pluralists do that the condition exists
in reality. The allocation of power resources
in the United States is too uneven for anything
like true competition to exist. The political
situation is comparable to two adolescent car
mechanics producing their own automobiles in
their backyard garage: they may sell enough
to make a profit, they may be written up in news
magazines, but no realistic observer expects
them to pose a genuine threat to the economic
survival of General Motors. Minority groups,
consumer and environmentalist organizations,
and "public interest" organizations likewise
may score successes in politics and receive
adoring press notice, but these achievements
actually only obscure how little their power
is in contrast to the influence wielded by the
giant corporations and the economic elites who
run them.

Given this power imbalance, then, the
elite theorist insists that real competition
does not exist and in the absence of a genuine
competition, the functional role of pressure
groups does not follow. "Pressure group politics"
becomes a euphemism for elite rule, a system
in which the great mass of the citizenry does

not participate, elections are controlled by
the wealthy behind-the-scenes wire-pullers, and
public officials are obedient to the desires
of the elite, not to any concept of the public
interest.

As a consequence, the second condition
of pluralist theory becomes dangerous to the
society as well. Elite theorists argue that
tolerance of "free competition" can be carried
to an extreme, especially when that free competition does not exist. They would point out that
there is a moral difference between the arms
manufacturer who seeks to profit from governmental investment in instruments of mass slaughter
and the civil rights group seeking to gain equal
opportunities for all. The claimed "moral
neutrality" of the pluralist becomes a moral
bias in favor of those who are powerful and self-
seeking. This is, so the elitist might claim,
the very climate which makes "politics" a word
synonymous with corruption, generates the quest
for power for its own sake, and creates the kind
of moral blindness that led to the collapse of
the Nixon Administration.

Without pursuing the debate between pluralists and eilitists further, it becomes apparent that there are simply no clear, easy
generalizations about a phenomenon as complex
as that of the pressure group in a modern democratic society. Both elitists and pluralists
have perhaps often overstated their respective
cases, but both have raised serious points that
deserve future research and analysis. Until
more knowledge is available, it is probably wiser
to confine additional discussion to some of the
persistent problems associated with pressure
group politics and some of the apparent political
and social benefits that accrue to the system.
Both problems and benefits require attention
because they form the basis of efforts to improve
the working of the political system.

In Criticism of Group Politics

How democratic are group politics? The
answer is: Probably not very. Although reliable
data are hard to come by, it does seem true that
the higher a person's position on the wealth,
educational, and social scales the more likely
that person is to belong to a pressure group.
And if group pressure is one of the more important ways an American gains economic and other
benefits from government, this means that the
better off one is, the more he will further
acquire from government in terms of tax incentives, credits or deductions, contracts, better
services, and greater protection.

While as much as fifty percent of the
adult American population may belong to an interest group of one kind or another, a smaller
proportion than this belong to active pressure
groups and even fewer are themselves group
activists.[12] Although the iron law of oligarchy
is not absolute, groups are led and controlled
by relatively small number of people who are,
on balance, those who hope and expect to gain
the most from pressure group activities. Accordingly, pressure groups are not democratic
in the sense they embrace the participation of
all or most of the citizenry nor in the sense
their internal dynamics provide for equal participation of their members.

It is theoretically possible that undemocratic institutions can produce democratic results,
the Supreme Court being a case in point. Are
pressure groups functional to the system in
this sense? As we have seen, the answer is controversial, but on the negative side of the tally
sheet the following points need to be made.

First, despite the diversity of pressure
groups in America, it is by no means certain
that the entire spectrum of citizen interests is

represented or, even if enunciated, is represented accurately or conscientiously. Do "consumer" organizations actually speak for the consumer or do they speak for what the leaders of those groups believe ought to be the consumers' interests? Are civil rights organizations, often led by college educated, middle-class blacks, genuinely in touch with the needs of the impoverished ghetto dweller? Can the numerous trade and business associations, dominated as they so often are by only a small number of firms, legitimately articulate the problems of the small businessman? Similar questions can be asked of the professional associations, the labor unions, public employee organizations, and environmentalist groups, to say nothing of the numerous "taxpayers associations" which are frequently covers for business interests.

Impressive as the diversity and clamor of modern pressure group politics is, there is good reason to accept that in many, if not most, instances what is occurring is a struggle between "elites" and "counter-elites,"[13] or as the same authors phrased it, "Perhaps what we have in the United States is the politics of intense minorities. Individual groups press for selective benefits, leaving the unorganized to pick up the remains."[14] The "average" American asking: Who speaks for me? Often must answer his own question: No one.

Second, it must be acknowledged that one of the enduring sources of corruption in American politics is pressure group efforts to gain special consideration from government. The Watergate Scandals only forced on the nation's attention what was already well-known to be the case in several states. By no means do all pressure groups stoop to graft, pay-offs, kick-backs, and illegal gifts and campaign contributions in order to gain access to governmental decision-making, but it is sadly apparent that these practices are common, touching not just governors

324

and state legislatures but reaching into the national government as well.

Corruption, while distasteful enough because it is illegal, creates other distortions. It means that power goes to the big bankroll and to the crafty and unscrupulous. It means decisions are made not on the basis of need, merit, or public benefit but to satisfy the "obligations" created by money payments. It means, most seriously, that public officials act to fulfill the desires of a small number of individuals rather than to meet the responsibilities of their offices. Widespread and consistent enough, corruption serves to convince the citizen that he has no stake in his government because it is "owned"--by right of direct purchase-- by a small number of pressure groups.

Third, public policy which is shaped by the group struggle cannot be fairly labelled public policy. It is the product of alliances, bargains, compromises, and negotiations among only a few powerful actors, the "intense minorities." If it were possible to assume that these actors represented all the interests affected by legislative or executive action, the process would have the virtue of efficiency. But, as discussed in the first point, such an assumption is a highly risky one. The result, then, is the mass public is bound by law to policies hammered out by a few often acting in secrecy, almost always without reference to the needs and wishes of that mass public. It can be argued that the function of the elected official is to give due regard to the electorate, while it is the function of the pressure group to express interests ordinarily lost or obscured in the confusion of achieving electoral majorities. If pressure groups did not become involved in the electoral process, the argument would be more persuasive. As we have seen, however, this is not the case, with the effect that some elected officials are as much pressure group representatives as they are spokesmen for any "will of the people."

Fourth, pressure group politics has unmeasurable but nonetheless clearly poisonous
effects on the nature of politics itself. In
the clash of interests, in the effort to gain
special benefits, the aim of the game of politics
becomes one of winning out over the competition
rather than counting the costs or effects of
victories. Public employees, for example, will
desert hospital patients or leave the public
safety unguarded in defiance of the law and in
disregard of the helplessness of their real victims. And they may do so to demand salary or
fringe benefit packages which already overloaded
city or state budgets cannot support. Their
battle cry might well be that of British union-
ists (in slightly censored version): "To hell
with you, Jack. I'm all right." Their demands,
of course, are no more outrageous than those
of food processors who want to be free of "government interference" in marketing nutrition-empty
products through deceptive if not fraudulent
advertising, or pharmaceutical firms anxious
to avoid government supervision while the public
is used as a guinea pig to test previously un-
tried drugs, or automotive firms willing to see
the citizen breathe the cancer-causing byproducts
of their inefficient internal combustion engines.

In each case, the group goal is to achieve
immediate benefits for itself, regardless of
direct or long-term effects on others. And the
logic that is forced on others is one in which
each interest should make a selfish grab for
itself for fear someone else will get there sooner.
Politics becomes the unenlightening spectacle
of so many hogs squirming at the public trough.

In sum, without necessarily accepting
the elitist thesis, it remains possible to point
to a number of less desirable traits in the pattern of American pressure group politics. The
common theme of all these points of criticism
is the distortion of the democratic norms which

Americans proclaim is their intention to have
govern their society. Politics itself becomes
a dirty word, implying a calling for the skills
of the shrewd manipulator and ruthless corrupter
rather than the public servant.[15] To the extent
pressure group politics contributes to this distortion, politics as Americans know it late in
the twentieth century must be viewed as to that
degree dysfunctional. A blanket indictment is
inappropriate; not all groups are corrupt by
any means, some attempt to insure a degree of
internal democracy, not a few leaders are concerned with the consequences of unbridled self-
seeking. Even with these qualifications in mind,
however, the four characteristics of group
politics listed above fall far short of a politics concerned with "freedom and justice for
all."

In Defense of Group Politics

It is possible to deplore the failings
of pressure group politics without ignoring the
credit side of the ledger as far as a democratic
polity is concerned. Realistically viewed, any
political order must suffer from at least some
of the sins ascribed to pressure groups. Corruption, self-seeking, imbalances in power resources,
and the tendency of small numbers of people to
dominate the policy-making process are perhaps
unavoidable. The more basic questions are: Do
political forces and institutions exist which
help to check and mitigate these tendencies?
Is there a pattern of politics in which the
"ordinary citizen," if he chooses, can gain
access to the policy-making process? And, are
limits imposed on the development of inordinate
power?

In defense of group politics, it can
be argued that pressure groups in America do
much to provide an affirmative answer to these

327

questions. In brief summary, these credits to
pressure group politics can be listed as:

First, the pressure group, in all its
various forms, does provide a vehicle by which
concerned citizens can effectively exercise their
right to petition the government. Many, it must
be conceded, do not choose to exercise that option. Many may do so ineptly, but the opportunity
exists, as the emergence of the gay liberation
movement, the consumer movement, the women's
movement, welfare clients' organizations, and
student associations all testify.

Second, the group struggle is competitive.
It may often be, in the phrase of the economist,
a situation of "imperfect competition," but the
sheer existence of contending power forces acts
as a check on the power of all the actors, as
a source of information to the public and to
public officials, and as a means of guaranteeing
the airing of more than one side of any public
issue. In the United States, few sacred cows
go uncriticized, meaning that it is unusual for
any single set of interests to be completely
dominant for an extended period of time.

Third, as has been suggested several
times, the pressure group is an important complementary institution to the political party. And,
as important, there is sufficient difference
between party and group that the two frequently
stand in a competitive relationship. The citizen's
opportunities are thereby further maximized. He
can participate as party activist, or pressure
group activist, or both. He enjoys as a consequence increased chances of seeing the political
system serve his interests rather than ignore
them.

Finally, as has been mentioned, pressure
groups play a vital role in raising questions,
in helping to set "the national agenda." A
group's leadership may be seeking highly selfish

328

rewards but, in the pursuit of their goals, raise
questions about larger and more fundamental issues.
No doubt many labor leaders have hoped only to
guarantee their continued leadership, but in
doing so they have often reminded the public
and policy-makers of the miserable pay and working conditions of a large number of working
people. Quite possibly some environmentalist
or consumer organization leaders are merely on
an "ego trip," but they too have made us aware
of the human costs of an over-loaded environment
and of shoddy or even dangerous products.

That is, pressure group politics has
made a major contribution to a democratic order,
as flawed as those politics might be. To concentrate on the flaws is to overlook the benefits.

References for Chapter XIII

[1]For a good general discussion of power,
see A. A. Berle, Power (New York: Harcourt,
Brace, and World, 1969). Edward Keynes and David
M. Ricci, eds., Political Power, Community, and
Democracy (Chicago: Rand McNally, 1970) contains
several essays that struggle with conceptuali-
zing power. One of the more influential state-
ments on the subject remains Harold D. Lasswell,
Politics: Who Gets What, When, How (New York:
McGraw Hill, 1936).

[2]David B. Truman, The Governmental Pro-
cess (New York: Alfred A. Knopf, 1951; rev.
ed., 1971). Arnold Rose, The Power Structure
(New York: Oxford University Press, 1967);
Robert A. Dahl, Who Governs: Democracy and
Power in an American City (New Haven, Conn.:
Yale University Press, 1961); Wallace S. Sayre
and Herbert Kaufman, Governing New York City (New
York: Russell Sage, 1960); Nelson Polsby, Com-
munity Power and Political Theory (New Haven,
Conn.: Yale University Press, 1963).

[3]The rubric "elitists" is slightly confusing. It does not imply here that society
ought to be ruled by elites, although in other
contexts it does mean just that.

[4]G. William Domhoff, The Higher Circles:
The Governing Class in America (New York: Vintage,
1971).

[5]C. Wright Mills, The Power Elite (New
York: Oxford University Press, 1956).

[6]Michael Parenti, Democracy for the Few,
2d ed. (New York: St. Martin's Press, 1977);
Morton Mintz and Jerry S. Cohen, America, Inc.
(New York: Dell, 1971).

[7]Kenneth Prewitt and Alan Stone, The Ruling Elites (New York: Harper and Row, 1973), pp. 136-37. Thomas R. Dye, Who's Running America? Institutional Leadership in America (Englewood Cliffs, N.J.: Prentice-Hall, 1976) comes to a similar conclusion although he refuses to generalize from his data. He argues, however, that a relatively small number of persons, drawn in most instances from similar backgrounds, make the basic policy decisions for the nation.

[8]See Bureau of the Census, Statistical Abstract of the United States, 97th ed. (Washington, D.C.: U.S. Bureau of the Census, 1976), Table 651.

[9]Grant McConnell, Private Power and American Democracy (New York: Alfred A. Knopf, 1966) and Theodore Lowi, The End of Liberalism: Ideology, Policy, and the Crisis of Public Authority (New York: W. W. Norton, 1969) have launched one of the most effective attacks on the "pluralist" thesis, although neither precisely fits the "elitist" mold.

[10]Leslie Lipson, The Democratic Civilization (New York: Oxford University Press, 1964) is a rich and interesting examination of the roots and nature of democratic values and practices.

[11]The doctrine of "one man, one vote" for example, is an expression of political parity, insisting as it does that legislative districts should be drawn so that each person has an equally weighted vote in the selection of representatives.

[12]See Chapters II and III.

[13]Prewitt and Stone, p. 227.

[14]Ibid., p. 216.

[15]Robert Sherill, <u>Why They Call It Politics</u> (New York: Harcourt, Brace, Jovanovich, 1972).

CHAPTER XIV

REFORM AND PROSPECTS

The debate between "pluralist" and
"elitist" is largely one over who wields power
in the world of pressure group politics. A
troubling undercurrent in both positions, however, is how that power is gained. Pluralist
and elitist, and others, struggle with the difficult question of how the blind search for power
can be bridled. The issues rotate around two
major problems: first, are there effective reforms that can be instituted to check the worst
abuses of group politics? And, second, are there
trends in American politics likely to make those
reforms more, or less, urgent?

As we will see, both questions are difficult to answer. Before examining the possible
answers, however, it is necessary to put the
major issues in context.

A Glance Back

We began our discussion by pointing out
that the quest of the pressure group is to gain
"access" to the policy-making process. We have
seen, further, that access is built out of the
interaction of policy, interest, interest base,
and strategic position in relation to specific
political arenas and the targets within those
arenas. We are now in a position to represent
our previous "models" in a combined and more
generalized way. Illustration Seven presents
that combined model schematically.

As the illustration suggests, "access"
is a pattern of complex interactions. Group

333

ILLUSTRATION   SEVEN
ACCESS   AND PUBLIC POLICY

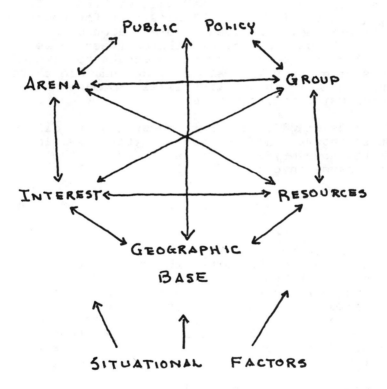

PUBLIC   POLICY

ARENA   GROUP

INTEREST   RESOURCES

GEOGRAPHIC
BASE

SITUATIONAL FACTORS

334

politics then is comprehensible only if we keep
constantly in mind the relationships among group,
arena, interest base, and resources. Each, more
or less directly, affects the others; each presents any group with advantages and disadvantages.

To take a very blunt example, we might
easily assume that all a group need do to gain
access is to buy a legislator. But, with our
model in mind, the questions begin to multiply.
Does the group have the money to pay a legislator's price? Does its geographic base include
a purchasable law-maker? Even if he can be found,
is he so placed within his arena (the legislature) that he can produce the policy wanted?
Is, for that matter, the policy even made in
that arena or is it actually made somewhere else
(the executive branch or the courts)? Will some
other group, a rival or opponent, undercut the
group's best efforts? And other questions could
be asked. In short, gaining access is more complex than it might initially seem. All of which
is no more than another way of saying that pressure politics in America is more complex than
is often assumed.

The Nature of Access

As was noted in Chapter I, moreover,
access has more than one meaning. It is possible
now to refine that generalization. Basically
five forms of access have appeared in the preceding pages.

First, there is access by persuasion.
Simply by the force of its arguments, the depth
of its research, and the logic of its position,
a pressure group may shape public policy by changing the minds of policy-makers. As we have seen,
legislative lobbyists and legislators claim that
rational argument can be effective. In the court
system, a good case often wins on its merits.

335

And, no doubt administrators can be persuaded
by information simply because the data shed new
light on a problem they are wrestling with.

Second, there is access by mutual interest. As in Congress's handling of distributive
policies, policy-maker and pressure group work
together because they share congruent goals.
The elected official who comes from an area in
which one interest is crucial can comfortably
satisfy his desire to be re-elected through the
satisfaction of group interests and feel, with
no qualms, that he is doing what he is supposed
to do: represent the interests of those who
have helped place him in office. As has been
stressed, the political geography of the American
federal system helps make access by mutual interest a common pattern.

A third form of group access is access
by established relationship. The "triple alliance"
of group-administrative agency-legislator is
the most important example. Significantly, the
alliance is built on mutual interest, but its
enduring, and self-protective, nature sets it
apart from access by mutual interest. We must
assume also that, as in any bargain, there are
occasional costs; the need to defend one of the
partners when attacked, for example. For those
within the partnership, however, access by established relationship has the enormous advantages of predictability and the exclusion of
competitors from the policy-making process.

Access by domination would represent
a fourth form of group access. In this instance,
the pressure group virtually monopolizes the
selection of policy-makers, their behavior, and
thus the policies themselves. It appears that
this pattern may apply to some independent regulatory agencies and perhaps to a number of local
governments. In effect the "public" policy-
making process is little more than "private"
decisions enacted into law and enforced as law.

336

Access by domination is probably limited to relatively small geographic areas and only a small number of administrative agencies.

Finally, there is access by purchase. Bribery, direct or indirect, can establish a relationship in which the policy-maker either sells his power to the group or feels he is sufficiently in debt to the group he will shape his decisions to favor their interests. Campaign contributions, gifts, entertainment, and of course direct pay-offs are the tools of access by purchase.

These five forms of access are not mutually exclusive. A group may follow a "mixed strategy," relying on one form of access in one arena and a different one in another. Further, it must be remembered that geographic base, interest, strategic position, policy type, and target all interact to create circumstances in which one form of access may be possible but another unavailable to a particular group.

It must also be recalled that the "pressure system" is a two-way street. Access does not simply mean "private" pressure groups reaching into the counsels of government; governmental actors--executives, administrative agencies, legislators--reach out to interest groups and apply pressure upon them. Pressure politics in America, then, is an interactive system and power may lie in the hands of a governmental pressure group rather than a private one.

Access: An Evaluation

It can be assumed that access by persuasion is the democratic goal. The tumult of competing argumentation might occasionally be deafening, but were groups to confine themselves

to appeals to reason, propaganda, and claims
that they best understand the "public interest,"
the policy-maker is free to weigh arguments,
consult public opinion polls, and balance one
set of data against another to finally make up
his own mind. Freedom of speech and of the press
are protected by the Bill of Rights for just
this purpose: to allow the free interchange
of ideas and information be the determining force
in political decisions. It can be hoped that
the best idea, not the most powerful pressure,
will prevail.

When one moves beyond the scope of rational debate, however, the problems become more
intricate. Access by mutual interest is built
into the very structure of American political
geography. It is clear that this is precisely
what Madison had in mind when he expressed his
anxieties about "factions" acting to "vex and
oppress each other [rather] than to cooperate
for the common good."[1] He saw the solution to
this problem in the size of the nation: a single
group might be able to find access with one legislator, but another would work out a pattern of
mutual interest with a different legislator,
and thus the latter would counterbalance the
former. And, it seemed quite possible that in
the process of give-and-take, of mutual interests
and their representation, some approximation
of the public welfare would manifest itself.

As Grant McConnell has cogently argued,
Madison's hope that the size of the republic
might be a counterforce to narrowly based interests has largely failed to materialize.[2] Madison omitted the possibility that less numerous
or widely scattered interests might well be
severely damaged by depending on pluralistic
competition. The black American long suffered
the consequences of access by mutual interest
and has yet to recover from its effects.

338

Nonetheless, access by mutual interest
is a political "reality" which cannot be denied.
The legislator especially does have some kind
of practical and moral obligation to represent
his district or state. This is also the role
in which he is apt to be most comfortable.[3]
Satisfying "the folks back home" is not only
a matter of realism for the man who wants to
be re-elected, it is perhaps the only reliable
way we have of discovering the "public interest."
As long as the legislator, or other policy-
maker, is sensitive to shifts in the needs and
desires of those whom he is supposed to represent,
mutual interest is an important way by which
these changes get translated into policy. In
this respect, the pressure group as an interest
articulator may help the policy-maker respond
to changing conditions.

It is through access by established relationship that the pressure group can be most
influential in meeting its interests.[4] It
is also this pattern which many critics see as
the most threatening to the American system.
McConnell, Theodore Lowi,[5] and John Kenneth
Galbraith[6] among others, regard the triple alliance, with its rigid exclusion of competition,
its massive control over policy-making in various
areas, its resistance to change, and its tendency
to satisfy narrow and short-run interests regardless of costs to the public as the Madisonian
nightmare come true, but in a form Madison and
other proponents of pluralism never dreamed
possible.

As Galbraith has argued, for example,
defense industries, the Department of Defense,
and the legislative committees and sub-committees
who "oversee" defense expenditures are so intimately interlocked, they are for all practical
purposes a single pressure group. Lowi points
out the same tendency in other policy areas.
He persuasively argues that a new kind of "feu-
dalism" is coming into being; one in which

jealous barons rule over their policy areas and beat back any attempt by "outsiders" (including the chief executive) to introduce innovation, rationality, or a sense of concern for the general welfare.[7] New York City, with its catastrophic problems, can be pointed to as the perfect example of the consequences of access by established relationship.[8]

Access by established relationship cannot be understood unless it is kept in mind that public servants act as pressure groups (a position "classic" group theory was reluctant to take). The power of the triple alliance springs from the meshing of different power bases: the outside pressure group's base in numbers, political geography, and money; the legislator's hold over key veto points in the policy-making process and his position of advantage in law-making; the administrator's control over rule-making, the carrying-out of laws, and information. Together, these resources are more awesome than when taken singly, because virtually all points of access to policy-making are closed off to other groups and interests.

Since the pattern of established relationships looks pluralistic--there are multiple centers of power, the appearance of jostling and conflict--the public and many trained observers are deceived into thinking that the system is "open." What they fail to see, however, is that as the smoke of pseudo-conflict slowly drifts away, it is almost invariably the triple alliances which retain control of the fields of battle.

Access by domination seems rare enough to be of small concern. No doubt it does occur with some local governments, but today much policy for local governments is made not only at the state level but at the national. Historical examples suggest that any such domination is almost always oppressive, which perhaps helps

340

explain why we can find so few examples currently.
With a mass electorate, a court system prepared
to apply constitutional standards to policy-
making, and an administrative system increasingly
free of "political" control, the very oppres-
siveness of domination means it cannot go unchallenged.

Little more needs to be added to the
remarks made in the preceding chapter about access
by purchase. When bribery, direct or indirect,
is the means through which policy is made, by
definition the policy will be narrowly self-
serving. We cannot overlook the possibility,
further, that access by purchase is a stage in
the development of access by established relationship. Once group, administrative agency, and
legislator are bound together by a network of
mutual obligations founded on money, favors,
and improper conduct, they may become virtual
captives of each other, much as the "corruptee"
is a necessary role in the structure of organized
crime. Accordingly, each partner must defend
the others, for if one falls prey to "outside
interference," all might find themselves subject
to investigation, criticism, loss of power, and
even prosecution. Thus in some instances, and
we cannot know how many, access by purchase creates
a bond of mutual interest that literally forces
an established relationship on the participants.

Attempts at Reform

These perspectives on access are important
because they provide a basis for evaluating efforts to reform or to control the worst excesses
of group politics.[9] Table 12 lists the most
significant reform efforts passed into law by
the U.S. Congress, or, as in the case of the
"Codes of Ethics," adopted as binding upon the
behavior of members of the executive branch and
the Congress.

341

TABLE 12

MAJOR NATIONAL REFORM EFFORTS

Date	Action
1907	Act prohibits corporate campaign contributions
1911	Act requires disclosure of campaign contributions
1925	Corrupt Practices Act: require candidates to report expenditures; set limits on expenditures
1939	Hatch Act: limit campaign contributions; limit political activities of federal employees
1944	Smith-Connally Act: prohibit union campaign contributions
1946	Lobby Registration Act: require lobbyists to register and report expenditures
1947	Taft-Hartley Act: repeated Smith-Connally provisions
1972	Federal Election Campaign Act: disclose contributions and contributors; limit expenditures on campaign advertising
1974	Federal Election Campaign Act Amendments: control presidential election expenditures; subsidize presidential campaigns; create the Federal Elections Commission
1977	Congressional and Executive Codes of Ethics to limit outside income, conflicts of interests.

SOURCES: Congressional Quarterly, The Washington Lobby, 2d ed. (Washington, D.C.: Congressional Quarterly, 1974). William J. Crotty, Political Reform and the American Experiment (New York: Thomas Y. Crowell, 1977).

Reform by Regulation

It is unnecessary to explore here in detail the various attempts listed in Table 12. We can safely generalize that they traditionally fit into the pattern of regulatory policies which overlap constituent policies. That is, the laws were generally stated in broad outline and left to the courts for detailed interpretation, which frequently had the effect of emasculating their provisions.[10] Additionally, their effectiveness has been diluted by administrative nonaction. Lobbyists before Congress, for example, register or not under the terms of the 1946 Lobby Registration Act, and no lobbyists are prosecuted for their failure to do so.[11]

The nearly seventy years of regulatory attempts culminated in the amendments to the 1972 Federal Election Campaign Act, passed into law in 1974 in response to the "Watergate" scandals. These amendments established specific criteria for the collection, expenditure, and reporting of campaign funds. Both the recipients of the money (the candidate and his campaign committee) and the donors must report their transactions. Additionally specific limits were placed on donations; a pressure group, for example, being allowed to donate no more than $5,000 in any one year to a candidate for federal office.

To discourage presidential aspirants from seeking money from pressure groups, provision was also made for public financing of elections. Each of the major parties could receive as much as $20 million; minor parties were allowed to receive subsidies in proportion to their total votes in the last election. A Federal Elections Commission was set up to administer the funds, publicize the lists of donors, and seek prosecution of those violating the Act.

343

The 1974 Amendments were, without question, the most significant attempt at reform to that time. From the perspective of the discussion of access, however, it must be recognized that the reforms were aimed at only one form of access--access by purchase--and that this is not necessarily the most important area of concern in the world of pressure politics.

If, as so many critics claim, access by established relationship is the more important, and more threatening, form of pressure group politics, regulatory policies such as the 1974 Amendments can do little more than scratch the surface. Some triple alliances may be weakened, if groups cannot buttress them with lavish spending to re-elect their legislative partners. Some future triple alliances, for the same reason, may be nipped in the bud. But, for those which already exist, campaign reform is probably little more than symbolic politics, useful for diverting the attention of the public away from the real centers of power.

Reform by Countervailing Power

Those sensitive to the power built into access by established relationship have generally looked beyond campaign reform for a means of limiting or breaking up triple alliances. Theodore Lowi has argued that the legislature itself could become a center of countervailing power.

His thesis is that one of the necessary ingredients for the successful functioning of the triple alliances is the discretion administrators have in executing policy, a discretion which they tend to share with their pressure group partners. By a return to a strict "rule by law," in which acts of Congress would be written in explicit, clear, and firm language,

344

policy-making at a minimum would be shifted back
to where it constitutionally belongs: in the
hands of legislators. At best, rule by law would
mean the public could identify and, if need be,
electorally punish those who made self-interested
policies.

Lowi's argument is more sophisticated
than any brief description can do credit; even
so, it must be accepted that the thrust of his
proposal runs counter to "traditional" legislative behavior. There are politically valid reasons
why legislators avoid certain kinds of decisions,
including the fear of angering powerful pressure
groups, damaging the relationships their col-
leagues may have worked out, and, by no means
least, the technical complexities of modern public
policy. Short of a major shift in the way legislators approach their tasks--which almost auto-
matically implies a major shift in the kind of
legislators chosen by the voters--Lowi's proposal
would appear to be more hopeful than practical.

The rise of "public interest" pressure
groups suggests another source of countervailing
power. Consumers' organizations, environmentalist
groups, civil liberties and some civil rights
groups are, in general, free of narrow geographic
bases, committed to ideological rather than economic interests, and avoid the classic pattern
of distributive policy-making. For these reasons,
they bring a different set of assumptions to
the pressure system, while relying on many of
the same resources.

Of these new "public interest" groups,
perhaps the most familiar is Common Cause.
Created in 1969, it claimed in 1977 over 250,000
members, many of whom were organized to bring
pressure to bear on state governments as well
as the federal government.[12]

Common Cause was the most vocal and significant supporter of the Federal Election Campaign

Act and not merely out of a desire to see greater
regulation of campaign expenditures and contributions. The organization's logic rotated around
the principle that by limiting the totals to
be spent and donated, the smaller contributor
would gain in significance or at least become
more nearly equal to the traditional "big spend-
ers." Further, it seemed likely that numbers,
organized and skillfully deployed, would become
more important than sheer dollars. The theory,
then, saw regulation as a handmaiden to the rise
of new groups speaking for a broader interest
base.

     Reform by countervailing power fits per-
fectly with the pluralist view of group politics
and can be seen as an important corrective to
any flaws inherent in pluralism. As these new
groups gain in skill and other resources, they
will be able to challenge the older triple alliances and act as a corrective to policy-making
for the benefit of narrow interests.

     Some critics, while admiring the political
resourcefulness of Common Cause and similar groups,
have been skeptical about their significance.
The rise of pressure groups based on "popular
interests" may be no more than the efforts of
"counter elites" to seize power for themselves.
Common Cause, for example, is occasionally cri-
ticized for having a "college educated, middle
class" bias and membership, committed to tinkering
with the system but never willing to face the
deeper-rooted sources of power-imbalances.[13]

     A balanced evaluation of efforts at reform
both by regulation and countervailing power seems
to lead to the conclusion arrived at by Grant
McConnell, "Quick or large-scale reform in the
United States is improbable."[14] Access by mutual
interest, and its extended form, access by established relationship, resist change because
they are built into "the system," indeed they
might be said to be the system.

346

Without doubt election reform will reduce
some corruption; how much remains to be seen.
As long as policy-makers need or want money,
and as long as pressure groups can purchase access
to policy-making with money, it seems safe to
say that the combination of greed and group interest will find a way to evade even the most
carefully written laws.

Prospects for the Future

There is one other possible source of
checks on the power of pressure groups: the
political party. Although by the mid-1970s the
word "politician" seemed more a term of contempt
than an occupational category, the parties have
produced men of stature, commitment, and with
the ability to look beyond limited goals and
parochial interests to some vision of a better
society.

The party system is, moreover, linked
in a complicated and only partly understood way
to the role of pressure groups. The two types
of activities are complementary, in theory and
in practice, yet it also seems to be true that
when and where there is a vigorous, competitive
two-party system, group influence is diminished.[15]
We do not know exactly why. Perhaps it is because
the parties, for all their faults, are more representative institutions than any number of pressure groups can ever be. Perhaps it is because
most Americans are not members of pressure groups
and would prefer to see their interests spoken
for through the electoral system when a real
choice exists. And, perhaps it is because policy-
makers who have a solid base of support in a
political party do not need to depend on pressure
groups for funds, electoral support, "cues,"
or information about consituents' attitudes,
since these are all supplied by the party.

347

As we have seen, party leaders do compete with pressure groups in certain critical arenas; administrative appointments, judicial selection, elections, and constituent policies are matters of deep concern to party activists. This competition may serve to limit the influence of groups, even to force them to work through the party organizations with the parties consequently performing their classic role as interest aggregators. As a counter-balance to group power, however, the political parties are effective only if they are vigorous and can hold the allegiance and involvement of the mass of citizens.

The Disarray of the Parties

The general thrust of present analysis is that the two-party system as we have known it is in deep difficulties, if it has not actually begun to disintegrate. Three interrelated trends appear to be at work.

First, both the Democratic and Republican parties have failed in a number of serious respects to maintain themselves as organizations.[16] The crucial state and local "chapters" of the national organizations have lost contact with the voters, fallen into the hands of lazy or indifferent leaders, and refused to recruit new leaders. Accordingly, candidates for office have found they can ignore--are in fact better off ignoring--the formal party organization. Instead, each aspirant for office builds his own personal organization, fuels it with money raised outside the party structure, and once in office feels no obligation to party "leaders" nor loyalty to party program.

Second, the voters themselves have changed.[17] "Classic" analysis of voting behavior held that the American voter was only mildly

348

involved in politics, had little concern with most issues, and could be counted upon to consistently vote his traditional party identification. Recent research has shown that the contemporary voter is very different in every respect. His involvement in politics has intensified; he is sharply aware of the issues and takes a position on them; and he votes his traditional party identification less and less, seeking instead the candidates which best satisfy his view of the issues, regardless of party labels.

Third, American society has changed in major ways and the party is adapted to a political order that existed before those changes took place.[18] The parties have shown themselves unable to adjust to a society in which technology (such as television), demographic changes (such as the movement of families from one area to another), and issue complexity (such as the energy crisis) make it almost impossible for party leaders to engage in their familiar practices of putting together coalitions of relatively unaware, stable, and easily led blocs of voters.

These three trends, taken together, mean the parties as we know them are no longer able to act as the necessary and sufficient avenues to political power and leadership in America. It could be noted in support of this view that the behavior of recent presidential candidates shows at best a veiled indifference to the party organizations. John F. Kennedy led the way by creating his own personal organization; Lyndon Johnson ran as the "leader of all the people" (not the Democrats); Richard Nixon deliberately dissociated his own campaigns from the party structure; it could be said that Jimmy Carter virtually ran against the parties in 1976.

Not all analysts agree with this assessment.[19] The "hard data" are difficult to refute, however. The American voter is not as loyal

349

to or as willing to follow the cues of the political parties as he once was. One implication
is that in the absence of the parties as aggregating mechanisms, pressure groups will become
increasingly more important as interest articu-
lators, especially for a population that is
deeply concerned with issues.

The Rise of Pressure Group Democracy?

The future may hold, then, a major change
for the American system. "Politics" could come
to mean not the party struggle but the pressure
group struggle.

A scenario for the future can be blocked
out. The disintegration of the parties will
continue, possibly at a more rapid rate. Candidates for office will increasingly speak to the
issues and thereby become interest group spokesmen rather than party spokesmen. The same candidates will seek the support of pressure groups
which share their interest concerns and build
enduring alliances with those groups. Interest
groups themselves will see they must organize
as pressure groups to field their own candidates,
influence those who have already offered themselves to the voters, and gain access to the
policy-making system. Groups will also devote
more effort and skill to shaping public opinion
and electoral choices.

Politics will accordingly become a struggle
between those who have built up established relationships and those who have not. The tendency
will be for pressure groups to multiply so as
to represent the various and complex shadings
of interests which exist in a "mass" society.

American politics will increasingly re-
semble European "multi-party" systems, with

divisions among the people occurring not on a
"Democrat-Republican" dichotomy, or even along
a "liberal-conservative" scale, but on the basis
of organized interests. Eventually fundamental
changes in constituent policies will become necessary to accommodate the diversity of interests,
in arrangements made for elections and for
appointments to important administrative agencies, for example.

The scenario can be extended without
reaching into the realm of fantasy. There are
others, however, which are equally possible.
One or more new parties may emerge and reassert
the party struggle as the dominant form of American politics. The current disarray of the
parties may be over-estimated; it could turn
out to be a short-run adjustment rather than
an inevitable decline. Perhaps some new, and
thus far unseen, pattern will appear: a return
to politics based on geographic sectionalism,
for example, as was manifested in the pre-Civil
War Era.

We are in the awkward position that we
cannot say with any certainty whether pressure
group politics is becoming more or less important in the total scheme of American politics.
To begin with, we simply do not know how many
pressure groups there are in the United States
or whether the number has increased or declined
over any recent time period.[20] We do not know
whether more or fewer Americans belong to pressure groups, nor, with any confidence how many
who do belong are activists. Thus there is no
"base line" of data from which we can make comparisons and projections.

Intuitive judgments would lead us to
believe that the number and range of groups and
interests has indeed increased. The emergence
of numerous minority, women's, and "public interest" groups all seem to point in that direction.

As social scientists have long been aware, however, what seems to be true may not be so when systematically tested.

We can safely predict that pressure group strategies and tactics will become more sophisticated. The computer, for example, is becoming as much a tool of the pressure group as the lobbyist and serves the same purpose: to collect data on policy-makers, their personal backgrounds, their voting records, their likes and dislikes, their weaknesses, and where they might be vulnerable to pressure. Groups, moreover, are made up of people, and people learn from their own experiences and the experiences of others. Group leaders watch the techniques of other leaders and learn what works and what does not.

If we remember, once again, that public policy interacts with group behavior, the increasing complexity of public policy-making demands more sophisticated approaches from group leaders. These trends and these demands for greater skills, often for greater money resources, always for more information can lead to a widening gap between the affluent group and the less well-to-do. Thus, pressure group power may actually tend to clot in fewer and fewer hands, whether the number of groups increases or not.

A democratic order built on pressure group politics might well turn out to be a hazardous undertaking, then. As the "elitists" have asserted, the results could well be not very democratic at all. To end where we began, the threat is a real one. As Madison said, "Men of factious tempers, of local prejudices, or of sinister designs, may, by intrigue, by corruption, or by other means, first obtain the suffrages, and then betray the interests, of the people."[21]

References for Chapter XIV

[1] James Madison, "Federalist No. 10," The Federalist, Modern Library Edition (New York: Random House, N.D.), p. 56.

[2] Grant McConnell, Private Power and American Democracy (New York: Alfred A. Knopf, 1966), especially Chapter 4.

[3] David R. Mayhew, Congress: The Electoral Connection (New Haven, Conn.: Yale University Press, 1974), pp. 53-56. John W. Kingdon, Congressmen's Voting Decisions (New York: Harper and Row, 1973) comes to much the same conclusion.

[4] Harmon Ziegler and Michael Baer, Lobbying: Interaction and Influence in American State Legislatures (Belmont, Cal.: Wadsworth, 1969), Chapter 1.

[5] Theodore Lowi, The End of Liberalism: Ideology, Policy, and the Crisis of Public Authority (New York: W. W. Norton, 1969).

[6] John Kenneth Galbraith, Economics and the Public Purpose (Boston: Houghton Mifflin, 1973).

[7] Lowi; the concept of "functional feudalities" was first fully enunciated by Lowi in "Machine Politics--Old and New," The Public Interest 9 (Fall 1967): 83-92.

[8] David Rogers, The Management of Big Cities: Interest Groups and Social Change Strategies (Beverly Hills, Cal.: Russell Sage, 1971), Chapter 2.

[9] Much of what follows is drawn from William J. Crotty's excellent book Political Reform and the American Experiment (New York: Thomas Y. Crowell, 1977).

353

[10]Congressional Quarterly, The Washington
Lobby, 2d ed. (Washington, D.C.: Congressional
Quarterly, 1974) discusses the specific court
decisions and their effects on reform efforts.

[11]Robert W. Miller and Jimmy D. Johnson,
Corporate Ambassadors to Washington (Washington,
D.C.: The American University Press, 1970),
Chapter 1.

[12]Andrew S. McFarland, Public Interest
Lobbies (Washington, D.C.: American Enterprise
Institute, 1976) contains an interesting discus-
sion of Common Cause. See also Andrew Glass,
"Common Cause," in Political Brokers: Money,
Organizations, Power and People, ed. Judith G.
Smith (New York: Liveright, 1972), pp. 260-
301.

[13]McFarland, pp. 3-4; David Broder, "Common Cause Opens the System," New Orleans States-
Item (April 26, 1977), p. A-8. Broder refers
to Common Cause as a "model of elitism," but
goes on to speak of it with high praise.

[14]McConnell, p. 367.

[15]McConnell, pp. 351-53; Ziegler and
Baer, p. 199.

[16]David S. Broder, The Party's Over:
The Failure of Politics in America (New York:
Harper and Row, 1971); Walter Karp, Indispen-
sable Enemies: The Politics of Misrule in
America (Baltimore: Penguin, 1973).

[17]Norman H. Nie, Sidney Verba, and John
R. Petrocik, The Changing American Voter (Cambridge, Mass.: The Harvard University Press,
1976).

[18]Walter Dean Burnham, Critical Elections
and the Mainsprings of American Politics (New

York: W. W. Norton, 1970); Everett Carll Ladd,
Jr. with Charles D. Hadley, Transformations of
the American Party System (New York: W. W.
Norton, 1975).

[19]James L. Sundquist, Dynamics of the
Party System: Alignment and Realignment of
Political Parties in the United States (Washing-
ton, D.C.:   The Brookings Institution, 1973);
Michael Margolis, "From Confusion to Confusion:
Issues and the American Voter," American Political
Science Review 71 (March 1977): 31-43.

[20]McConnell, p. 127, notes the problems
of counting pressure groups.   Although Sidney
Verba and Norman H. Nie, Participation in America:
Political Democracy and Social Equality (New
York: Harper and Row, 1972) provide valuable
indicators of group activity, the data simply
are not specific enough to give us an accurate
assessment of pressure group membership or numbers.   See Jerrold G. Rusk, "Political Participation in America: A Review Essay," American
Political Science Review 70 (June 1976): 583-91.

[21]Madison, p. 59.

INDEX

358

NAACP, 28, 99, 279; and judicial strategy, 291-94
National Association of Manufacturers, 109

Opinion leaders, 213-14
Opposition, and pressure groups, 102-3
Organization, forms, 53-54; and policy, 52;
  as power resource, 92-93

Parenti, Michael, 5
Party politics, and interest aggregation, 15;
  See also Political Parties
Peltason, Jack, 279
Plessy vs. Ferguson, 291
Pluralism, 315ff.
Policy, classified, 26-28; and democracy, 325-26;
  and legislative politics, 247-49; and organi-
  zation, 52
Political action committees, 50
Political interest, see Interest
Political Interest group, see Pressure Group
Political Participation, 13-14
Political Parties, decline, 224; disarray, 348-49;
  and elections, 216-18; and executive
  branch, 267-68, and legislature, 245
Political questions, as legal doctrine, 284-85
Power, generally, 313-15; and group resources, 89
Presidency, 255
Pressure groups, and agenda-setting, 6; and
  appointment process, 261-62, 266; and
  corruption, 2-3; defined, 18; factions, 60;
  membership criteria, 41-42; opposition, 102-3;
  rivals, 104-5; resources, 89ff.
Primary elections, 216, 219-220
Propaganda, 209-11; and judicial decisions, 302;
  and legislators, 234-35
Public policies, see Policies
Public Relations, 212-13

Redistributive policies, defined, 27
Regulatory policies, defined, 27-28
Ripeness, as legal doctrine, 283
Rivals, and pressure groups, 104-5

Securities and Exchange Commission, 134
Sherman Antitrust Act, 134
Sierra Club, 55, 59
Skill, as power resource, 97
Staff, role in pressure group, 79; as power
  resource, 98-99
Standing to sue, as legal doctrine, 281-82
Status and image, as power resource, 99-100
State attorneys general, 296-97
Strikes, as propaganda, 212; and public
  employees, 195-96
Subsidies, 23

Trade associations, 55
"Triple alliances," 269-70, 336
Truman, David B., 315

Unitary organization, 53
United Farm Workers Organization, 109

Veto Points, 206-7

Weber, Max, 80
Wilson, James Q., 81-82